EASY HIKING
IN SOUTHERN CALIFORNIA

EASY HIKING
IN SOUTHERN CALIFORNIA

SECOND EDITION

Ann Marie Brown

AVALON
TRAVEL

FOGHORN OUTDOORS EASY HIKING IN SOUTHERN CALIFORNIA

Second Edition

Ann Marie Brown

Text © 2004 by Ann Marie Brown.
All rights reserved.
Maps © 2004 by Avalon Travel Publishing.
All rights reserved.

Please send all feedback about this book to:

ⒻOGHORN OUTDOORS®
Easy Hiking in Southern California
Avalon Travel Publishing
1400 65th Street, Suite 250
Emeryville, CA 94608, USA
atpfeedback@avalonpub.com
www.foghorn.com

Some photos and illustrations are used by permission
and are the property of the original copyright owners.

ISBN: 1-56691-660-7
ISSN: 1099-5110

Printing History
1st edition—1998
2nd edition—April 2004
5 4 3 2 1

Editor: Mia Lipman
Series Manager: Marisa Solís
Copy Editor: Emily McManus
Proofreader: Candace English
Graphics Coordinator: Deb Dutcher
Production Coordinator: Jacob Goolkasian
Cover and Interior Designer: Darren Alessi
Map Editor: Olivia Solís
Cartographers: Mike Morgenfeld, Kat Kalamaras, and Suzanne Service
Indexers: Marie Nuchols and Peter Brigaitis

Front cover photo: Hiking sand dunes in Death Valley National Park © Mark Gibson

Printed in the United States of America by Malloy

ABOUT THE AUTHOR

© BILL RHODES

The author of 12 outdoors guide-books, Ann Marie Brown is a dedicated California outdoorswoman. She hikes, bikes, and camps more than 150 days each year in a dedicated effort to avoid routine, complacency, and getting a real job.

Ann Marie's work has appeared in *Sunset, VIA, Backpacker,* and *California* magazines. As a way of giving back a bit of what she gets from her outdoor experiences, she writes and edits for several environmental groups, including the Sierra Club and Natural Resources Defense Council.

When not hiking or riding along a California trail, Ann Marie can be found at her home near Yosemite National Park.

In addition to *Foghorn Outdoors Easy Hiking in Southern California,* Ann Marie's outdoors guidebooks include:

Foghorn Outdoors 101 Great Hikes of the San Francisco Bay Area
Foghorn Outdoors 250 Great Hikes in California's National Parks
Foghorn Outdoors Bay Area Biking
Foghorn Outdoors California Waterfalls
Foghorn Outdoors Easy Biking in Northern California
Foghorn Outdoors Easy Camping in Southern California
Foghorn Outdoors Easy Hiking in Northern California
Foghorn Outdoors Northern California Biking
Foghorn Outdoors Southern California Cabins & Cottages
Moon Handbooks Yosemite
Foghorn Outdoors California Hiking (with Tom Stienstra)

For more information on these titles, visit Ann Marie's website at www.annmariebrown.com.

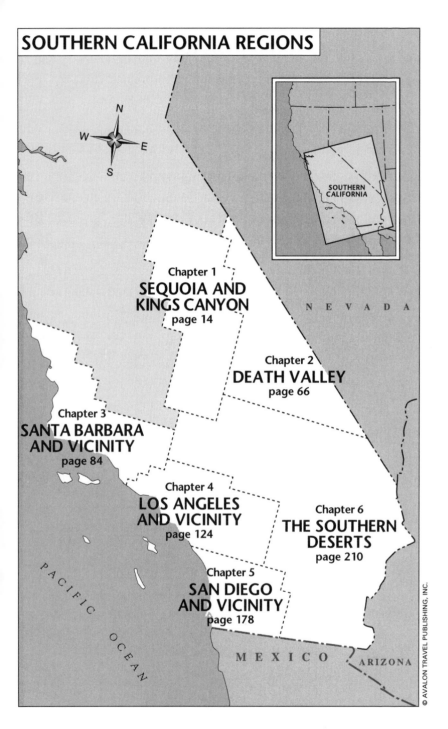

SOUTHERN CALIFORNIA REGIONS

SOUTHERN
CALIFORNIA

NEVADA

Chapter 1
**SEQUOIA AND
KINGS CANYON**
page 14

Chapter 2
DEATH VALLEY
page 66

Chapter 3
**SANTA BARBARA
AND VICINITY**
page 84

Chapter 4
**LOS ANGELES
AND VICINITY**
page 124

Chapter 6
**THE SOUTHERN
DESERTS**
page 210

Chapter 5
**SAN DIEGO
AND VICINITY**
page 178

PACIFIC OCEAN

MEXICO   ARIZONA

© AVALON TRAVEL PUBLISHING, INC.

CONTENTS

HOW TO USE THIS BOOK

This book is organized geographically, with the trails listed in numerical order from west to east and north to south within a region (numbering begins again at 1 in each new chapter). Using the overview map at the beginning of this book or the region map at the start of each chapter, locate the area in Southern California where you want to hike. Then find the trail descriptions for that area by checking the table of contents or the index—or by turning to the chapter covering the region where you'd like to hike, and reading all the trail descriptions in that chapter.

Each trail has an icon or a series of icons provided at the top of the listing. These icons give you a snapshot of the trail's features, as follows:

 The trail visits a beach.

 The trail travels to a waterfall.

 The trail leads to a lake.

 The trail passes through a special forest.

 The trail travels through desert terrain.

 The trail climbs to a high overlook with wide views.

 The trail features wildflower displays in spring.

 The trail offers an opportunity for wildlife-watching.

The trail visits a historic site.

Leashed dogs are permitted on the trail.

Each of the trails in this book is rated for round-trip distance and hiking time. Although the mileage is as accurate as possible, the time required is more subjective, and you may find that you require more or less time to complete the hike. Each of these trails was selected for its ease, but due to the variation in mileage, some hikes are easier and shorter than others.

At the end of most trail descriptions, you'll find additional information under the heading Options. This section gives you some choices for other hikes in the same park or public land. Also watch for the "Best season" information at the top of each listing—this tells you the optimal time of year to hike each trail. In an area as diverse as Southern California, with its snow-covered peaks, high and low deserts, inland grasslands, and temperate coastline, it's smart to keep an eye on the calendar. That way, you'll be sure to have great hiking adventures year-round.

Our Commitment

We are committed to making *Foghorn Outdoors Easy Hiking in Southern California* the most accurate, thorough, and enjoyable hiking guide to the area. With this second edition, you can rest assured that every trail in this book has been carefully reviewed and is accompanied by the most up-to-date information. Please be aware that with the passing of time, some of the fees listed herein may have changed, and trails may have closed unexpectedly. If you have a specific need or concern, it's best to call the location ahead of time.

If you would like to comment on the book, whether it's to suggest a trail we overlooked or to let us know about any noteworthy experience—good or bad—that occurred while using *Foghorn Outdoors Easy Hiking in Southern California* as your guide, we would appreciate hearing from you. Please address correspondence to:

Foghorn Outdoors Easy Hiking in Southern California, 2nd edition
Avalon Travel Publishing
1400 65th Street, Suite 250
Emeryville, CA 94608
email: atpfeedback@avalonpub.com

If you send us an email, please put "Easy Hiking in Southern California" in the subject line.

Introduction

INTRODUCTION

I admit it; the idea for this book came from my own selfish perspective. Like so many of my friends and acquaintances, for years I had been working long hours in an office five or more days a week, putting in plenty of overtime and spending way too much time indoors. When I had time off, I tried to get out in the wilderness as much as possible, but with all of life's demands, I rarely had more than a free morning or afternoon to spend outside.

In response to the complexity and demands of my life, I decided to take up a weekly ritual: Every Sunday morning, no matter what else was happening, I would take a couple of hours to go for a walk in a beautiful outdoor place. I did this almost without fail for three years, only rarely missing a Sunday, and it was during one of those walks that the idea for this book was born: A guide to 100 great easy hiking trails, for those of us who want to feel the peace of the wilderness but are short on time and also frequently short on energy.

What is great about the trails in this book is that they are suitable and fun for almost everybody. Bring along your children, your grandma, or your spouse who thinks the outdoors is all mosquitoes and poison oak. Every trail in this book was chosen because it offers a good payoff, a reason for going besides merely exercise. These trails lead you away from pavement, exhaust fumes, and crowds to places where you'd rather be: sparkling waterfalls, scenic viewpoints, and peaceful forests. The best test for these trails is to try hiking one of them with someone who says they hate hiking, and just see if they don't have a good time.

To choose these 100 hikes, I walked every trail in this book, some many times over. I also hiked plenty of other trails that didn't make the cut, often because they were too difficult or too dull to ensure that everybody would have fun. Sometimes I brought my less-than-enthusiastic-about-hiking friends with me. Sometimes I borrowed my friends' kids and took them along to see if they liked the hikes. Sometimes I met new friends on the trail—solitary female hikers, older hikers, hikers with babies in backpacks, hikers with dogs—and I asked them to suggest fun and easy trails.

What I found in researching this book is that there are plenty of Southern California trails designed for ordinary people, not just Mr. and Ms. Hardcore Outdoors Enthusiast, and when people hike them, they feel good. It seems that fundamentally, we aren't all that different from our canine companions, whom we call man's (and woman's) best friend. We seem to be happiest when we get to go for a good walk.

Hope to see you (and your children, grandmas, and spouses) out there.

HIKING TIPS
What to Carry with You

1. Food and Water

There's nothing like being hungry or thirsty to spoil a good time, or to make you anxious about getting back to the car. Even if you aren't the least bit hungry or thirsty when you park at the trailhead, you may feel completely different after 45 minutes or more of walking. A small day-pack or fannypack can keep you happily supplied with a quart or so of water and a few snacks. Always carry more than you think you'll need. If you don't bring your own water, make sure you carry a water filter or purifier so you can obtain water from a natural source, such as a stream or lake. Never, ever drink water from a natural source without first filtering, purifying, or boiling it. The risk to your health (from *Giardia lamblia* and other microorganisms) is too great.

2. Trail Map

Get a current map of the park or public land you're visiting. Most of the trails featured in this book are thoroughly signed, but that isn't always enough to keep you on track. Signs get knocked down or disappear with alarming frequency, due to rain, wind, or park visitors looking for souvenirs. Also, signs will sometimes state the name of the trail you're walking on and sometimes state the name of a destination you're heading toward, but it isn't necessarily the information you need at that moment.

Maps are available from the managing agency of the place you're visiting. All their names and phone numbers are in this book. At state and national parks, you can usually pick up a map when you drive into the park entrance. If it costs a buck or so, pay it. At national parks, maps are included free with your entrance fee. For national forest lands, purchase maps at the ranger district offices noted for each trail, or order maps at the website: www.fs.fed.us/r5/maps.

Also, if you're planning to hike in a Southern California national forest, see the information below about obtaining a National Forest Adventure Pass.

3. Extra Clothing

On the trail, conditions can change at any time. Not only can the weather suddenly turn windy, foggy, or rainy, but your own body conditions also change: You'll perspire as you hike up a sunny hill, then get chilled at the top of a windy ridge or when you head into shade. Always carry a lightweight jacket with you, preferably one that is waterproof and wind-resistant. Put it in your daypack or tie it around your waist. If your jacket isn't waterproof, pack along one of the $2 single-use rain ponchos that come in a package the size of a deck of cards (available at most drugstores and outdoors stores). If you can't part with two bucks, carry an extra-large garbage bag instead. If you need to, you can poke a hole in the bottom of the bag, stick your head through, and stay dry.

If you are hiking in the mountains, carry gloves and a hat as well. You never know when you might need them.

4. Sunglasses and Sunscreen
The dangers of the sun are well-known. Wear both sunglasses and sun-screen, and/or a hat with a wide brim. Put on your sunscreen 30 minutes before you go outdoors so it has time to take effect, and don't forget about your lips. Coat them with lip balm with a high SPF to protect them.

5. Flashlight
Just in case your hike takes a little longer than you planned and darkness falls, bring at least one flashlight. Mini-flashlights are available every-where, weigh almost nothing, and can save the day—or night. I especially like the tiny squeeze flashlights, about the shape and size of a quarter, which you can clip on to any key ring (the Photon Micro-Light is a popu-lar brand). Since these flashlights are so small, carry two or three. That way you never have to worry about the batteries running out of juice.

6. First Aid Kit and Emergency Supplies
Unless you're trained in first aid, nothing major is required here, but a few large and small Band-Aids and moleskin for blisters, antibiotic oint-ment, ibuprofen, and an Ace bandage can be valuable tools. If anyone in your party is allergic to bee stings or anything in the outdoors, carry their medication. If you are hiking where you might be bothered by mosqui-toes, bring a small bottle of insect repellent.

For emergencies, always carry a Swiss Army–style pocket knife—one with several blades, a can opener, scissors, and tweezers on it. Matches in a waterproof container and a candle will ensure you can always build a fire if you need to. A whistle and small signal mirror can help you get found if you ever get lost. And if you know how to use a com-pass, carry one.

About the National Forest Adventure Pass

Beginning in 1997, a fee was instituted in Angeles, San Bernardino, Cleveland, and Los Padres National Forests to raise revenue to cover the costs of recreation on national forest land. The fee policy states that any vehicle parked on land in those four national forests must display a National Forest Adventure Pass. Visitors are free to drive through these national forest lands without a pass, but if you park your car at a trailhead, day-use area, or any other no-fee recreation site, you must have one.

Passes are available for $5 per day or $30 per year, and the same pass is valid in all four national forests. Passes can be purchased at all Angeles, San Bernardino, Cleveland, and Los Padres National Forest visitors centers and ranger stations. They are also available at many commercial establishments (such as grocery stores and minimarts) on or near national forest land. For more information about the Adventure Pass program, visit www.fsadventurepass.org.

Hiking Boots

Hiking boots are not always imperative for the trails in this book, but they can make your experience a lot more pleasant. Hiking boots offer more foot and ankle protection than running or athletic shoes (or most other types of footwear), and they provide better traction and grip on a rocky, wet, or muddy trail. These days, you'll find lots of lightweight hiking boots on the market. They feel as comfortable as your old tennis shoes, but offer much more protection for your feet and joints. Don't make the mistake of purchasing heavy, expensive mountaineering or backpacking boots if you are simply going for day hikes. You can buy a decent pair of lightweight boots for $60 or so. If you plan to hike even once a month, they're worth it. They'll last a long time.

If you have hiking boots, don't forget to treat them with a waterproofing spray. You'll need to re-treat them every few months, especially if you've been out in the rain.

Bears, Mountain Lions, and Snakes

All three of these creatures deserve your respect, and it's good to know a little bit about them. Chances are high you will never see a mountain lion, but you just might run into a bear or a snake somewhere.

You'll only find bears in bear country. For the trails covered in this book, that's the San Gabriel, San Jacinto, and San Bernardino Mountains, and the Sierra Nevada. The only bears found in California are black bears (even though they are usually brown in color). They almost never harm human beings, but with their impressive size and strength, they can make your hair stand on end.

There's only one important thing to remember about bears: They love snacks. Anytime you see a bear, it's almost guaranteed that he's looking for food, preferably something sweet. When you are camping, keep your food—and anything scented, including toiletry items that a bear might mistake for food—packed away in bearproof containers. Get an update from the rangers in the park you're visiting about suitable bear precautions. You're most likely to see a bear in or near a campground; it's less common to encounter one on a trail. When you're hiking, bears will usually hear you coming and avoid you.

Mountain lions are almost everywhere in California, but they are very shy and secretive animals, and thus rarely seen. When they do show themselves, they get a lot of media attention. If you're hiking in an area where mountain lions or their tracks have been spotted, remember to keep your children close to you on the trail and your dog leashed. If you see a mountain lion, it will most likely vanish into the landscape as soon as it notices you. If it doesn't, make yourself appear as large and aggressive as possible. Raise your arms, open your jacket, wave a big stick, and speak loudly and firmly or shout. If you have children with you, pick them up off the ground, but try to do so without crouching down or leaning over. (Crouching makes you appear smaller and more submissive, like prey.) Don't turn your back on the cat or run from it, but rather back away slowly and deliberately, always retaining your aggressive pose and continuing to speak loudly.

Rattlesnakes live where it's warm, and usually at elevations below 6,000 feet. If you see one, give it plenty of space to get away without feeling threatened. If you're hiking on a nice day, when rattlesnakes are often out sunning themselves, keep your eyes open for them so you don't step on one. Be especially on the lookout for rattlesnakes in the spring, when they leave their winter burrows and come out in the sun. They tend to prefer rocky, exposed areas. Although rattlesnake bites are painful, they are very rarely fatal. In the rare event that you should get bitten by a rattlesnake, your car key—and the nearest telephone (remember that cell phones may not work in many rural areas)—are your best first aid. Don't panic or run, which can speed the circulation of venom through your system. Call 911 as soon as you can, or drive to the nearest hospital.

Except for a handful of rattlesnake species, all Southern California snakes are nonpoisonous. Just give them room to slither by.

Ticks and Poison Oak

Most hikers would say that these two are far worse than a whole convention of bears, mountain lions, and snakes. But you can avoid them with a little common sense. The easiest way to stay clear of ticks is to wear long pants and long sleeves when you hike. If it's too hot to be covered up, make sure you check yourself thoroughly when you leave the trail, and remove anything that's crawling on you. Check your clothes, and also your skin underneath. A good friend can be a useful assistant in this endeavor.

If you find a tick on your skin, remember that the larger brown ones are harmless. It's the tiny brown-black ones that are deer ticks and can carry Lyme disease. Deer ticks about as small as the tip of a sharpened pencil. If you find a very small tick on you that's not crawling around but actually biting into your skin, do the following: Remove the tick very slowly and gently with a tweezers or other tool, put it in a plastic bag, and take it to your doctor for examination to see if it is carrying Lyme disease.

Most tick bites cause a painful sting that will get your attention. But rarely, ticks will bite you without you noticing. If you've been in the outdoors, and then a few days or a week later you start to experience headaches, fever, nausea, or rashes, see a doctor immediately. Tell the doctor you are concerned about possible exposure to ticks and Lyme disease. Caught in its early stages, Lyme disease is easily treated with antibiotics.

If you stay on the trails when you hike, and if you perform tick checks faithfully after every trip outdoors, you should have few problems with ticks.

And as for poison oak, that old Boy Scout motto holds true: Leaves of three, let them be. If you can't readily identify poison oak, learn how. Poison oak disguises itself in different seasons. In spring and summer when in full leaf, it looks somewhat like wild blackberry bushes. In late summer, its leaves turn bright red. But in winter, the plant loses all or most of its leaves and looks like clusters of bare sticks. Poison oak is poisonous year-round. To avoid it, stay on the trail and watch what you brush up against. If you're severely allergic to poison oak, wear long pants and long sleeves, and remove and wash your clothes immediately after hiking.

Hiking with Kids

Taking children along on a hiking trip can be immensely rewarding, for them and for you. That's the best scenario. In the worst scenario, hiking with kids can turn your day trip into a nightmare. Avoid the latter experience by following a few simple tips:

1. *Choose your trail wisely.* If you pick a trail that is too difficult for the age and ability level of your kids, no one will have fun. All of the trails in this book are rated "easy," but they aren't equally easy. If you have small children with you, a one- or two-mile hike will be challenging and time-consuming enough (see "5 Best Hikes for Toddlers" suggestions under Best Easy Hikes). If your children are age six or older, and eager to experience the outdoors, they can probably hike five or six miles round-trip quite comfortably. When in doubt, choose a shorter trail. If the kids are disappointed when the hike is over so quickly, choose a longer trail next time.

2. *Bring more snacks than you think you will need.* Adults burn a lot of calories while exercising, but kids burn even more. Offer them a variety of snacks—both salty and sweet—and don't forget to have them drink plenty of water. You'll have to carry most of the foodstuffs in your own pack, but let your kids carry their own small daypacks filled with snacks and a small bottle of water. Just make sure their packs are not too heavy.

3. *Let your child take the lead.* Kids love to be out in front on the trail. If you have more than one child with you, rotate leaders from time to time. Don't let anyone get too far out in front—or too far behind, either. For safety's sake, the entire group should always stay close together.

4. *Distract when necessary.* Remember that kids' attention spans are shorter than yours, and children are not always enthralled by scenery and fresh air the way adults are. To keep your child interested and motivated on the trail, distract him or her by singing songs, making up games, or telling stories. If necessary, use the promise of snacks or rest stops as an impetus for continuing up the trail (but make sure you deliver on the promise). Education also makes an excellent distraction, if it is accomplished in a fun, nonlecturing manner. Teach children about what they are seeing along the trail. Show them the difference between various types of conifer cones. Let them smell the scent of the Jeffrey pine's bark. Have them look for fish in streams or lakes, and birds in the high branches of trees.

5. *Have children keep a scrapbook of their outdoor experiences.* This could include feathers or leaves found along the trail, photographs taken on hiking trips, or a list of the birds or animals they have seen. At the same time, teach children that some things, like wildflowers and pinecones, should always be left where they are, and not taken home as souvenirs.

6. *Slow down.* Let your children determine the hiking pace, which may be a lot slower than you would like. Take plenty of stops for rests and

snacks. If you don't make it to your chosen destination, who cares? With children, the joy is in the going, not in the getting there.

7. *Set ground rules.* Teach children that hiking is fun, but that nature is no place for yelling loudly, running ahead of the group, or destroying plants or wildlife. Make these rules clear before you set out on the trail, so everyone understands what is acceptable. Children can easily learn respect for nature at an early age, but they must be taught.

8. *Offer praise, not nagging.* Give plenty of positive reinforcement when a child makes it up a hill or reaches a destination. The words "Wow, you're a great hiker" go a long way with children. If your kids don't perform as well as you would like them to, keep it to yourself. The goal is to keep their feelings about outdoor adventures positive so they will be willing to try again on the next trail.

Getting Lost and Getting Found

If you're hiking with a family or group, make sure everybody knows to stay together. If anyone decides to split off from the group for any reason, make sure he or she has a trail map and knows how to read it. Also, be sure that everyone in your group knows what to do if they get lost:

- Whistle or shout loudly at regular intervals.
- "Hug" a tree, or a big rock or bush. Find a noticeable landmark, sit down next to it, and don't move. Continue to whistle or shout loudly. A lost person is easier to find if he or she stays in one place.

Protecting the Outdoors

Take good care of this beautiful land you're hiking on. The basics are simple: Leave no trace of your visit. Pack out all your trash. Do your best not to disturb animal or plant life. Don't collect specimens of plants, wildlife, or even pinecones. Never, ever carve anything into the trunks of trees. If you're following a trail, don't cut the switchbacks. Leave everything in nature exactly as you found it, because each tiny piece has its place in the great scheme of things.

You can go the extra mile, too. Pick up any litter that you see on the trail. Teach your children to do this as well. Carry an extra bag to hold picked-up litter until you get to a trash receptacle, or just keep an empty pocket for that purpose in your daypack or fannypack.

If you have the extra time or energy, join a trail organization in your area or spend some time volunteering in your local park. Anything you do to help this beautiful planet will be repaid to you many times over.

BEST EASY HIKES

Of all the easy hikes in this book, here are my favorites in the following categories:

5 Best Waterfall Hikes

Rancheria Falls, Sierra National Forest, p. 36
Tokopah Falls, Sequoia National Park, p. 50
Nojoqui Falls, Nojoqui Falls County Park, p. 105
Rose Valley Falls, Los Padres National Forest, p. 120
Sturtevant Falls, Angeles National Forest, p. 139

5 Best Summit Hikes

Fresno Dome, Sierra National Forest, p. 30
Little Baldy, Sequoia National Park, p. 48
Mount Waterman, Angeles National Forest, p. 144
Garnet Peak, Cleveland National Forest, p. 196
Ryan Mountain Trail, Joshua Tree National Park, p. 239

5 Best Hikes with Dogs

Little Lakes Valley, John Muir Wilderness, p. 17
Inspiration Point, Los Padres National Forest, p. 111
Holy Jim Falls, Cleveland National Forest, p. 156
Ernie Maxwell Scenic Trail, San Bernardino National Forest, p. 173
Garnet Peak, Cleveland National Forest, p. 196
Anywhere in our national forests (but almost nowhere in our national and state parks!)

5 Best Hikes to See Wildlife

Tokopah Falls, Sequoia National Park, p. 50
Farewell Gap Trail to Aspen Flat, Sequoia National Park, p. 56
Wildwood Canyon Loop, Wildwood Park, p. 131
Mount Waterman, Angeles National Forest, p. 144
Cabrillo Tidepools, Cabrillo National Monument, p. 185

5 Best Hikes to See Birds

Painted Rock Trail, Carrizo Plain National Monument, p. 99
Oso Flaco Lake, Oceano Dunes State Vehicular Recreation Area, p. 102
McGrath Nature Trail & Beach Walk, McGrath State Beach, p. 121
Big Morongo Canyon Loop, Big Morongo Canyon Preserve, p. 227
Rock Hill Trail, Sonny Bono Salton Sea National Wildlife Refuge, p. 245

5 Best Hikes with Toddlers

Nojoqui Falls, Nojoqui Falls County Park, p. 105
Rose Valley Falls, Los Padres National Forest, p. 120
Millard Canyon, Angeles National Forest, p. 137
Monrovia Canyon, Monrovia Canyon Park, p. 141
Cabrillo Tidepools, Cabrillo National Monument, p. 185

5 Best Coastal Hikes

Moonstone Beach Trail, San Simeon State Beach, p. 92
Bluffs Trail, Montaña de Oro State Park, p. 93
Two Harbors to Cherry Cove, Two Harbors, Catalina Island, p. 152
Razor Point & Beach Trail Loop, Torrey Pines State Reserve, p. 181
Cabrillo Tidepools, Cabrillo National Monument, p. 185

5 Best Streamside Hikes

Indian Pools, Sierra National Forest, p. 38
Zumwalt Meadow Loop, Kings Canyon National Park, p. 42
Limekiln Trail, Limekiln State Park, p. 90
Little Falls Canyon, Santa Lucia Wilderness, p. 97
San Ysidro Trail, Los Padres National Forest, p. 116

5 Best Lakeside Hikes

Little Lakes Valley, John Muir Wilderness, p. 17
Ruby Lake, John Muir Wilderness, p. 19
Blue Lake, John Muir Wilderness, p. 21
Twin Lakes, Kaiser Wilderness, p. 34
Oso Flaco Lake, Oceano Dunes State Vehicular Recreation Area, p. 102

5 Best Wildflower Hikes

Bluffs Trail, Montaña de Oro State Park, p. 93
Painted Rock Trail, Carrizo Plain National Monument, p. 99
Big Sycamore Canyon & Old Boney Trails, Santa Monica Mountains, p. 133
Pictograph Trail to Overlook, Anza-Borrego Desert State Park, p. 207
South & North Poppy Loop, Antelope Valley California
    Poppy Reserve, p. 213

5 Most Unusual Hikes

Fossil Falls, Bureau of Land Management Ridgecrest Area, p. 81
Bear Gulch Caves & Overlook, Pinnacles National Monument, p. 87

Painted Rock Trail, Carrizo Plain National Monument, p. 99
Mitchell Caverns & Crystal Springs, Providence Mountains State
    Recreation Area, p. 223
Rings Trail, Mojave National Preserve, p. 225

5 Most Interesting Tree Hikes

Shadow of the Giants, Sierra National Forest, p. 28
Trail of 100 Giants, Giant Sequoia National Monument, p. 61
Los Osos Oaks Trails, Los Osos Oaks State Reserve, p. 95
Champion Lodgepole Pine, San Bernardino National Forest, p. 167
Elephant Tree Trail, Anza-Borrego Desert State Park, p. 202

5 Best Desert Hikes

Mosaic Canyon, Death Valley National Park, p. 75
Ghost Mountain/Marshal South Home, Anza-Borrego Desert
    State Park, p. 205
Teutonia Peak Trail, Mojave National Preserve, p. 219
Kelso Dunes, Mojave National Preserve, p. 221
Ryan Mountain Trail, Joshua Tree National Park, p. 239

© ANN MARIE BROWN

Chapter 1

Sequoia and Kings Canyon

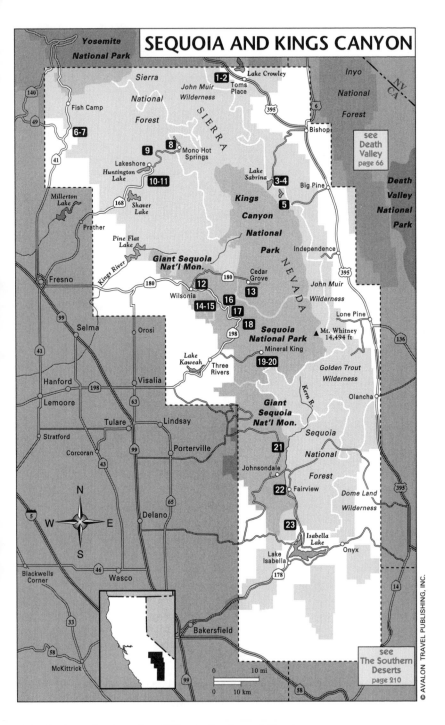

SEQUOIA AND KINGS CANYON

CHAPTER 1—SEQUOIA AND KINGS CANYON

Located on the western slope of the Sierra Nevada, Kings Canyon, and Sequoia National Parks are famous for their giant sequoia groves, tall mountains, deep canyons, roaring rivers, and spectacular hiking trails with views of the jagged peaks of the Great Western Divide. Often referred to as "Yosemite without the masses," these two side-by-side national parks offer classic Sierra scenery without the infamous overcrowding that plagues that great park to the north.

Managed jointly by the National Park Service since 1943, Kings Canyon and Sequoia abound with superlatives. The highest peak in the contiguous United States, Mount Whitney at 14,494 feet, is located in Sequoia National Park, although most people hike to its lofty summit from the east side in Inyo National Forest. Several other park peaks top out at more than 14,000 feet. The Sherman Tree, the largest living tree in the world at 275 feet tall and with a 103-foot circumference at the ground, is also found in Sequoia National Park. This massive tree is still growing; every year it adds enough wood to make another 60-foot-tall tree. Many other record-setting trees are found in the two parks. No nature experience is quite as awe-inspiring, and as humbling, as hiking through a grove of these giant sequoias.

Since December 2000, a new park joins the borders of Sequoia and Kings Canyon: Giant Sequoia National Monument. Administered by the Forest Service, not the National Park Service, the national monument contains two noncontiguous land areas, both designated to increase protection for the last remaining giant sequoia groves in the world.

The hiking options don't stop at the national park and monument borders. Visitors seeking the polished granite landscape of the national parks without the accompanying crowds can find it along the trails of the Kaiser Pass area near Huntington Lake, or in the Sierra National Forest lands north of Kings Canyon. And far across the Sierra Nevada, on the U.S. 395 corridor in the Eastern Sierra, hikers can access one trailhead after another at the end of almost every road leading west off the highway. From Tom's Place to Bishop to Big Pine, each mountain-bound road is a gateway to the John Muir Wilderness and a world of hiking opportunities.

1. LITTLE LAKES VALLEY

John Muir Wilderness, off U.S. 395 near Tom's Place

Total distance: 5.0 miles round-trip

Type of trail: Rolling terrain

Hiking time: 2.5 hours

Best season: June–October

There's a place in the Eastern Sierra with some of the easiest hiking you can find in the high country. The place is Little Lakes Valley, and the trail through it is darn near flat—a rarity in this land of steep escarpments and pointy peaks.

Better still, the trailhead at Mosquito Flat is at 10,300 feet in elevation, so you don't have to hike for miles to reach high mountain scenery. Your car whisks you uphill, and your feet start walking in heavenly paradise.

On the trail, you find that Little Lakes Valley is a land of water, water, everywhere. If you're not gazing at a beautiful alpine lake, then you're crossing or walking alongside melodious Rock Creek. The main trail through the valley, Morgan Pass Trail, undulates along, climbing a few feet and then losing them again. It traces alongside the creek, passing a

llamas, dogs, and hikers on the trail in Little Lakes Valley

proliferation of lakes, sometimes as little as a quarter-mile apart. Through it all you are treated to a dramatic backdrop of snow-covered mountains at the head of the glacial valley. Most of the peaks are in the 13,000-foot range—Mount Mills, Mount Dade, Mount Abbott, and Bear Creek Spire among them. The white-topped summits create a brilliant contrast against Sierra blue skies and glacial lakes.

After an initial brief ascent on the Morgan Pass Trail, you reach a junction at .3 mile and stay left. Spur trails cut off from the trail so you can explore each lake individually if you wish. The first lake you come to is Mack Lake at .5 mile; the trail runs high above it. It's closely followed by Marsh Lake, then Heart Lake at 1.5 miles. For true romantics, Heart Lake is indeed shaped like a heart.

A quarter-mile farther is larger Box Lake. Two smaller lakes to the east are called the Hidden Lakes. They're "hidden" because they're not readily visible from the main trail; you hike around the edge of Box Lake and beyond it to reach them. Back on the Morgan Pass Trail, .3 mile past Box Lake is still larger Long Lake, a total of two miles from the trailhead. A highly photogenic stretch of trail runs alongside its granite-lined eastern edge. Most easy hikers will be satisfied with this lake as their destination, although you can hike farther to more lakes, if you wish (see Options, below).

Because of the easy access to this high-elevation trailhead, the mellow trail, and the exquisite beauty of Little Lakes Valley, the Morgan Pass Trail is extremely popular with beginning backpackers, day-hikers, dog walkers, and trout anglers. If you want to avoid the crowds, start your hike as early in the morning as possible, and try to plan your visit for a weekday instead of a weekend. Otherwise, just smile at everyone as they go past, because they'll be smiling right back at you.

Options

Those with more stamina can continue on the Morgan Pass Trail to Chickenfoot Lake at three miles out, or the Gem Lakes at 3.5 miles. The Gem Lakes are the most beautiful of all the lakes along the trail.

Information and Contact

There is no fee. For more information and/or a map of Inyo National Forest, contact the White Mountain Ranger Station, 798 North Main Street, Bishop, CA 93514, 760/873-2500, website: www.fs.fed.us/r5/inyo.

Directions

From U.S. 395 in Bishop, drive 24 miles north to Tom's Place and the Rock Creek Road turnoff on the left. Follow Rock Creek Road southwest for 10.5 miles to its end at the Mosquito Flat parking area. The trail begins at the west end of the parking lot.

2. RUBY LAKE

John Muir Wilderness, off U.S. 395 near Tom's Place

Total distance: 4.5 miles round-trip   **Hiking time:** 2.5 hours

Type of trail: Some steep terrain   **Best season:** June–October

---

The Little Lakes Valley is a spectacularly beautiful, glacially carved canyon that is littered with lakes, both large and small, and framed by frosted white peaks. There are enough hiking options along this one trail to keep most lake lovers busy for a week. (See the preceding hike for details.)

The valley's only drawback is its popularity, which increases dramatically on summer weekends. If, when you visit, the Little Lakes Valley looks like a freeway of hikers and backpackers, a right turn on the Mono Pass Trail to Ruby Lake will provide you with some peace and quiet, plus a unique bird's-eye perspective on the Little Lakes Valley.

Ruby Lake, on the Mono Pass Trail

The reason there are fewer people on the Mono Pass Trail is simple: the trail climbs. The cardinal rule of getting away from the hiking crowds: Just go uphill. Although plenty of hearty backpackers use the Mono Pass Trail to access the pass and the Pioneer Basin beyond, most don't bother with a side trip to Ruby Lake, .5 mile off the trail. That leaves you with a chance for a seat at your own private lake.

Follow the main pathway (Morgan Pass Trail) into Little Lakes Valley for .3 mile, then take the right fork signed for Ruby Lake and Mono Pass. You'll quickly switchback uphill, and as you rise above the Little Lakes Valley, you're rewarded with one picture-perfect view after another. Don't use up all your film on the lower reaches of trail, because with every uphill switchback, a wider vista appears. You can point out each of the lakes in Little Lakes Valley—Mack, Marsh, Heart, Box, and Long—and name the snow-covered peaks in the background—Mount Morgan, Bear Creek Spire, Mount Abbott, and Mount Dade.

Near the top of the climb, you pass a pothole pond on your left, which creates a sparking blue foreground for a wide-angle view of Morgan Pass and the Little Lakes Valley. Soon afterward you reach the spur trail to Ruby Lake on the left, two miles from the trailhead. Leave the Mono Pass Trail and follow the path alongside Ruby Lake's outlet stream. In a matter of minutes, you'll be gazing at a small turquoise lake set at 11,120 feet.

Ruby Lake is simply stunning. Almost completely encircled by rocky cliffs, it is a gemlike expanse of sparkling blue-green. The lake's full pleasures are revealed only when you make your way to its shoreline, then find a flat piece of granite to sit on. Very little foliage grows at this high elevation, so you'll find only a few shrubby whitebark pines and some chinquapin. Otherwise, there is just granite, blue water, and a few lingering patches of snow, even at the end of summer.

Not surprisingly, the lake is very cold, but the brook trout seem to like it. Some people fish in Ruby Lake; others try their luck in its outlet stream.

Options
You can continue hiking on the Mono Pass Trail to 12,600-foot Mono Pass, where William Brewer and his party crossed the Sierra in 1864. The panoramic view from the pass includes a series of 13,000-foot peaks, plus the Pioneer Basin and the Mono Recesses. The pass is another 1.7 miles beyond the Ruby Lake turnoff, and it's uphill all the way.

Information and Contact
There is no fee. For more information and/or a map of Inyo National For-

est, contact the White Mountain Ranger Station, 798 North Main Street, Bishop, CA 93514, 760/873-2500, website: www.fs.fed.us/r5/inyo.

Directions

From U.S. 395 in Bishop, drive 24 miles north to Tom's Place and the Rock Creek Road turnoff on the left. Follow Rock Creek Road southwest for 10.5 miles to its end at the Mosquito Flat parking area. The trail begins at the west end of the parking lot.

3. BLUE LAKE

John Muir Wilderness, off U.S. 395 near Bishop

Total distance: 6.0 miles round-trip   **Hiking time:** 3.0 hours
Type of trail: Some steep terrain   **Best season:** June–October

---

First, a warning: The trail to Blue Lake is more difficult than you might think, given how many novice hikers and families you'll see traveling on it on summer weekends. But if you pace yourself on the high-elevation climb and carry plenty of water and snacks, you will find yourself on the shores of 10,400-foot Blue Lake, framed by Mount Thompson and the Thompson Ridge, in less than two hours of hiking. That's why many Bishop Canyon vacationers are willing to make the trip, despite the 1,300-foot climb.

This is a trail for good hiking boots; the path is quite rocky and steep, although you won't know it in the first mile. You follow the Sabrina Basin Trail from Sabrina Lake, climbing very gently along the aspen-lined lakeshore while enjoying nonstop water views. At .5 mile you pass a John Muir Wilderness boundary sign, and as you begin to ascend, you can turn around and see the desert, far to the east.

At Sabrina Lake's western edge, the Sabrina Basin Trail enters some very tight, steep switchbacks, but a noisy waterfall across the canyon provides distraction from the physical strain. The rocky, switchbacked climb goes on for a solid mile, so just sweat it out. The trail was constructed to accommodate pack animals, so the steeper grades follow well-built rock staircases. Somewhere on this stretch I passed a six-year-old girl who kept yelling, "Look! Thousands and thousands of more

along the trail to Blue Lake

stairsteps!" I understood how she felt.

At last you gain the ridge and the trail levels out for the last mile to the lake, except for a final brief climb on, yes, still more rock stairsteps. The ascent is over when your vista suddenly opens up to a large lake bowl with Thompson Ridge and Thompson Peak in the background. Behind you, you can see the reddish crags of the Piutes. Rock-hop across the lake's outlet stream to walk along the shore, then just branch off anywhere and pick your lakeside spot.

Blue Lake is surprisingly large and punctuated by several rock islands. Although it's a deservedly popular destination, there is more than enough shoreline for everybody to spread out and have their own space.

It would be good planning, and very good fortune, to hike this trail in late September or early October. Then you'll get to see an incredibly vivid aspen display along the shores of Lake Sabrina. It's a sight you won't forget.

Options
If you get inspired to see more, you can continue onward from Blue Lake to Donkey Lake and the Baboon Lakes, 1.5 miles farther.

Information and Contact
There is no fee. For more information and/or a map of Inyo National Forest, contact the White Mountain Ranger Station, 798 North Main Street, Bishop, CA 93514, 760/873-2500, website: www.fs.fed.us/r5/inyo.

Directions

From Bishop on U.S. 395, turn west on Line Street (Highway 168) and drive 18.5 miles to Lake Sabrina. Day-use parking for the Sabrina Basin Trail is at the end of the road.

4. LOCH LEVEN LAKE

John Muir Wilderness, off U.S. 395 near Bishop

Total distance: 5.6 miles round-trip   **Hiking time:** 3.0 hours

Type of trail: Some steep terrain   **Best season:** June–October

---

It's hard to say which is the best part of the trip to Loch Leven Lake. The dancing leaves of the aspen trees at the trail's start? The views of Mount Emerson and the Piute Crags, appearing as colorful as Death Valley at sunset? Or the lake itself—a windswept wisp of blue in a glacial tarn, surrounded by rock and snow?

The truth is, every part is the best part. The only thing you might complain about is that the trail begins at North Lake Campground, but if you're not camping there, you have to leave your car .5 mile away at the North Lake day-use area and walk in. A stay at North Lake Campground shortens this to a 4.6-mile round-trip.

Visiting Loch Leven Lake does require a climb. The total elevation change is 1,400 feet, but fortunately it is spread out over a couple of miles. The toughest ascent is in the first mile uphill from North Lake Campground. If you can make it through that, the rest is relatively easy. Remember that the air is thin here at 9,300 feet, so stopping to catch your breath is perfectly acceptable.

If you aren't camping at North Lake Campground, park at the lot near North Lake signed as Hiker Parking. Then walk up the road to access North Lake Campground and the Piute Pass trailhead.

Follow the trail past a few walk-in campsites, then pass the wilderness entry sign and take the right fork for Piute Pass. Hike steadily uphill through quaking aspens and lodgepole pines. Amazingly, there are almost no switchbacks in the first mile—the trail just goes up and up. The sound of Bishop Creek's North Fork will cheer you on. Along its streambanks in July, you'll find columbine and leopard lilies in bloom.

looking toward Piute Pass from Loch Leven Lake

The second mile of the climb is much easier than the first, and this is where your views start to open up. Leaving the forest behind, you now enter stark, exposed granite country, interspersed with a few lonely whitebark pines. The red-colored Piute Crags tower above you. Turn around occasionally to take in the sweeping views at your back. The valley below you appears so vast and deep, it's hard to imagine that you climbed out of it so quickly.

Soon you'll spy the rock wall that forms the basin for Loch Leven Lake, and hear its outlet creek pouring down. But even though the lake's basin looks close, it takes a while to reach it as the trail curves through a half-dozen long, sweeping switchbacks. It's as if the trail-builders were over-compensating for that initial steep, beeline mile of trail.

The final quarter-mile is an interesting feat of trail building, with rocky stairsteps spaced perfectly about two strides apart. A tiny pothole pond lies just before the lake; continue past it to the much larger Loch Leven Lake. At 10,740 feet in elevation, the lake has a very distinct shape—long and narrow, and about the size of a football field. There is very little accessible shoreline; the lake's west side is bordered by a wall of barren rock and talus and partially covered by snow fields. The scene is so stark that it's easy to imagine the glaciers grinding through here eons ago. A few whitebark pines cling to life at the lake's north end. Small trout are plentiful; the same is true of sunshine and solitude.

Options
Continue hiking from Loch Leven Lake to Piute Lake, another 1.2 miles farther. There is little elevation gain between the two lakes; you've already done most of the climbing.

Information and Contact
There is no fee. For more information and/or a map of Inyo National Forest, contact the White Mountain Ranger Station, 798 North Main Street, Bishop, CA 93514, 760/873-2500, website: www.fs.fed.us/r5/inyo.

Directions
From Bishop on U.S. 395, turn west on Line Street (Highway 168) and drive 18 miles toward Lake Sabrina. Just before reaching the lake, turn right at the sign for North Lake. Drive 1.5 miles and turn right to park in the hiker parking lot by North Lake. Walk down the road for .5 mile to the Piute Pass trailhead at North Lake Campground.

5. NORTH FORK BIG PINE CANYON

John Muir Wilderness, off U.S. 395 near Big Pine

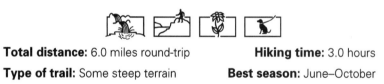

Total distance: 6.0 miles round-trip   **Hiking time:** 3.0 hours

Type of trail: Some steep terrain   **Best season:** June–October

---

If you're anywhere near the town of Big Pine on U.S. 395, there's a hike you should take that leads into the North Fork of Big Pine Canyon. It's home to two waterfalls, a historic rock-walled cabin, and a wildflower-filled meadow.

Park in the day-use parking lot by Glacier Lodge (not the backpackers' parking lot), then walk west from the lot. Go around the gate and follow the wide road past some private cabins. In a few footsteps you'll cross a bridge over First Falls, a noisy, 200-foot-long whitewater cascade. Then bear right on a narrower trail and start switchbacking uphill, paralleling the cascade. You must negotiate a dozen or more tight curves to get above the falls. Your lungs will feel the elevation if you aren't acclimated. As you climb, you get awesome views into Big Pine Canyon's South Fork, but that's not where you're headed—you're going into the North Fork.

At the top of First Falls, cross another bridge over the creek, then take a hard left onto a dirt road, staying along the creek. Don't take the trail signed as Upper Trail, or you'll miss out on the good stuff ahead. A third option, the dirt road to the right, goes to a small walk-in campground, an excellent place to spend the night.

Now you have a mellow stroll into the North Fork of Big Pine Canyon. Your destination is Second Falls, a larger, more impressive cascade than First Falls, less than one mile away and clearly visible from the trail. You travel along the canyon bottom, which is lined with ancient lodgepole pines and mountain wildflowers. A mixed profusion of plant life thrives here, including mountain mahogany, aspens, sagebrush, Indian paintbrush, and even some scrubby-looking cacti.

In short order, the trail switchbacks to the right to climb out of the canyon, heading up and over Second Falls. (If you want to get closer to Second Falls, a spur trail will take you to its edge.) Once you're above the falls, take the trail on the left signed for Big Pine Lakes. You stay along the North Fork of Big Pine Creek and pass a John Muir Wilderness boundary sign. Cutoff trails lead to fishing and swimming holes.

view of Big Pine Canyon from the trail near First Falls

One mile from Second Falls you reach your final destination at Cienega Mirth, a lush, meadowy area that is rife with lupine, larkspur, and leopard lilies in July. The mirth is fed by a spring, which, in conjunction with the proximity of the creek, can make the area quite swampy until late summer. The wetness produces spectacular wildflowers but also, alas, prolific mosquitoes. Near the creek at Cienega Mirth is a beautiful stone cabin that was built by movie star Lon Chaney. Today, it's a backcountry ranger residence.

If you notice other hikers in North Fork Big Pine Canyon carrying axes and climbing equipment, it's because they are following this same route to Palisades Glacier, the southernmost glacier in the United States and the largest in the Sierra Nevada. The glacier is about two miles long, one mile wide, and several hundred feet thick. The route to the upper reaches of the glacier is for experienced alpine climbers only; it's a nine-mile one-way trip just to its lower edge. If you think you were out of breath on your trip, consider this: The total elevation gain from the trailhead to the glacier's edge is a whopping 5,000 feet.

Options
At 1.5 miles past Cienega Mirth is the first of the Big Pine Canyon lakes, called simply First Lake. Second Lake lies .25 mile beyond. Both of these glacially fed lakes are worth seeing, but keep in mind this means a nine-mile round-trip.

Information and Contact
There is no fee. For more information and/or a map of Inyo National Forest, contact the White Mountain Ranger Station, 798 North Main Street, Bishop, CA 93514, 760/873-2500, website: www.fs.fed.us/r5/inyo.

Directions
From Bishop, drive 15 miles south on U.S. 395 to Big Pine. Turn right (west) on Crocker Street, which becomes Glacier Lodge Road, and drive 10.5 miles to Glacier Lodge and the Big Pine Canyon Trailhead at the end of the road. Day-hikers may park in the day-use area near the lodge store.

6. SHADOW OF THE GIANTS

Sierra National Forest, off Highway 41 near Oakhurst

Total distance: 1.2 miles round-trip
Type of trail: Rolling terrain

Hiking time: 30 minutes
Best season: May–October

If you're vacationing in the Bass Lake area and you want to see the giant sequoias, you have two choices: Drive to the southern entrance of Yosemite National Park and get in the long line of cars to see the Mariposa Grove, or drive to the Nelder Grove in Sierra National Forest and take a peaceful hike on Shadow of the Giants Trail.

Because of its unique resources and features, Shadow of the Giants is a federally designated National Recreation Trail. Less than 100 of these trails are found in California. That's one way to know that the hike will be good before you even get there. In addition, for sheer numbers of big trees and blissful peace and quiet, the trail beats the heck out of the sequoia groves in Yosemite National Park.

A variety of plants grows in the understory of giant sequoias.

It's not uncommon to walk the one-mile interpretive trail completely alone. The self-guided signs along the trail are interesting and informative, and the babble of Nelder Creek is the perfect accompaniment to the huge, majestic trees. In addition to the sequoias, the forest is filled with western azaleas, dogwoods, incense cedars, wild rose, sugar pines, and white firs.

The trailhead elevation is 5,000 feet, where the air is cool and the trees grow big. How big? You probably already know that sequoias are the largest living things on earth in terms of volume—no other tree combines the great height and diameter of the sequoia. One of the mature trees along this trail is 270 feet tall (about as tall as a 25-story building), and has a circumference at its base of 71 feet. If it were cut down, it would provide 170,000 board-feet of lumber, about enough to build a small town.

Luckily for the giant sequoias, they make lousy lumber. Unlike the giant sequoias' cousins, the coastal redwoods, giant sequoias do not submit well to the lumberman's saw. When felled, they hit the ground with such force that their wood usually shatters. Lumberjacks of the 19th century tried making soft supports for the toppled trees to land on, but the technique wasn't very effective. Although thousands of sequoias were felled in the 1800s, many of the great trees were simply left to waste, or their wood was used for scrap items like fenceposts and pencils.

The Shadow of the Giants Trail makes an easy loop, heading up one side of Nelder Creek, crossing it on a footbridge, and then circling back on the far side. In early summer, you'll find sweet-smelling ceanothus blooming along the trail, plus wild iris and wild rose. You won't see a lot of sequoias at the start of the trail, but by the time you get to the loop's far end, they are everywhere you look.

The largest trees along this trail are between 2,000 and 3,000 years old, which doesn't make them the oldest living things on earth (the ancient bristlecone pine has them beat by a couple thousand years), but it certainly puts them in the venerable category. On the oldest sequoias, the cinnamon-colored bark can grow up to two feet thick, which insulates the tree from cold and helps to protect it from fire.

My favorite fact gleaned from the trail's interpretive signs: The bark of mature sequoias is so soft that squirrels use it to line their nests.

Information and Contact

There is no fee. For more information and/or a map of Sierra National Forest, contact the Bass Lake Ranger Station, 57003 Road 225, North Fork, CA 93643, 559/877-2218, website: www.fs.fed.us/r5/sierra.

Directions

From Oakhurst, drive north on Highway 41 for five miles to Sky Ranch Road (Road 632). Turn east on Sky Ranch Road and drive six miles to the turnoff for Nelder Grove (Sky Ranch Road becomes Road 6S10). Turn left, drive 1.5 miles, then take the left fork signed for Shadow of the Giants. Drive .5 mile to the trailhead.

7. FRESNO DOME

Sierra National Forest, off Highway 41 near Oakhurst

Total distance: 2.0 miles round-trip   **Hiking time:** 1.0 hour

Type of trail: Rolling terrain   **Best season:** May–October

The trail to Fresno Dome is drop-dead gorgeous from the start and gets better as it goes. The stunning vista from this 8,300-foot granite dome is the main attraction on this hike, but you may find it takes you an unusually long time to get there because there is so much beauty to examine along the way.

Trailhead elevation is 8,000 feet, a considerable height for those who are not acclimated. The path begins by traversing a verdant meadow filled with corn lilies, quaking aspens, and lavender shooting stars pointing head-down toward the earth. It's a perfect subalpine meadow, the kind you'd expect to find in Yosemite or the Eastern Sierra. You're only 100 yards from your parked car and already you will feel compelled to stop, observe, and admire.

Soon you enter an old-growth white fir forest, with staghorn moss clinging eight feet off the ground on the trees' fat trunks. The pungently scented bush growing alongside the trail is mountain misery. Because bears like to munch on it, it is also known as bear clover.

When you reach the back side of Fresno Dome, you'll leave the firs behind and find big old Jeffrey pines growing in their place. These perseverant trees are impervious to the wind and exposed slopes; harsh weather doesn't bother them a bit.

The first half-mile of trail is completely level; in the second half-mile, you ascend the dome's sloped back side. Trail cairns (piles of rocks) mark the route where it crosses granite slabs. Children and out-of-shape hikers might have to go a little slow on the ascent, but when they reach the top, they'll feel like champions.

The reward at the summit of Fresno Dome is a top-of-the-world, 360-degree view. Your field of vision is mostly filled with wavelike masses of deep green conifers covering the slopes and valleys of Sierra National Forest. You can just make out a bright blue corner of Bass Lake, as well as the town of Oakhurst and the Central Valley to the west. The real surprise is on the edge of the horizon to the east: a far-off glimpse of the snow-covered peaks of the John Muir Wilderness. From up on top of Fresno Dome, it all looks like heaven.

tree snag on top of Fresno Dome

Information and Contact
There is no fee. For more information and/or a map of Sierra National Forest, contact the Bass Lake Ranger Station, 57003 Road 225, North Fork, CA 93643, 559/877-2218, website: www.fs.fed.us/r5/sierra.

Directions
From Oakhurst, drive north on Highway 41 for five miles to Sky Ranch Road (Road 632). Turn east on Sky Ranch Road, drive approximately 12 miles (Sky Ranch Road becomes Road 6S10 and turns to dirt), then turn left at the sign for Fresno Dome Campground and drive 4.8 miles to the trailhead (it's 2.8 miles past the camp).

8. MONO MEADOW, DORIS & TULE LAKES

Ansel Adams Wilderness, off Kaiser Pass Road near
Mono Hot Springs

Total distance: 5.5 miles round-trip   **Hiking time:** 3.0 hours

Type of trail: Rolling terrain   **Best season:** June–October

---

If you're vacationing anywhere in the vicinity of Mono Hot Springs or
Lake Thomas A. Edison, you are already far away from civilization. If you
want to get a little farther away, take this easy hike to one, two, or three
scenic destinations—all within about five miles. A bonus is that the trailhead is at Mono Hot Springs Resort, so you can end your hike with a soak
in a hot springs bath.

From the trailhead at the resort, just outside the entrance to Mono Hot
Springs Campground, walk .25 mile down a dirt road and enter the Ansel
Adams Wilderness, a land of huge granite boulders, giant conifers, rush-
ing creeks, and high mountain lakes.

You can tailor your trip any way you like, hiking only 1.5 miles round-
trip to Doris Lake, or two miles round-trip to Mono Meadow, or three
miles round-trip to Tule Lake, or combining all of them for a 5.5-mile
jaunt that connects all three destinations. The first trail junction is
reached a half-mile from the end of the dirt road, after a brief climb up a
rocky, sage-covered slope. Turn right there, and in 10 minutes of easy
walking, you're at the rocky shore of Doris Lake.

The lake is long and narrow, and bordered by big, smooth granite boulders, perfect for picnicking or sunbathing. It's difficult, although not impossible, to walk around the entire lake, because much of the shore is
lined with tules and quite boggy. Most people don't bother circumnavi-
gating—instead, they just pick a spot on a boulder and stay there. On
warm days, swimming is popular.

From Doris Lake, backtrack to the trail junction and take the opposite
fork for Tule Lake. You'll gain another low ridge, passing two smaller, un-
named lakes along the way. (They're a few dozen yards off the trail.) At a
second trail junction, bear left for Tule Lake and arrive at its shores in another 15 minutes of walking.

rickety footbridge over Mono Creek

Tule Lake is similar in appearance to Doris Lake, although smaller and with more tules and less granite. It has one standout boulder on its far shore, as wide as a city block and about 10 stories high, with small trees growing out of its rocky perches. Some people fish at Tule Lake, with mixed results. We sat near the lake's edge and watched a flotilla of coots skitter across the lake's surface, their feet never quite leaving the water.

From Tule Lake, backtrack to the second trail junction, and this time take the fork signed for Mono Meadow and Edison Lake. A sign states that Mono Meadow is a mile away, but it's actually slightly less. The meadow is wide, lush, and filled with wildflowers as late as July. At its far end you'll find a trapper's cabin, which was built early in the 20th century and has been restored by the Forest Service.

Just beyond the cabin is Mono Creek, crossed via an old wooden suspension footbridge that sways precariously over the stream. It's begging to be photographed.

When you get back to Mono Hot Springs Resort, pay the day-use fee and take a long soak in one of the natural hot springs tubs, either indoors or out. If that doesn't suit your fancy, have lunch in Mono Hot Springs' funky café instead. The service is decidedly casual, so they won't mind your dirty hiking boots.

Options
The trail continues past the suspension bridge over Mono Creek for two miles to Thomas A. Edison Lake.

Information and Contact

There is no fee. For more information and/or a map of Sierra National Forest, contact the High Sierra Ranger District, P.O. Box 559, Prather, CA 93651, 559/855-5360, website: www.fs.fed.us/r5/sierra.

Directions

From Highway 168 at the eastern edge of Huntington Lake, turn right on Kaiser Pass Road and drive 17 narrow and winding miles to a fork in the road. (Trailers and motor homes are not recommended.) Bear left at the fork for Mono Hot Springs and Edison Lake, drive 1.6 miles, and turn left again. You'll reach Mono Hot Springs Resort in .3 mile. Park your car at the resort, walk past the spa building, and turn right on the dirt road just before the entrance to Mono Hot Springs Campground.

9. TWIN LAKES

Kaiser Wilderness, off Highway 168 near
Huntington Lake

Total distance: 6.4 miles round-trip   **Hiking time:** 3.5 hours

Type of trail: Some steep terrain   **Best season:** June–October

Trails into the Kaiser Wilderness always seem to come with a climb, and the route to Twin Lakes is no exception. But if you're willing to work your heart and lungs a bit, your reward is a spectacular day hike over the top of Kaiser Ridge to scenic Twin Lakes. Although the mileage is greater on this trail than on most others in this book, the well-graded trail and the mountain scenery make the travel distance painless.

The trail is up and down in both directions. You climb from the Highway 168 trailhead to Kaiser Ridge, gaining 800 feet in elevation, then you descend into Twin Lakes' basin, losing 500 feet in elevation. The return trip is just the reverse. Both the ups and the downs are moderate, with plenty of switchbacks, and the reward for topping Kaiser Ridge is a knockout view from Potter Pass.

Begin hiking through a mixed conifer forest, slowly ascending 8,980-foot Kaiser Ridge. Since trailhead elevation is 8,200 feet, you may find that you are breathing harder than you would expect, especially if you

Upper Twin Lake

aren't acclimated. Luckily, abundant red firs and lodgepole pines provide welcome shade.

You'll finish out your climb after two miles, where the trail crosses over the ridge at Potter Pass. Stop at the pass to catch your breath and enjoy the classic Sierra view. Far off to the east, you can see the back side of the Minarets and 13,000-foot Mount Ritter.

It's almost all downhill from the pass to the granite-lined Twin Lakes. The first part of the descent leads you past a flower-filled meadow, with a small stream carving perfect S-turns through its center. Watch for a junction at 2.5 miles; bear left for Twin Lakes. The first Twin Lake (Lower) is reached .5 mile from the junction, but just admire it and keep walking, because Upper Twin Lake is far lovelier and only .2 mile farther. Large Upper Twin Lake is backed by a wall of granite and has a big rock island in its center. Take a walk around the edges of the lake, find a private spot among the boulders and wildflowers, and call it your own.

Options
The hike to Potter Pass alone is rewarding for its wide vistas and excellent wildflower viewing (usually in July). This makes a four-mile round-trip. On the other hand, if you have energy to burn, you can continue past Upper Twin Lake to George Lake, 1.3 miles farther.

Information and Contact

There is no fee. For more information and/or a map of Sierra National Forest, contact the High Sierra Ranger District, P.O. Box 559, Prather, CA 93651, 559/855-5360, website: www.fs.fed.us/r5/sierra.

Directions

From Fresno, drive northeast on Highway 168 through Clovis for 70 miles to Huntington Lake, then turn right on Kaiser Pass Road and drive 4.8 miles. A large parking area is located on the south side of the road; the trail begins on the north side.

10. RANCHERIA FALLS

Sierra National Forest, off Highway 168 near
Huntington Lake

Total distance: 2.0 miles round-trip   **Hiking time:** 1.0 hour

Type of trail: Rolling terrain

Best season: Good whenever the trail is snow-free, but best from snowmelt until mid-July

The Rancheria Falls National Recreation Trail is so well-groomed, it's hike-able in tennis shoes—even little four-inch-long Reeboks made for three-year-old feet. I know, because I found one alongside the trail, and a few moments later, I came upon its owner, walking along with one shoe on and one shoe off. She seemed nonplussed by the missing sneaker, but feigned gratitude for its return.

Why worry about footwear when you're hiking to Rancheria Falls? There's so much else to concern yourself with. This smooth and wide path follows a gentle uphill grade to the waterfall. You'll share the trail with a mélange of butterflies and noisy cicadas flitting by. The mostly sun-filled route leads through an understory of gooseberry, chinquapin, and colorful wildflowers—purple lupine, pink larkspur, and fiery red Indian paintbrush. Occasional fir trees provide shade.

You don't see or hear any water until you are 100 yards from Rancheria Falls. Your first view of it can take your breath away—the waterfall plummets 150 feet over a wide rock ledge, then continues down-canyon in a long, boisterous cascade. During high water, as Rancheria Creek's flow hits smaller ledges below its lip, the water pushes off and sprays outward like fireworks exploding. It's the kind of sight you can watch for a long, long time.

From the trail's end, you can climb over rocks and pick your viewing spot, either closer to or farther from the voluminous spray. Even if there's a small crowd here (typical in summer because of Rancheria Falls' proximity to popular Huntington Lake), you can usually find a private spot downstream. Did you pack along your sandwiches? Now that's good planning.

© ANN MARIE BROWN

Rancheria Falls is an easy-to-reach destination near Huntington Lake.

Options

Several easy hiking trails exist around the shore of Huntington Lake. Try the Coarsegrass Meadow Trail that begins near Huntington Lake Resort's marina (west end of the lake). A five-mile round-trip leads to flower-lined Coarsegrass Meadow.

Information and Contact

There is no fee. For more information and/or a map of Sierra National Forest, contact the High Sierra Ranger District, P.O. Box 559, Prather, CA 93651, 559/855-5360, website: www.fs.fed.us/r5/sierra.

Directions

From Fresno, drive northeast on Highway 168 through Clovis for 70 miles, past Shaver Lake. At .5 mile past Sierra Summit Ski Area (and .5 mile before reaching Huntington Lake), take the right turnoff signed for Rancheria Falls (Road 8S31). Follow the dirt road 1.3 miles to the signed trailhead at a sharp curve in the road. Park off the road.

11. INDIAN POOLS

Sierra National Forest, off Highway 168 near
Huntington Lake

Total distance: 2.0 miles round-trip | **Hiking time:** 1.0 hour
Type of trail: Mostly flat terrain | **Best season:** June–October

---

Some days are swimming hole days, the kind of days when nothing feels as good as a dip in a cool mountain pool. If you're vacationing in the Huntington Lake area, the Indian Pools by Sierra Summit Ski Area are just the place to take an easy hike, then dive into a refreshing mountain stream.

The trail requires something more like a walk than a hike. It skirts along the edge of Big Creek in Sierra National Forest, one of the major feeder streams for popular Huntington Lake. Locating the trail can be a little tricky for first-timers, because the path starts at the back end of Sierra Summit Ski Area. You have to drive a half-mile through the ski resort complex to find the trailhead, and while doing this, most people become convinced they are in the wrong place. Keep driving to the end of the very last parking lot, near some mobile homes and trailers, and you'll see the trail sign. Occasionally the ski resort parking area is closed. Then you must park along Highway 168 and walk in.

At the trailhead, follow the single-track trail signed as Indian Pools (not the wide dirt road). The trail is perfectly level for the first quarter-mile as it ambles through the forest. It meets the creek, then climbs almost imperceptibly alongside it. Flowers bloom in profusion along Big Creek's streambanks, particularly Indian paintbrush and larkspur. You'll likely pass some anglers on this trail, and it's easy to see why: Small trout ply the waters of Big Creek.

The official trail ends at a huge, clear pool at .75 mile. You can watch people dive off the rocks into this deep pool while you work up the courage to plunge in and join them. If you can't convince yourself to brave the chilly water just yet, follow the informal use trail that continues upstream. Boy Scouts have carefully marked the path with piles of stones. A short distance farther are quieter, more private pools.

swimming in the Indian Pools near Huntington Lake

Options

For a look at more pools and cascades, follow the easy Lower Kaiser Loop Trail along Line Creek in early to midsummer. The trailhead is at Upper Billy Creek Campground on Huntington Lake.

Information and Contact

There is no fee. For more information and/or a map of Sierra National Forest, contact the High Sierra Ranger District, P.O. Box 559, Prather, CA 93651, 559/855-5360, website: www.fs.fed.us/r5/sierra.

Directions

From Fresno, drive northeast on Highway 168 through Clovis for 70 miles, past Shaver Lake. One mile before reaching Huntington Lake, turn right at the signed Sierra Summit Ski Area. Drive .5 mile to the far end of the ski area parking lot, near some mobile homes and trailers. The signed trailhead is on the back side of the last parking lot.

12. PANORAMIC POINT & PARK RIDGE

Kings Canyon National Park, off Highway 180
near Grant Grove

Total distance: 4.6 miles round-trip   **Hiking time:** 2.5 hours

Type of trail: Rolling terrain   **Best season:** May–October

---

You've driven a long way from home, you've just arrived in Grant Grove in Kings Canyon National Park, and you want to get out of the car and start hiking immediately. If you drive just two miles more, following the road behind Grant Grove's cabins and restaurant to the Panoramic Point parking area, you can say adios to your automobile and set out on the trail.

Start your hike with a warm-up: Take the 300-yard paved walk uphill to Panoramic Point, elevation 7,250 feet. The point delivers what its name implies: a stunning panoramic vista. An interpretive display names the many peaks and valleys you can see across Kings Canyon and Sequoia National Parks, including the big pointy one, Mount Goddard, at 13,560 feet.

From Panoramic Point, take the dirt trail that leads to the right along the ridge. The trail starts out level and then switchbacks uphill for a couple of turns, following the ridgeline. Plenty of boulders provide spots where you can sit and enjoy the view. The ridge is peppered with wildflower blooms in June and July.

At a junction with a dirt road, follow the road to the left for about 50 yards, then pick up the trail again (on your left). If you want to cut some distance off your trip, you can stay on the road and follow it all the way to the Park Ridge Fire Lookout. The road and trail run roughly parallel, but the road is more direct. The trail, however, has much finer views.

Following the trail, you'll meet the dirt road again about 100 yards below the lookout. Turn left and walk the final uphill stretch. At the fire lookout, check out the nifty outdoor shower at its base. If someone is stationed in the tower, he or she may give you permission to come upstairs. You can chat with the nice lookout person, sign the visitor register, and enjoy a view surprisingly different from what you saw at Panoramic Point. Your field of vision includes the postcardlike Sierra Crest to the east, but you can also look down at the town of Pinehurst and the Central

Valley to the west. On the clearest days, you can see all the way to the Coast Range, 100 miles westward. The lookout tower is operated only during the fire season, usually from May to October.

For your return trip, you can walk back down the dirt road and then take the trail back to Panoramic Point, or follow the dirt road all the way downhill to the parking lot. If you're surprised to see some recent logging activity alongside this road, it's because you've crossed the border of the national park and entered Giant Sequoia National Monument, where logging is still permitted.

Options
Follow the dirt road up to the lookout tower and back, which will cut 1.5 miles off your round-trip.

Information and Contact
There is a $10 entrance fee per vehicle at Sequoia and Kings Canyon National Parks, good for seven days. Maps are available at park entrance stations or at the address below. For more information, contact Sequoia and Kings Canyon National Parks, 47050 Generals Highway, Three Rivers, CA 93271-9651, 559/565-3341 or 559/335-2856 (Grant Grove Visitors Center), website: www.nps.gov/seki.

Directions
From Fresno, drive east on Highway 180 for 55 miles to the Big Stump Entrance Station at Kings Canyon National Park. Continue 1.5 miles and turn left for Grant Grove. Drive 1.5 miles to Grant Grove Village and turn right by the visitors center and store. Follow the road past some cabins, then take the right fork for Panoramic Point. It's 2.3 miles from the visitors center to Panoramic Point.

13. ZUMWALT MEADOW LOOP

Kings Canyon National Park, off Highway 180
near Cedar Grove

Total distance: 1.5 miles round-trip
Type of trail: Mostly flat terrain

Hiking time: 1.0 hour
Best season: May–October

What's the prettiest easy hike in Kings Canyon National Park? Zumwalt Meadow Loop Trail wins hands down. Starting with the incredible scenery on the drive from Grant Grove to the Zumwalt Meadow trailhead deep in Kings Canyon, you know you're in for something special. Then you amble down a scenic trail alongside the South Fork Kings River. It's a delightfully easy walk, suitable for hikers of all abilities, with surprises at every curve and turn of the trail.

From the parking area, walk downstream along the river to a picturesque suspension footbridge, then cross it and walk back upstream. The loop begins at an obvious fork, and you can hike it in either direction. Bear right at the fork; the path traverses a boulder field of jumbled rocks, the evidence of a powerful rockslide. The trail is cut right through the rubble, which tumbled down from the Grand Sentinel, elevation 8,504 feet.

As you walk among the rocks, you have lovely views across the meadow and river of the cliffs on the far side of the canyon. Vistas of 8,717-foot North Dome are as awe-inspiring as the views of the Grand Sentinel on your side of the canyon.

Looping back on the north side of the trail, you come out at the edge of a meadow in a dense, waist-high fern forest. We were surprised by a deer who was standing up to her neck in the ferns, nearly hidden from view. Walk downstream alongside the river with the meadow on your left. Where the trail reaches a marshy area, it leads up and over a wooden walkway, and sadly, you've finished out the loop.

Options

To extend your walk, you can continue 1.6 miles downstream to Roaring River Falls. From the suspension bridge, follow the trail downstream instead of crossing the bridge to the parking lot.

South Fork Kings River by Zumwalt Meadow

Information and Contact

There is a $10 entrance fee per vehicle at Sequoia and Kings Canyon National Parks, good for seven days. Maps are available at park entrance stations or at the address below. For more information, contact Sequoia and Kings Canyon National Parks, 47050 Generals Highway, Three Rivers, CA 93271-9651, 559/565-3341, or 559/335-2856 (Grant Grove Visitors Center), website: www.nps.gov/seki.

Directions

From Fresno, drive east on Highway 180 for 55 miles to the Big Stump Entrance Station at Kings Canyon National Park. Continue 1.5 miles and turn left for Grant Grove and Cedar Grove. Continue 36 miles on Highway 180 to the parking area for Zumwalt Meadow on the right side of the road.

14. REDWOOD CANYON

Kings Canyon National Park, off Highway 180
near Grant Grove

Total distance: 4.0 miles round-trip **Hiking time:** 2.0 hours

Type of trail: Rolling terrain **Best season:** May–October

You visited the General Sherman Tree, the Washington Tree, and the General Grant Tree in Sequoia and Kings Canyon National Parks—the three largest trees on earth. You were impressed, of course. But now you'd like to see some giant sequoias that are free of asphalt and fences, and thriving in the same unaltered woodland that they've known for two or three thousand years.

Head for Redwood Canyon in Kings Canyon National Park, a short drive from Grant Grove and the Highway 180 park entrance. Several loop trips are possible in this sequoia-laden area, but one of the best hikes is just an out-and-back walk on Redwood Canyon Trail, paralleling Redwood Creek. The beauty begins before you even start walking. On the last mile of the drive to the trailhead, the road winds through giant sequoias that are so close, you can reach out your car window and touch them.

From the parking area, the Redwood Canyon Trail leads downhill. In .3 mile, you reach a junction and head right. You may notice that this giant sequoia grove is far more lush with foliage than others you've seen. Because the grove is situated alongside Redwood Creek, the sequoias grow amid a dense background of dogwoods, firs, ceanothus, and mountain misery. The canyon is reminiscent of the damp coastal redwood forests of northwestern California, instead of the typically drier mountain slopes that are home to Sierra redwoods or sequoias.

Although the standing sequoias in Redwood Canyon are impressive, some of the fallen ones along the trail are really amazing. Since they are laying down, you get a close-up look at their immense girth and thick bark. It's easy to see how the trees could shatter under their own weight when they hit the ground.

As you hike, consider this: The first giant sequoias started growing about 130 million years ago. For many thousands of years, the trees ranged widely all over the Sierra, but climate changes slowly reduced their habitat to only 70 small groves. Each giant sequoia you see here in Redwood Canyon is one in a total population of less than 60,000 mature trees.

It's a humbling experience to stand among the giants in Redwood Canyon.

Be sure to hike the full two miles to the stream crossing of Redwood Creek. Some of the best tree specimens are there by the crossing; others are near a junction with Sugar Bowl Loop Trail. (Look for a cluster of about 10 giant sequoias, grouped close together like ancient friends.)

In late June, we saw many wildflowers blooming on the forest floor: orange and yellow paintbrush, pink wild rose, and purple lupine. Hummingbirds were slaking their thirst with nectar from the plentiful blossoms. Keep your eyes open for wildlife sightings, too. As we hiked, we surprised two black bears who were drinking from the stream; they dashed off when they heard us coming.

No bridge crosses Redwood Creek; hikers looping through the canyon have to ford the stream. But for this hike, you needn't bother. Instead, just turn around and retrace your steps. The return trip is all uphill, but it's easier than you'd expect.

Options
Rockhop across or ford Redwood Creek and return via a loop around Redwood Canyon, a 6.5-mile round-trip. Highlights along the return leg of the loop include the Hart Tree, the largest tree in the grove, and the Tunnel Log, which you can walk through.

Information and Contact

There is a $10 entrance fee per vehicle at Sequoia and Kings Canyon National Parks, good for seven days. Maps are available at park entrance stations or at the address below. For more information, contact Sequoia and Kings Canyon National Parks, 47050 Generals Highway, Three Rivers, CA 93271-9651, 559/565-3341, or 559/335-2856 (Grant Grove Visitors Center), website: www.nps.gov/seki.

Directions

From Fresno, drive east on Highway 180 for 55 miles to the Big Stump Entrance Station at Kings Canyon National Park. Continue 1.5 miles and turn right on the Generals Highway, heading for Sequoia National Park. Drive approximately three miles on the Generals Highway to Quail Flat (signed for Hume Lake to the left). Turn right on the dirt road to Redwood Saddle and drive 1.5 miles to the parking lot. Start hiking on the Redwood Canyon Trail.

15. BUENA VISTA PEAK

Kings Canyon National Park, off Highway 180
near Grant Grove

Total distance: 2.0 miles round-trip   **Hiking time:** 1.0 hour

Type of trail: Rolling terrain   **Best season:** May–October

Most park visitors stop at the drive-up Kings Canyon Overlook, where they get out of their cars (or just roll down the windows) and admire the roadside vista of "the second largest roadless landscape in the lower 48 states." That's what the sign says, and without question, it's an awesome view encompassing much of the John Muir and Monarch Wildernesses. Some of the highlights you see from the overlook include Spanish Mountain, Mount McGee, Mount Goddard, and Finger Peak, each attaining heights of 10,000 to 12,000 feet. The summit that everyone points out is the phallus-shaped Obelisk at 9,700 feet (it's easy to tell which one that is).

But with all the people stopping at the Kings Canyon Overlook, few bother to hike the easy trail to Buena Vista Peak located just across the road. On the Buena Vista Peak Trail, you get all the same views as at the

A hiker stands atop the boulder-lined summit of Buena Vista Peak.

roadside vista (and more), plus a chance at a private picnic spot on a wide slab of granite overlooking the scene.

Buena Vista Peak is a granite dome, topping out at 7,603 feet, one of the highest points west of the Generals Highway. (East of the Generals Highway, the peaks fall into a much taller category.) The dome's summit offers 360-degree views, including a sea of conifers and the hazy, sometimes smoggy foothills and valley to the southwest, and the snow-capped peaks of the John Muir and Monarch Wildernesses to the east. Pick your vista; once on top of the dome, you can situate yourself so you are looking in any direction you please.

It's an easy half-hour walk up the gently sloped back side of the dome, passing through a forest of pine and fir, manzanita, ceanothus, and sage. The most interesting feature along the short trail, aside from its first-class destination, is the odd piles of granite scattered here and there. Check out the giant boulder sculpture in the first .2 mile of trail—it's a big flat rock with three large round rocks balanced side-by-side on top, looking as if they were placed there on display.

At the top of the dome, you can walk around on its wide summit, taking in all possible perspectives. Pick your spot for picnicking, sunbathing, or philosophizing, all of which are good activities on Buena Vista Peak.

Options
Drive 2.5 miles south on the Generals Highway and hike the trail to Big Baldy, a mostly level five-mile round-trip. More views await from the top of this even larger granite dome.

Information and Contact
There is a $10 entrance fee per vehicle at Sequoia and Kings Canyon National Parks, good for seven days. Maps are available at park entrance stations or at the address below. For more information, contact Sequoia and Kings Canyon National Parks, 47050 Generals Highway, Three Rivers, CA 93271-9651, 559/565-3341, or 559/335-2856 (Grant Grove Visitors Center), website: www.nps.gov/seki.

Directions
From Fresno, drive east on Highway 180 for 55 miles to the Big Stump Entrance Station at Kings Canyon National Park. Continue 1.5 miles and turn right on the Generals Highway, heading for Sequoia National Park. Drive approximately five miles on the Generals Highway to the Buena Vista Peak Trailhead on the right, across the road and slightly beyond the large pullout for the Kings Canyon Overlook.

16. LITTLE BALDY

Sequoia National Park, off the Generals Highway
near Lodgepole

Total distance: 3.6 miles round-trip   **Hiking time:** 2.0 hours
Type of trail: Rolling terrain   **Best season:** May–October

Along this stretch of the Generals Highway, there are so many big pieces of granite you can hike on, it's hard to know where to begin. The Little Baldy Trail is an excellent starting point. It's a little more challenging than the Buena Vista Peak Trail (see Hike 15 in this chapter), but less so than the nearby Big Baldy Trail, and it offers similar mind-boggling views.

In fact, some claim that Little Baldy's view of the Silliman Crest, the

Great Western Divide, Castle Rocks, Moro Rock, the Kaweah River canyon, and the San Joaquin foothills is the best panorama in the park. A bonus is that you can also view Big Baldy to the northeast from this trail—a perspective that you don't get from anywhere else.

Like other peaks in the area, Little Baldy is a granite dome, with a smooth rounded summit that tops out at 8,044 feet. The trail to reach it has several long switchbacks that make the 600-foot gain from the trailhead quite manageable.

Start your trip at Little Baldy Saddle, right along the highway at 7,400 feet in elevation. The only disappointment on this trail is that you can hear some road noise, which doesn't leave you for almost a half-hour of hiking. You're compensated with a fine view of Big Baldy about .3 mile up the trail (look over your left shoulder), and by the lovely wildflowers and ferns that grow enthusiastically alongside the path. This trail rates high for having an exemplary display of lupine in early summer. The flowers bloom dark purple right alongside the trail, close enough to lean over and put your nose in.

As you climb, Little Baldy Trail gets rockier and more exposed, and you start to see the harbingers of the high country—Jeffrey pines. Although your trail initially headed north, the switchbacks you've tackled have actually deposited you south of your starting point. Vistas open up wider, giving you a look at far-off snow-covered peaks.

Before you know it, you're on Little Baldy's summit, with a front-row view of the high mountains of the national parks. Look for well-named Chimney Rock, an easy landmark to spot. In addition, there's an excellent view of the massive Great Western Divide, as well as Tokopah Valley to the east and the San Joaquin Valley to the west.

Options
Drive north for 1.5 miles to Dorst Campground and take a hike out and back on the Muir Grove Trail, a 4.6-mile round-trip. The trail leads from the far west end of the campground to a peaceful grove of giant sequoias.

Information and Contact
There is a $10 entrance fee per vehicle at Sequoia and Kings Canyon National Parks, good for seven days. Maps are available at park entrance stations or at the address below. For more information, contact Sequoia and Kings Canyon National Parks, 47050 Generals Highway, Three Rivers, CA 93271-9651, 559/565-3341, or 559/335-2856 (Grant Grove Visitors Center), website: www.nps.gov/seki.

Directions

From Fresno, drive east on Highway 180 for 55 miles to the Big Stump Entrance Station at Kings Canyon National Park. Continue 1.5 miles and turn right on the Generals Highway, heading for Sequoia National Park. Drive approximately 18 miles south on the Generals Highway to the Little Baldy trailhead on the left, 1.5 miles past Dorst Campground.

17. TOKOPAH FALLS

Sequoia National Park, off the Generals Highway near Lodgepole

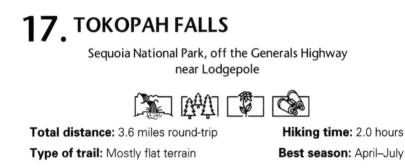

Total distance: 3.6 miles round-trip

Hiking time: 2.0 hours

Type of trail: Mostly flat terrain

Best season: April–July

Tokopah Falls is hands-down the best waterfall in Sequoia and Kings Canyon National Parks. To get the most out of your hike to the falls, head to Lodgepole Campground and the Tokopah Falls trailhead in late spring or early summer, when the waterfall is a showering spectacle.

Sure, the trail can be crowded. Why wouldn't it be? The walk to the falls is only 1.8 miles of level trail through gorgeous High Sierra scenery, culminating at the base of 1,200-foot-high Tokopah Falls. But if you follow the cardinal rule for popular outdoor destinations and start hiking early in the morning, the crowds will still be sleeping in their tents. You can be out to the falls and back before most people have finished brushing their teeth.

The trail offers almost as many rewards as its destination. In a little more than a mile and a half, you get incredible views of the Watchtower, a 1,600-foot-tall glacially carved cliff on the south side of Tokopah Valley. Your perspective on the Watchtower changes with every few steps you take. Then there's Tokopah Valley itself, with Tokopah Falls pouring down the smooth back wall of its U-shape. Tokopah Valley is similar in geological type and appearance to Yosemite Valley, formed partially by the river flowing in its center but mostly by slow-moving glaciers.

The Tokopah Falls Trail also provides a near guarantee of seeing some wildlife, specifically yellow-bellied marmots, the largest and most charming member of the squirrel family. The marmots' great abundance in this area is due in part to the proximity of Lodgepole Campground and the furry creatures' great love of food. (Don't give them any handouts.) You'll have dozens of chances to photograph the cute little guys, or just to admire their beautiful blond coats as they sun themselves on boulders or stand on their back legs and whistle.

The trail is a mix of conifers and granite and follows close to the Marble Fork of the Kaweah River. It leads gently uphill all the way to the falls, then downhill all the way back. If the route seems rather rocky at the start, don't fret; its surface changes. Sometimes the trail winds along a soft forest floor of conifer needles, other times

yellow-bellied marmot, Tokopah Falls Trail

it travels over bridges that cross tiny feeder creeks, and still other times it traverses meadows overflowing with ferns, orange columbine, yellow violets, and purple nightshade. The trail passes through so many different habitats, you can find 40 different kinds of wildflowers along its brief length.

The final .25 mile crosses a rockslide area and gives you wide-open views of Tokopah Falls' impressive 1,200-foot height. The trail has been dynamited into the granite; in one section you must duck your head as you walk under a ledge. The trail ends just before the edge of the waterfall, which drops over fractured granite. Choose a rock to sit on and marvel at the cacophony of cascading water, but don't get too close. Tokopah flows fast, and can be dangerous in springtime.

Options

Drive three miles south of the Lodgepole Campground turnoff on the Generals Highway to the Wolverton trailhead and parking area. From

Wolverton, you can hike the five-mile Alta Trail Loop by combining Lakes Trail and Alta Trail.

Information and Contact

There is a $10 entrance fee per vehicle at Sequoia and Kings Canyon National Parks, good for seven days. Maps are available at park entrance stations or at the address below. For more information, contact Sequoia and Kings Canyon National Parks, 47050 Generals Highway, Three Rivers, CA 93271-9651, 559/565-3341, or 559/335-2856 (Grant Grove Visitors Center), website: www.nps.gov/seki.

Directions

From Fresno, drive east on Highway 180 for 55 miles to the Big Stump Entrance Station at Kings Canyon National Park. Continue 1.5 miles and turn right on the Generals Highway, heading for Sequoia National Park. Drive approximately 25 miles on the Generals Highway to the Lodgepole Campground turnoff, then drive .7 mile to the Log Bridge Area of Lodgepole Camp. Park in the large lot just before the bridge over the Marble Fork Kaweah River. Walk across the bridge to the trailhead on your right.

18. CRESCENT MEADOW & EAGLE VIEW

Sequoia National Park, off the Generals Highway
near Giant Forest

Total distance: 4.5 miles round-trip   **Hiking time:** 2.5 hours
Type of trail: Rolling terrain   **Best season:** May–October

John Muir called Crescent Meadow "the gem of the Sierras," and when you see it, you'll know why. The meadow is more than a mile long and surrounded by giant sequoias, and it sits almost side by side with equally large and beautiful Log Meadow. With a short hike from the dual meadows' lush, grassy edges, you can find yourself at aptly named Eagle View, looking out over the peaks and valleys of the Great Western Divide.

From the eastern edge of the parking area, follow the paved trail for 200 yards, and quickly you're at the southern edge of Crescent Meadow. Take the right fork and head for Log Meadow, saving Crescent Meadow

view of Moro Rock from Eagle View on the High Sierra Trail

for later. Bear right again, heading around the far side of Log Meadow. Big ferns line the path, and magnificent giant sequoias stand guard at the meadow's edges. Where you cross Log Meadow's tiny stream on a footbridge, look closely and you may see small trout swimming by.

At Log Meadow's far end, you'll find Tharp's Log. A big downed sequoia log was the homestead of Hale Tharp, the first white man to enter this forest. Accompanied by two Yokut Indians, Tharp arrived here in 1858. He grazed cattle and horses in the meadows and built his modest home inside this fire-hollowed sequoia. Tharp lived in his log during almost 30 summers, from 1861 to 1890. You can look inside it and see his bed, fireplace, and dining room table, and the door and windows he fashioned.

From Tharp's Log, continue your loop back to Crescent Meadow and around its west side. Instead of heading back to the parking lot, finish out your loop by returning to the first junction you passed at the southern edge of Crescent Meadow. Take the signed fork that leads up the ridge on the High Sierra Trail, heading to your left. The High Sierra Trail is a popular trans-Sierra route that eventually leads to Mount Whitney, the highest peak in the contiguous United States. You'll follow it for .5 mile to Eagle View, gaining the ridge and edge-of-the-world vistas.

Eagle View is only .25 mile down the ridgeline at an unsigned but obvious lookout. From this high point, you get a fascinating look at Moro Rock to your right, Castle Rocks straight ahead, and dozens of peaks and ridges of the Great Western Divide far across the canyon. The vistas are so inspiring that you might just decide someday to keep walking all the way to Mount Whitney.

Options
Hike as far as you like on the High Sierra Trail. Views are exceptional and the trail stays mostly level for several miles.

Information and Contact
There is a $10 entrance fee per vehicle at Sequoia and Kings Canyon National Parks, good for seven days. Maps are available at park entrance stations or at the address below. For more information, contact Sequoia and Kings Canyon National Parks, 47050 Generals Highway, Three Rivers, CA 93271-9651, 559/565-3341 or 559/565-3135 (Foothills Visitors Center), website: www.nps.gov/seki.

Directions
From Fresno, drive east on Highway 180 for 55 miles to the Big Stump Entrance Station at Kings Canyon National Park. Continue 1.5 miles and turn right on the Generals Highway, heading for Sequoia National Park. Drive approximately 30 miles on the Generals Highway, past Lodgepole and Wolverton, to the Giant Forest area of Sequoia National Park. Just beyond the Giant Forest museum, turn left on Crescent Meadow Road and drive 3.5 miles to the Crescent Meadow parking area. Begin hiking from the trailhead on the east (right) side of the parking lot.

19. COLD SPRINGS NATURE TRAIL

Sequoia National Park, off Highway 198 in Mineral King

Total distance: 2.5 miles round-trip

Type of trail: Mostly flat terrain

Hiking time: 1.5 hours

Best season: June–October

The first thing you need to know about Cold Springs Nature Trail is that it's set in the Mineral King Valley in the southern reaches of Sequoia National Park. Access to Mineral King is limited to one long and winding 25-mile road, so the area doesn't see the heavy visitation that Grant Grove and Giant Forest get. You have to make an effort to get to Mineral King, but whatever it takes, it's worth it.

Surrounded by 12,000-foot granite and shale peaks, Mineral King is a glacial-cut valley and home to the headwaters of the East Fork Kaweah River. The area was slated for development as a ski resort in the 1960s, but through one of the great conservation battles of our time, the proposal was defeated and Mineral King became a part of Sequoia National Park.

Now, you might not expect much from a campground nature trail, but because this is Mineral King, Cold Springs Nature Trail will far exceed your expectations. Not only is it lined with wildflowers along the East Fork Kaweah River and informative signposts that teach you to identify junipers, red and white firs, cottonwoods, and aspens, but the views of the high peaks of the Sawtooth Ridge are glorious. The nature trail is only .5 mile long, but from the end of it a path continues along the East Fork Kaweah River, heading into the heart of Mineral King Valley.

If you are camping at Cold Springs Campground, just start hiking by campsite 6. If you're not, park your car by the ranger station across the road, then walk in to the campground. Along the short interpretive section of the trail, you'll learn about native gooseberries or currants, how to identify red and white firs by their cones, and that the junipers along the trail are as much as 1,000 years old.

When you reach the last interpretive sign, continue hiking along the river. Wildflowers found along the streambanks include asters, columbine, and bog orchids. There are many lovely pools and cascades to admire when the stream flow is high, accented by colorful rocks shimmering just beneath the surface.

If you like the color show from the flowers and the rocky riverbed, try taking this walk right before sunset, when the peaks surrounding the valley turn every imaginable shade of pink, orange, and coral, reflecting the sun setting in the west. This is the kind of sight that will keep you coming back to Mineral King year after year.

Options

Another easy hiking trail in the Mineral King area is the Hockett Trail that begins at Atwell Mill Campground (near site number 16). A two-mile hike leads to the East Fork Kaweah River Bridge, a scenic spot with many sculptured granite pools, small cascades, and giant sequoias growing along the streambanks.

Information and Contact

There is a $10 entrance fee per vehicle at Sequoia and Kings Canyon National Parks, good for seven days. Maps are available at park entrance stations or at the address below. For more information, contact Sequoia and Kings Canyon National Parks, 47050 Generals Highway, Three Rivers, CA 93271-9651, 559/565-3341, or 559/565-3135 (Foothills Visitors Center), website: www.nps.gov/seki.

Directions

From Visalia, drive east on Highway 198 for 38 miles to Mineral King Road, 2.5 miles east of Three Rivers. (If you reach the Ash Mountain Entrance Station, you've gone too far.) Turn right on Mineral King Road and drive 23.5 miles to Cold Springs Campground on the right. The trail begins near campsite 6. If you aren't staying in the camp, park your car by the Mineral King Ranger Station across the road.

20. FAREWELL GAP TRAIL TO ASPEN FLAT

Sequoia National Park, off Highway 198 in
Mineral King Valley

Total distance: 2.0 miles round-trip

Hiking time: 1.0 hour

Type of trail: Mostly flat terrain

Best season: May–October

The glacial-cut Mineral King Valley, a peaceful paradise of meadows, streams, and historic cabins, has to be one of the most scenic places in the West, possibly the world. By following Farewell Gap Trail on an easy stroll along Mineral King's canyon floor, you meander past waterfalls and alongside the headwaters of the East Fork Kaweah River, in the shelter of thousand-foot cliffs.

You park your car a short distance from the actual trailhead, which is located by the Mineral King pack station. Leave your car at the Eagle/Mosquito parking area, then walk back down the road and cross the bridge over the East Fork Kaweah River. Turn right on the dirt road to the pack station, walk past the corral, and you'll see the trailhead for Farewell Gap Trail.

The path begins as a wide dirt road, heading straight into the heart of the canyon, with the headwaters of the East Fork Kaweah River flowing by on your right. You may see anglers working the river, mostly fly-fishing.

It's almost a guarantee that you'll see deer munching the grasses along the riverbanks or grazing on the mountain slopes. Mineral King Valley is famous for having an abundance of wildlife, most notably deer, yellow-bellied marmots, and sage grouse. The latter are large, bold birds who are likely to stare at you instead of flying away.

You see and hear a waterfall almost immediately—it's Tufa Falls on Spring Creek, dashing off the far canyon wall just across from the pack station. A series of 12,000-foot peaks tower over the canyon, their shale and granite surfaces colored rust, red, white, and black. The proximity of the river and the plentiful summer sunshine encourage many wildflowers to bloom in the canyon. Is this paradise? Maybe, just maybe.

Farewell Gap Trail stays level as it traces a path up the canyon. At one mile from the trailhead, Crystal Creek pours down the mountainside on your left. Your destination is close at hand; shortly after crossing Crystal Creek, take the right fork off the main trail. (It may have branches or logs across it; just go around the logs.)

The spur trail brings you closer to the river, where you follow a narrow path to Aspen Flat, a lovely grove of quaking aspens. Nearby is Soda Springs, situated right along the river's edge, where mineral springs bubble up from the ground, turning the damp earth bright orange.

Sit yourself down in the verdant grasses, either in the shade of the aspens or in the sun by Soda Springs.

© ANN MARIE BROWN

Mineral King Valley

Count the wildflowers, try to discern every hue in the canyon walls, and listen to the music of the river.

Options
Return to the main Farewell Gap Trail and hike farther back into the canyon. The trail begins to climb after the Aspen Flat turnoff. Less than one mile away is a series of cascades on Franklin Creek.

Information and Contact
There is a $10 entrance fee per vehicle at Sequoia and Kings Canyon National Parks, good for seven days. Maps are available at park entrance stations or at the address below. For more information, contact Sequoia and Kings Canyon National Parks, 47050 Generals Highway, Three Rivers, CA 93271-9651, 559/565-3341, or 559/565-3135 (Foothills Visitors Center), website: www.nps.gov/seki.

Directions
From Visalia, drive east on Highway 198 for 38 miles to Mineral King Road, 2.5 miles east of Three Rivers. (If you reach the Ash Mountain Entrance Station, you've gone too far.) Turn right on Mineral King Road and drive 25 miles to the end of the road and the Eagle/Mosquito trailhead. (Take the right fork at the end of the road to the parking area.) Walk back out of the parking lot and follow the road to the pack station; the Farewell Gap Trail begins just beyond it.

21. NEEDLES LOOKOUT
Giant Sequoia National Monument, off the Western Divide Highway near Quaking Aspen

Total distance: 5.0 miles round-trip   **Hiking time:** 2.5 hours
Type of trail: Some steep terrain   **Best season:** May–October

This may be the most perfect easy day hike in the southern Sierra. Needles Lookout Trail is just long enough and has just enough of a climb to be challenging, but not overly demanding. More important, it's chockfull of visual rewards.

The trail starts at a sign bearing an old black-and-white photo that shows the fire lookout on top of the Needles rock formation in the 1930s. The first time you see it, even in a photograph, it's hard to believe. The Needles are a pinnacle-like granite formation of towering spires and smooth, narrow domes. You probably noticed their distinctive shape as you drove in on the Western Divide Highway. The Needles Lookout is perched on a series of spindly metal legs high on top of the Needles formation, at elevation 8,228 feet. "Precarious" is the word that comes to mind, but the lookout has stood its ground, or rather its rock, for more than 60 years.

The trail begins in the trees, but in a few hundred yards you leave the forest and come out to two wooden benches, suitably placed for gazing at the view of the Kern River Basin before you. Looking ahead, you have a brief glimpse of the fire lookout straddling the Needles' tall spires. As you continue on the trail, you'll lose your view of the Needles temporarily.

The trail undulates through a forest of firs, ponderosa and sugar pines, occasionally passing over granite slabs and sandy stretches. The path is never monotonous; every hill and curve is delightfully different from the last.

The big surprise comes when you round the corner and see the lookout tower straight ahead of you, perched way up high on the far western spire. The trail starts to descend, which seems unfair, and you lose elevation before going uphill again on the final set of switchbacks. Lizards cross the trail and chipmunks scurry past, encouraging you.

The final ascent is the only part that's genuinely steep; you may have to stop to catch your breath a few times on the switchbacks. Fortunately, there are plenty of granite boulders to lean against, or sit on, while you admire the increasingly wide views.

The trail ends at a series of stairs and catwalks that ascend to the lookout. After you reach the first catwalk, the rest is a cakewalk, although not for those who are afraid of heights. A sign states whether the tower is open, and if you may come up and visit. Generally, it's open Wednesday through Sunday, 9 A.M.–6 P.M., but it is closed during fires or lightning storms so the lookout person can concentrate on his or her duties. If it's closed, just scramble up on any boulder to admire the vista.

If the tower is open, ascend the metal stairways and catwalks to the top, introduce yourself to the lookout person, and get ready for an unforgettable view. Your scope includes Lloyd Meadow, the southern half of the Golden Trout Wilderness to the north, and the Dome Lands Wilderness to the southeast. On clear days, you can make out Mount Whitney far to the northeast and the San Joaquin Valley to the west. Add in the close-up peaks—Olancha Peak, Jordan Peak, Slate Mountain, and Dome Rock—and this is a sight you'll long remember.

Options
Drive south on the Western Divide Highway for 2.5 miles to Road 21S69, across from the Peppermint Work Center. Turn left and follow the dirt road to the Dome Rock Trailhead. This short hike is less than a quarter-mile in length, but the views of the Needles will take your breath away.

Information and Contact
There is no fee. For more information and/or a map of Giant Sequoia National Monument and Sequoia National Forest, contact the Tule River Ranger District, 32588 Highway 190, Springville, CA 93265, 559/539-2607, website: www.fs.fed.us/r5/sequoia.

Directions
From Porterville, drive 46 miles east on Highway 190, which becomes the Western Divide Highway, to Forest Service Road 21S05, .5 mile south of Quaking Aspen Campground. Turn east (left) on Road 21S05, the Needles Road, and drive 2.8 miles to the trailhead.

long distance view of the Needles' spires from on top of Dome Rock

22. TRAIL OF 100 GIANTS

Giant Sequoia National Monument, off the Western
Divide Highway near Johnsondale

Total distance: .5 mile round-trip   **Hiking time:** 30 minutes

Type of trail: Rolling terrain   **Best season:** May–October

---

You've been practicing saying *"Sequoiadendron giganteum"* on the long drive to the trailhead. Whether you've come east from Porterville or north from Kernville, you've been in the car too long and you're ready to get out and hike among the giant sequoias. If you've made it to this trailhead, your wishes will soon be granted. Prepare to walk the Trail of 100 Giants and be awed.

This sequoia trail is easily as good as the showpiece sequoia trails in Sequoia and Kings Canyon National Parks, but it's located here, in Giant Sequoia National Monument, at a 6,400-foot elevation. The giant sequoias are dense in this grove, situated amid a mixed forest of cedars and pines. The path is an easy and nearly level loop that is suitable for wheelchairs and baby strollers.

As you walk in from the parking lot across the road, the first sequoia tree on your right is a doozy—possibly the best one on the loop. Squeeze past it, then continue hiking into the grove, taking note of all the big trees.

You'll see a few fallen sequoias, which allows you to get a close-up view of their immense girth. These fallen trees can stay in nearly perfect condition, laying on the ground for decades or even centuries, with little evidence of decay. Tannic acid in the trees' wood prevents the growth of fungi and bacteria and stops or slows decay. This tannic acid, combined with the sequoias' resistance to fire, disease, and insects, allows the trees to survive for thousands of years. Only after a tree has been down for a few hundred years will rain and melting snow leach the tannin from the tree, allowing decay to begin.

Of the many sequoia groves in the southern Sierra, the Trail of 100 Giants grove stands out because it contains an unusual number of twins—two sequoias that are growing tightly side by side in order to share resources. Eventually the twins will fuse together. This grove even has one set of twins that rangers call a "sequedar." It's a sequoia and cedar that have grown together.

Options

Drive back to the Western Divide Highway, turn left, and drive 2.5 miles farther north to the signed turnoff for Mule Peak at Road 22S03. Turn left and drive five miles to the Mule Peak Trailhead. The hike leads .5 mile to a Forest Service fire lookout with excellent views.

Information and Contact

There is no fee. For more information and/or a map of Giant Sequoia National Monument and Sequoia National Forest, contact the Tule River Ranger District, 32588 Highway 190, Springville, CA 93265, 559/539-2607, website: www.fs.fed.us/r5/sequoia.

giant sequoia, Trail of 100 Giants

Directions

From Kernville on the north end of Lake Isabella, drive north on Sierra Way/Road 99 for 27 miles to Johnsondale R-Ranch. Continue west (the road becomes Road 50), then in 5.5 miles, turn right on the Western Divide Highway. Drive 2.4 miles to the trailhead parking area on the right, just before Redwood Meadow Campground. The trail begins across the road.

23. UNAL TRAIL

Sequoia National Forest, off Highway 155
near Wofford Heights

Total distance: 3.0 miles round-trip　　**Hiking time:** 1.5 hours

Type of trail: Rolling terrain　　**Best season:** May–October

Unal Trail in the Greenhorn Mountains is dedicated to the early Native Americans who once lived in this area. The trail ascends Unal Peak and pays tribute to the Tubatulabal culture and a way of life long gone.

The trail is a three-mile loop that climbs gently to the peak. Where the trail forks at .1 mile, be sure to take the left fork and hike the trail clockwise. Traveling in this direction, the 700-foot climb to the summit is spread out over two miles on an excellent grade. Children can easily manage this trail, and along the way, they'll learn about Native American culture. Pick up an interpretive brochure at the trailhead.

The route is heavily forested, with a healthy mix of incense cedars, white fir, ponderosa pines, sugar pines, and black oaks. Although this was once an old-growth cedar forest, the biggest trees were cut in the 1950s and 1960s for lumber. What you see today is second- and third-growth. Deer roam the forested hillsides.

At the top of Unal Peak, you may be surprised at the strong breeze. A few trees have been cut on the summit, which improves the view but exposes the area to wind. The view is blissfully free of buildings, roads, and people—just forest and mountains as far as the eye can see, which is much of the appeal of the Greenhorn Mountains. The Tubatulabal Indians considered this summit to be a sacred place.

The trail passes a Native American cultural site on the return of the loop. Maintained by local Native Americans, the site includes a re-created Tubatulabal homestead. In addition to the manufactured artifacts, you can see real bedrock mortars in the granite, where Tubatulabal women ground acorns into meal.

Are you wondering what "unal" means? Bear. They eat the gooseberries, currants, and elderberries that grow in these woods, and were key figures in the stories of the Tubatulabal Indians.

deer on the Unal Trail in the Greenhorn Mountains

Information and Contact

There is no fee. For more information and/or a map of Sequoia National Forest, contact the Greenhorn Ranger District, c/o Lake Isabella Visitors Center, P.O. Box 3810, Lake Isabella, CA 93240, 760/379-5646, website: www.fs.fed.us/r5/sequoia.

Directions

From Wofford Heights on the west side of Lake Isabella, turn west on Highway 155 and drive eight miles to Greenhorn Summit. Turn left at the sign for Shirley Meadows Ski Area and drive 100 yards to the Greenhorn Fire Station and Unal trailhead, on the right side of the road.

© ANN MARIE BROWN

Chapter 2

Death Valley

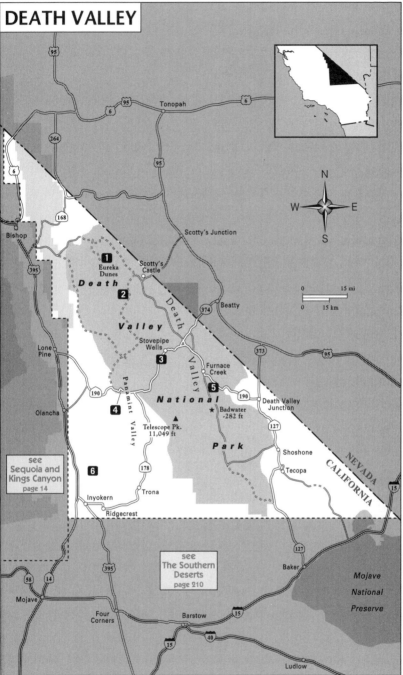

DEATH VALLEY

Tonopah

Scotty's Junction

1 Eureka Dunes

Scotty's Castle

Death

2

Valley

Stovepipe Wells

Beatty

3

Furnace Creek

National

5

Badwater -282 ft

Death Valley Junction

4

Telescope Pk. 11,049 ft

Park

Shoshone

Tecopa

see
Sequoia and
Kings Canyon
page 14

6

Inyokern

Trona

Ridgecrest

NEVADA

CALIFORNIA

see
The Southern
Deserts
page 210

Baker

Mojave

National

Preserve

Four Corners

Barstow

Mojave

Ludlow

Bishop

Lone Pine

Olancha

Panamint Valley

N
W E
S

0   15 mi
0   15 km

© AVALON TRAVEL PUBLISHING, INC.

CHAPTER 2—DEATH VALLEY

The Death Valley region includes our largest national park outside of Alaska, plus seemingly endless acres of land managed by Inyo National Forest and the Bureau of Land Management. The landscape in this far eastern part of California is dramatically different from anywhere else in the United States and, in fact, most of the world.

Although its name is foreboding, Death Valley National Park comprises a vast land of desert beauty, from soaring sand dunes and mountain ranges to below-sea-level salt flats. In summer, the park is the hottest place in North America—temperatures over 120°F are common—but in winter, the weather is cool and mild.

Simply put, Death Valley is a land of extremes. It is home to the lowest point in elevation in the western hemisphere, Badwater at 282 feet below sea level. In stark contrast, it's also home to Telescope Peak, elevation 11,048 feet, which is snow-covered six months of the year. In between these extremes are a wide range of ecological communities, from desert scrub to piñon and juniper woodlands. More than 900 plant species and 50 mammal species live in Death Valley. Hikers can choose from an amazing diversity of trails that lead to destinations such as 700-foot-high sand dunes, colorful badlands, towering rock walls, volcanic craters, old mining ruins, and even a waterfall in the desert.

Plan ahead before making a trip to the park. Because of its immense size, hikers need at least a few days to best experience it. Driving from one trailhead to another can take up half a day. Accommodations, services, and towns are few and far between.

If the desert landscape appeals to you, don't miss exploring some of the public lands just south of Death Valley. One of many fascinating geological features to be seen is Fossil Falls, an ancient lava field lined with polished rock. After an hour spent hiking in this strangely beautiful landscape, you'll come away marveling at the diversity of the Death Valley region.

1. EUREKA DUNES

Death Valley National Park, off Highway 190
near Scotty's Castle

Total distance: 2.0 miles round-trip   **Hiking time:** 1.0 hour

Type of trail: Some steep terrain   **Best season:** November–April

Let's talk sand dunes, those great icons of the desert. Here in California we are blessed with several sets of them—Kelso Dunes in Mojave National Preserve, Mesquite Flat Sand Dunes near Stovepipe Wells, and Ibex Dunes in the southern end of Death Valley. But the king of them all is Eureka Dunes, one of the shining stars of Death Valley National Park.

The Eureka Dunes are the tallest sand dunes in California, and arguably also the tallest in North America. They rise nearly 700 feet from their base and are home to several rare and endangered plants, including Eureka dune grass, Eureka evening primrose, and shining locoweed. When you visit the dunes, use great caution not to step on any of these special plants.

hiker on top of Eureka Dunes

For photographers, Eureka Dunes are a must-see in Death Valley. If you can keep the sand out of your camera, you'll go home with many weird and wonderful photographs of wind patterns on sand, and your hiking partner posing on swirling dune ridgetops. Yet the dunes' most alluring feature has little to do with their immense size or immeasurable beauty, but rather with their musical talent. When sand tumbles down one of the steep faces of the dune, usually provoked by the clumsy weight of some hiker's footsteps, it can emit a deep bass tone, like the drone of a distant engine. Some compare it to a meditator's mystical "om." Unfortunately, the dune music doesn't occur all the time. The sand must be completely dry to create enough friction between the sliding grains; only then can the magical sound can be heard.

Eureka Dunes were tacked on to the rest of Death Valley National Park in 1994. You'll see when you drive to the trailhead that the dunes are really far out there, even by Death Valley standards, where driving for hundreds of miles each day is commonplace. Do not attempt this trip unless you have a high-clearance vehicle. Although plenty of people seem to make it in a passenger car, it's not a good idea. As with anywhere in Death Valley, be absolutely certain that you have plenty of water with you, both in your car and in your daypack when you hike. And do not make the trip in summertime under any circumstances. It is simply too hot to be safe or enjoyable.

The best way to make the long trip to Eureka Dunes is to get a very early start and try to combine it with the first morning tour of Scotty's Castle, or a brief visit to Ubehebe Crater. Either of these will break up the long drive to Eureka Dunes, which, if you are starting from Furnace Creek or Stovepipe Wells, is about 90 miles one-way, with a whopping 44 miles of dirt road. It's slow going (about three hours each way).

When you finally reach the trailhead, just walk any which way you please, heading for the nearby dunes. There isn't any marked trail because of the continuously shifting desert sands, so just make a beeline to any point that interests you. It's best to climb to the top of the tallest dune you see, and then trace a narrow ridgeline path from dune to dune. It's like being on the narrowest backbone trail you can imagine, with steep slopes dropping off on both sides. But the difference is that this trail conforms to your footsteps, and the sand cushions you and supports your weight as you walk. There's no way to fall off the narrow ridge, and even if you did, the sand is silky soft.

The only difficult hiking is where you head steeply uphill. On some ascents you do the old, familiar dance: Two steps forward, one step back. Just take your time and enjoy the uniqueness of the experience. We stopped to rest for a moment and noticed the tiny tracks of a kangaroo rat in the dunes. If we hadn't paused to catch our breath, we surely would have missed this delicate sight.

Options
Forget the long drive to Eureka Dunes and visit the smaller Mesquite Flat Sand Dunes, 2.2 miles east of Stovepipe Wells Village on Highway 190. These 100-foot-tall dunes can be reached via a one-mile hike.

Information and Contact
There is a $10 entrance fee per vehicle at Death Valley National Park, good for seven days. Park maps are available at entrance stations. For more information, contact Death Valley National Park, P.O. Box 579, Death Valley, CA 92328, 760/786-3200, website: www.nps.gov/deva.

Directions
From the Furnace Creek Visitors Center in Death Valley, drive north on Highway 190 for 17 miles, then bear right on Scotty's Castle Road. In 32 miles, you will reach the Grapevine entrance station. A quarter-mile beyond it, bear left at the fork with Scotty's Castle Road. Continue northwest for three miles to the dirt road on the right signed for Eureka Dunes (Big Pine Road). (If you reach Ubehebe Crater, you've missed the turnoff.) Turn right and drive 34 miles to the South Eureka Valley Road turnoff. Turn left and drive 10 miles to the Eureka Dunes parking area. A high-clearance vehicle is recommended; call to check on road conditions before heading out.

2. UBEHEBE & LITTLE HEBE CRATERS

Death Valley National Park, off Highway 190
near Scotty's Castle

Total distance: 1.5 miles round-trip   **Hiking time:** 30 minutes

Type of trail: Rolling terrain   **Best season:** November–April

---

Ubehebe Crater is a volcanic fossil, a giant scar in the earth left from an act of volcanism that occurred about 2,000 years ago. Visitors who stand on its broad cinder-and-gravel rim are often seen shaking their heads in wonder. It's strangely beautiful, and yet so large that it is frustratingly difficult to photograph. Memories of the crater's yawning abyss tend to stay with you for a long time.

The crater was born when molten magma rising from deep beneath the earth's crust came in contact with groundwater. Like a cup of water poured on hot rocks in a sauna, the groundwater turned instantly to steam, which exploded from the earth. The energy from this superheating process was many times stronger than that of a nuclear blast.

The resultant Ubehebe Crater is 500 feet deep and .5 mile wide from rim to rim. Considering that it is surrounded by absolutely nothing—only in Death Valley is the true definition of nothingness understood—it's an awesome sight. No trees or foliage line its edges; nothing mars your view of the giant, gravelly abyss, except the trail sign at the parking lot. The crater is mostly black and ash-colored inside, but its eroded walls reveal a colorful blend of orange and rust from the minerals in the rock.

Many visitors make a beeline for the bottom of the crater, 500 feet down, and then find themselves a bit dismayed at the uphill return trip. Fewer people hike the trail from Ubehebe's rim to the edge of Little Hebe Crater, one of Ubehebe's smaller (and younger) siblings, then make a loop return around the far side of Ubehebe. This is the more interesting hike. Although the trail is covered in fine volcanic gravel, which has the annoying habit of finding its way into your hiking boots, it is relatively easy to walk, with only a few short, steep sections. (The gravel is some of the debris left from the volcanic explosion. The force of the blast is believed to have caused 100-mile-per-hour winds, which in turn scattered ash and fine gravel over an area of six square miles.)

Ubehebe Crater

From the parking area at the edge of Ubehebe Crater, head to your right along the trail, which leads uphill. Walk along Ubehebe Crater's southwest rim, then veer right off the main trail toward Little Hebe Crater. (A sign points the way.) The trail curves and winds for .25 mile around the strange, arid landscape. Your shoes will sink into the gravel somewhat, and you may face a headwind, so the going can be slower than you expect.

When you arrive, you see that Little Hebe Crater looks a lot like Ubehebe Crater, only it's much smaller. It was formed by the same chain of events that formed the larger crater, but with a less powerful explosion. Scientists guess that Little Hebe is much younger than Ubehebe, perhaps only 400 years old. Several other small craters can be seen along the trail, although none are as impressive as these two.

For your return, hike back to the junction bearing the Little Hebe trail sign, and continue on the main trail to the north. This leads you back uphill to the rim of Ubehebe Crater, which you can circumnavigate. If you take your eyes off the huge crater's interior, you have nice views of the far-off Last Chance Range from Ubehebe's high rim.

So, what does Ubehebe mean? Nobody's quite sure. The popular misinterpretation is that Ubehebe means "big basket" in the Shoshone Indian language. The Shoshone Indians called Ubehebe Crater *Tempin-ttaa Wo'sah,* which translates to "basket in the rock." The word Ubehebe was first applied to a mountain peak 20 miles away, and no one knows why the crater came to share the name.

Options
Since you've already driven this far from the main visitor areas in Death Valley, you're in an ideal spot to continue onward to see the park's famous Racetrack, where large rocks are pushed across the mudflats by mysterious forces. Drive out of the Ubehebe Crater parking lot, then go left on the dirt road signed for the Racetrack. You have 28 miles to go, all on dirt road (turn right at Teakettle Junction). When you reach the interpretive sign announcing the Racetrack, walk across the mudflats until you come upon the "moving rocks."

Information and Contact
There is a $10 entrance fee per vehicle at Death Valley National Park, good for seven days. Park maps are available at entrance stations. For more information, contact Death Valley National Park, P.O. Box 579, Death Valley, CA 92328, 760/786-3200, website: www.nps.gov/deva.

Directions
From the Furnace Creek Visitors Center in Death Valley, drive north on Highway 190 for 17 miles, then bear right on Scotty's Castle Road. In 32 miles, you will reach the Grapevine entrance station. A quarter-mile beyond it, bear left at the fork with Scotty's Castle Road. Continue northwest for six miles to the end of the pavement at the parking area for Ubehebe Crater.

3. MOSAIC CANYON

Death Valley National Park, off Highway 190 near
Stovepipe Wells

Total distance: 3.0 miles round-trip   **Hiking time:** 1.5 hours

Type of trail: Mostly flat terrain   **Best season:** November–April

---

Mosaic Canyon is one of the crown jewels of Death Valley, accessible to
all kinds of hikers. Its gemlike marble walls are known as a "geologic outdoor museum." The trail through the colorful, smooth-walled canyon is
easy to follow, and the hiking is relatively easy. Given these facts, the
canyon should be on every hiker's itinerary.

The trailhead is just two miles from Stovepipe Wells and 25 miles from
Furnace Creek. Unlike so many trails in Death Valley, which require a
long, arduous drive to reach their trailheads, Mosaic Canyon is an easy-
access destination, perfect for an after-dinner or early-morning stroll.
Once you're on the trail, you can walk as little or as much as you like,
heading gently uphill through the gorgeous marble-lined canyon.

If you've hiked in Golden Canyon in Death Valley (see Hike 5 in this
chapter), don't make the mistake of bypassing this trail because you think
you've already seen similar sights. The pastel-colored rock in Mosaic
Canyon is far different from that of other desert canyons. The trail shows
off smooth, water-polished marble from ancient lakebeds as it winds its
way up the narrow, high-walled canyon, which was formed by a fault
zone. Particularly unique are the "mosaics" on the canyon walls: Multi-
colored rock fragments that appear to be cemented together are visible in
several areas, especially in the first .25 mile of trail. This is a rock formation known as mosaic breccia. It's a gorgeous mix of red, white, black,
and gray stone.

Occasionally, the trail requires a little easy scrambling over foot-high
boulders and small dry waterfalls—the kind of scrambling that makes the
trip seem like a real adventure, but in fact it's quite easy and safe. Kids
have a ball on this trail.

From the trailhead, the route enters the canyon almost immediately, so
the fun begins right away. In some places, Mosaic Canyon's smooth marble walls close in around you, then the fissure you're walking through
suddenly opens wider into "rooms" lined with marble walls. At various

points the canyon walls are as little as 10 feet apart, and there are good spots for safe rock scrambling. If you choose to stay on the ground, the trail surface is gravel—ground-up bits of the canyon walls—and easy to walk on.

If you're wondering exactly what kind of rock this is, most of the canyon is a limestone called noonday dolomite. It was formed hundreds of millions of years ago when the desert was undersea. After being buried by other types of rocks and subjected to pressures and temperature swings, the limestone slowly metamorphosed into marble. Eventually, erosion and running water channeling through the layers of rock and soil carved out and reexposed the limestone, creating the canyon we see today.

After .25 mile, the canyon opens out to a wide alluvial fan, which is not quite as fascinating as the narrows. Many people just turn around and head back through the narrows again, but if you wish, you can continue hiking for another mile or two. Mosaic Canyon tapers once more, and with some easy to moderate scrambling you can reach a second narrows area, 1.2 miles from the trailhead, which shows off more stream-polished marble. Eventually the canyon becomes impassable, at a dry waterfall too high to be scaled.

Options

If you enjoy this type of desert canyon hiking, pay a visit to much less traveled Fall Canyon. The trailhead is found on Titus Canyon Road, 2.7 miles east of Scotty's Castle Road (just before Titus Canyon Road becomes one-way). You can hike up to three miles in this colorful, high-walled canyon before your path is blocked by a 20-foot-high dry waterfall.

Mosaic Canyon

Information and Contact

There is a $10 entrance fee per vehicle at Death Valley National Park, good for seven days. Park maps are available at entrance stations. For more information, contact Death Valley National Park, P.O. Box 579, Death Valley, CA 92328, 760/786-3200, website: www.nps.gov/deva.

Directions

From the Furnace Creek Visitors Center in Death Valley National Park, drive north on Highway 190 for 15 miles, then turn left to stay on Highway 190 toward Stovepipe Wells. Drive 10 miles, or .1 mile past Stovepipe Wells Village, to the left turnoff for Mosaic Canyon. Turn left and drive 2.2 miles to the trailhead parking lot.

4. DARWIN FALLS

Death Valley National Park, off Highway 190 near
Panamint Springs

Total distance: 2.2 miles round-trip   **Hiking time:** 1.0 hour

Type of trail: Mostly flat terrain   **Best season:** November–April

Darwin Falls is a must-do desert hike. A waterfall in the desert is a rare and precious thing, a miracle of life in a harsh world. As you hike into a narrow desert canyon, you follow the trail of a tiny trickle of water as it slowly expands into a fully flowing stream. You trace the stream's path, and at the back of the canyon you discover that it drops over a 30-foot-high cliff to create Darwin Falls. The slender waterfall is perfectly show-cased in a rock gallery.

The hike to the falls is just over one mile each way, and except on hot summer days it is well-suited for families. Be sure to carry plenty of water with you.

At its start the path is not well-defined; it's more like a well-used route that parallels some water pipes through a wash, then turns into single-track. At several points you must cross the narrow stream to follow the trail, but rocks are conveniently placed for easy crossing. Route-finding is simple because you just walk up-canyon, following the stream. Canyon walls on both sides keep you channeled in the correct direction.

The stream flow increases and the canyon walls narrow as you approach the waterfall, requiring some minor scrambling. The amount of vegetation also increases as you near the fall; notice the proliferation of willows, cattails, and reeds jockeying for position next to the running water. If it's spring, you may have some winged companions. More than 80 species of resident and migrating birds have been sighted in this canyon.

Darwin Falls streams over a 30-foot cliff in Death Valley.

You pass a small stream-gauging station right before you reach Darwin Falls, then round a corner and enter a box canyon. The walls around you have become more colorful as you've progressed; now you are completely surrounded by shades of yellow, coral, orange, and crimson. Darwin Falls drops over a rock cliff with a large cottonwood tree growing at its lip. The water pours down and then forks into two separate streams, giving life to ferns and colorful mosses growing alongside the fall.

Some intrepid explorers choose to scramble above Darwin Falls and head farther back in the canyon, where more than a dozen small cascades can be found, but this requires advanced scrambling skills. Darwin is the largest and loveliest of the falls, so your best bet is to stay right here and savor the miracle of this desert oasis.

Options
While you're in the neighborhood, drive to the nearby "town" of Darwin, and take a walk around this living ghost town.

Information and Contact
There is a $10 entrance fee per vehicle at Death Valley National Park, good for seven days. Park maps are available at entrance stations. For more information, contact Death Valley National Park, P.O. Box 579, Death Valley, CA 92328, 760/786-3200, website: www.nps.gov/deva.

Directions
From Stovepipe Wells Village at Death Valley, drive west on Highway 190 for 28 miles to Panamint Springs Resort. Continue past the resort for one mile to the left (south) turnoff for Darwin Falls. Turn left and drive 2.5 miles on the dirt road to a fork, then bear right and park at the signed trailhead.

Alternatively, from Lone Pine on U.S. 395, drive east on Highway 136 for 18 miles, then continue straight on Highway 190 for 30 miles. The right (south) turnoff for Darwin Falls is exactly one mile before you reach Panamint Springs Resort.

5. GOLDEN CANYON TO RED CATHEDRAL
Death Valley National Park, off Highway 190 near Furnace Creek

Total distance: 2.5 miles round-trip   **Hiking time:** 1.0 hour

Type of trail: Mostly flat terrain   **Best season:** November–April

---

Many hikers say that there are too many roads and too few trails in Death Valley National Park. Golden Canyon Trail is Mother Nature's revenge on this state of affairs, because the trail exists where a paved road was destroyed in a flash flood in 1976.

As the saying goes, Mother Nature always bats last. Where park visitors in cars once drove up Golden Canyon to park near the base of Red Cathedral and view its majesty, today hikers get to walk the distance. No one's complaining; it's much better this way.

The interpretive trail is a perfect path for first-timers in Death Valley National Park. Be sure to purchase an interpretive brochure at the trailhead or visitors center so that you understand what you see as you hike. The trail leads up a gently sloped alluvial fan that displays a colorful array of volcanic rocks, sand, and gravel. Golden Canyon's cliffs exhibit every

Golden Canyon and Red Cathedral

shade of gold you can imagine, from yellow to orange to apricot. In fact, you see almost nothing but yellow and gold rock as you hike, except for scarlet Red Cathedral looming in the background.

As you walk, notice the occasional evidence of an old paved road that once traveled up this canyon. It seems inconceivable that cars could have fit through some of the narrower sections—they must have just squeezed by.

Travel slowly and admire the colorful rock walls, which are crumbly and sandy. These walls are the layers of ancient lakebeds, tilted upward on their sides by earthquakes and fault activity. The beautiful colors are caused by minerals in the ancient lakebed soils mixing with minerals in the volcanic ash that settled over this area. All of this is ancient history, of course. Golden Canyon has looked as it does today for a few thousand years.

At one mile out, you'll reach the last numbered marker of the interpretive trail (number 10). Continue beyond it, bearing left for Red Cathedral. You'll pass numerous side canyons, but just continue straight ahead for .3 mile to the huge red cliff. Its lovely hue is caused by the weathering of its rocks, which contain large quantities of iron compounds.

If you want to see Golden Canyon at its best, visit either first thing in the morning or right around sunset. Not only will the national park crowds be someplace else, but the colors are more vivid at the edges of the day. The golds and yellows are more saturated; everything seems to glow.

Options
When you reach the last interpretive trail marker on the Golden Canyon Trail, take the right fork for Zabriskie Point, 2.2 miles away. Hike across the face of Manly Beacon (a big sandstone hill with lovely views), then continue to Zabriskie Point, with its colorful vista of the badlands and Panamint Mountains.

Information and Contact
There is a $10 entrance fee per vehicle at Death Valley National Park, good for seven days. Park maps are available at entrance stations. For more information, contact Death Valley National Park, P.O. Box 579, Death Valley, CA 92328, 760/786-3200, website: www.nps.gov/deva.

Directions
From the Furnace Creek Visitors Center in Death Valley, drive southeast on Highway 190 for 1.3 miles to the right fork for Badwater. Bear right and drive south for two miles to the Golden Canyon parking area on the left side of the road.

6. FOSSIL FALLS
Bureau of Land Management Ridgecrest Area,
off U.S. 395 near Inyokern

Total distance: .5 mile round-trip   **Hiking time:** 30 minutes

Type of trail: Mostly flat terrain   **Best season:** November–April

A lot of Southern Californians think that when they drive to Mammoth Lakes or the Eastern Sierra, there's nothing to do but race as fast as possible on U.S. 395, just to get some miles behind them.

But people with "get-there-itis" miss out on this great short hike to Fossil Falls, only slightly more than a mile from the highway. You could take the exit for Fossil Falls, drive to the trailhead, hike the trail, and be back on the freeway in an hour, feeling a lot better than if you made a fast-food stop.

Don't let the name deceive you into believing you'll find a waterfall here. There's no water to be found at Fossil Falls, but there is an ancient lava field, which is home to two 40-foot-tall dry waterfalls and a series of polished rock formations.

The trail to Fossil Falls is well-maintained, completely level, and easy enough for children. However, shade is conspicuously absent here; you don't want to hike it on a hot day. The trail travels for a quarter-mile through a field of completely exposed black rocks, with some scraggly creosote bushes trying to eke out a living among them. In about 10 minutes you reach the edge of a giant fissure, where the colors in the rock change from pure black to black, gray, and red. This fissure is the channel of the now-dry Owens River. (It's dry only in these parts; farther north, the river still flows.)

Keep hiking "downstream" along the fissure's rim or, if you prefer, descend to its base and explore. In about 60 yards, you'll reach the first dry fall; the second fall is about 60 yards farther. If you're hiking in the canyon bottom, be careful not to slip over the 40-foot-high falls' lip.

The volcanic action that caused Fossil Falls occurred extremely recently in geologic time—about 20,000 years ago. Lava from several volcanic eruptions flowed into the Owens River channel, mixed with river water, and created the hard, smooth surface of the canyon walls. It's fascinating to stand at the dry falls' brink and listen to the desert wind whip around the smooth, rounded rocks below. It is presumed that the smooth polish on the lava occurred during the last Ice Age.

In addition to the volcanic history of the area, Fossil Falls has extensive human history. Although it can be difficult to fathom on a summer day, archaeologists believe that prehistoric people found this area a pleasant place to live. The climate in this area was once very different—the river flowed, surrounding lakes were filled with water, and animals roamed in a grassland savannah. The physical remains of 10,000 years of occupation can be found in various archaeological sites at Fossil Falls, including petroglyphs and rock rings built by the Paiute Indians.

Information and Contact
There is no fee. For more information, contact Bureau of Land Management Ridgecrest Field Office, 300 South Richmond Road, Ridgecrest, CA 93555, 760/384-5400, website: www.ca.blm.gov/ridgecrest.

Directions
From the junction of Highway 14 and U.S. 395 near Inyokern, drive north on U.S. 395 for 20 miles to just north of Little Lake and turn east on Cinder Road. Drive .6 mile, bear right at the fork, then drive another .6 mile to the Fossil Falls Trailhead.

Chapter 3

Santa Barbara and Vicinity

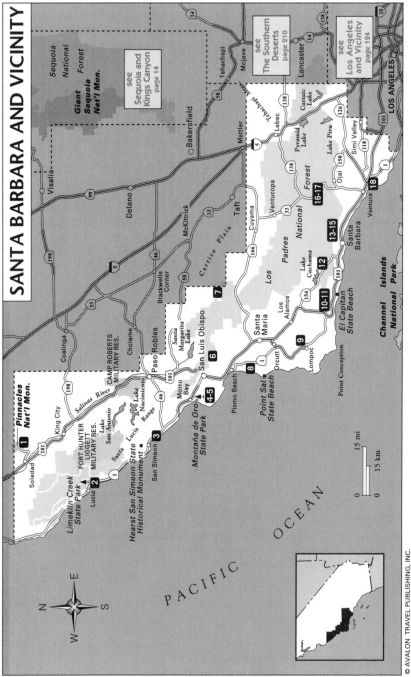

SANTA BARBARA AND VICINITY

© AVALON TRAVEL PUBLISHING, INC.

CHAPTER 3—SANTA BARBARA AND VICINITY

The Santa Barbara region, which extends 250 miles from just north of the artsy town of Cambria and the terraced vineyards of Paso Robles to the white sands of Ventura, encompasses what many consider to be Southern California's finest stretch of coast. The Santa Barbara County shoreline, curving up-coast from Carpinteria to Point Conception, has a southern, not western exposure, which results in exceptionally mild weather. To the south, Ventura County's coast offers 40 miles of fine sandy beaches. To the north, San Luis Obispo County offers miles of sand dunes and a wildlife-rich estuary at Morro Bay.

Hikers can explore this meeting of land and sea on a wealth of trails in state-protected lands: San Simeon State Beach, Los Osos State Reserve, Montaña de Oro State Park, Gaviota State Park, and McGrath State Beach. Trails wind along the tops of oceanside bluffs, across coastal grasslands gilded with wildflowers in the spring, and on top of boardwalks spanning coastal dunes and wetlands.

Lest you think the Santa Barbara region is all sun and sand, note that it also contains more than a million acres of national forest land in the Santa Barbara, San Luis Obispo, and Ojai backcountry—the southern section of Los Padres National Forest. This landscape is a conglomeration of pine-clad high mountain peaks, river-cut canyons, and chaparral-covered hillsides. The Santa Ynez Mountains, a centerpiece of southern Los Padres National Forest, are part of the unique Trans-verse Range, a system of mountains that defies the rules of California geography: They run from east to west, rather than north to south.

Not surprisingly, these mountains provide myriad hiking opportunities. Those seeking easily accessible day hikes will find Los Padres National Forest trails just beyond the town limits in Santa Barbara, Montecito, and Ojai. Paths lead to waterfalls, high overlooks of mountains and ocean, and sculpted sandstone formations. And best of all, many of these destinations can be visited with only a small investment of mileage and time.

1. BEAR GULCH CAVES & OVERLOOK

Pinnacles National Monument, off Highway 25
near King City

Total distance: 3.0 miles round-trip **Hiking time:** 1.5 hours

Type of trail: Rolling terrain **Best season:** November–May

Bear Gulch Caves are a crowd-pleaser at Pinnacles National Monument. Sure, the park has terrific hiking trails, hundreds of first-class rock-climbing sites, abundant spring wildflowers, and fascinating geological features. But what many Pinnacles visitors want to do is explore Bear Gulch Caves.

That's partly because they have waited so long to do so. From 1997 until 2003, the Bear Gulch Caves were closed continually, sometimes due to flooding, but mostly to protect the endangered bats that nest inside. But under a policy that goes into effect in 2004, the Park Service plans to use a system of gates to keep at least some portion of the caves open to visitors most of the year. As park biologists studied the cave-dwelling bats, they realized that the bats don't use the entire cave system year-round—only certain regions in certain seasons. With lockable gates, rangers will be able to close off the portion of the caves the bats are using, and allow visitors to explore the rest of the caves.

Your hike through the caves begins just beyond the Bear Gulch Visitors Center on Moses Spring Trail, also signed for Bear Gulch Caves. Pick up an interpretive brochure at the visitors center or the trailhead, and you'll learn to identify the flora of the Pinnacles. The first .25 mile is nothing out of the ordinary, just a pleasant walk through oaks, gray pines, and buckeye trees. In spring, the buckeye flowers smell so sweet, they can make you giddy.

Shortly you'll enter and exit a rock tunnel that was built by an ambitious trail crew in the 1930s. Just beyond it, at a fork, take leave of Moses Spring Trail, which goes up and over the Bear Gulch Caves instead of through them. Bear left for Bear Gulch Caves and turn on your flashlights. Now the fun begins: You'll squeeze through clefts in the rock, duck your head under ledges, and climb down rocky staircases. You'll walk into water-sculpted volcanic caverns where only occasional beams of sunlight flash through the ceiling. You'll twist and turn through narrow passageways in which the only sound is the dripping of water on the walls. If you don't have a good light with you, you may bump into a few boulders or tree roots, or get lost momentarily. But no worries—small painted arrows on the cave walls keep you going in the right direction. Every moment of this spelunking expedition feels like an adventure, even though it's easy enough for a six-year-old to accomplish. Adults love it as much as kids; these caves are just plain fun. If you were a bat, you might want to live here too.

These intriguing caves, and the surrounding rocky spires and crags of Pinnacles National Monument, are the result of an ancient volcano

A tunnel in the rock leads to the entrance to Bear Gulch Caves.

that erupted some 200 miles to the southeast, in the northern San Fernando Valley. Movement along the San Andreas Fault carried these rock formations many miles from the rest of the volcano's remains and deposited them in the smooth, grassy hills of this inland valley. Water erosion over many thousands of years did a final job on the Pinnacles' mighty rock formations, creating deep, tunnel-like canyons covered by and partially filled with huge boulders. These tunnels form the Bear Gulch Caves, and also the Balconies Caves on the park's west side.

After exiting Bear Gulch Caves, head back to the visitors center on Moses Spring Trail. At the visitors center, pick up the trail across the road, the Condor Gulch Trail to the High Peaks Trail and Overlook. It's a solid 30-minute uphill climb to the overlook on a comfortably graded trail. In spring, a cascading stream parallels the path. The scent of wild sage and rosemary is enticingly aromatic, and your eyes will be drawn to the fascinating colorful lichen growing on the equally colorful rocks. That is, until you start getting views of the high pinnacles, which will surely divert your attention. The overlook, a giant volcanic boulder with a metal railing, is a great place to stand and admire the high peaks of the Pinnacles and look down on the rocky valley below.

Options
Hike beyond the overlook on the Condor Gulch Trail. In .7 mile, you'll reach the High Peaks Trail, where you can turn left and access one of the most exciting trail stretches in the park. High Peaks Trail leads through a maze of cliffs and spires by utilizing handholds and footholds in the rock, stairsteps blasted out of the rock, and metal railings to hold you on the rock. It's great fun.

Information and Contact
There is a $5 entrance fee at Pinnacles National Monument, good for seven days. Park maps are available at the entrance station. For more information, contact Pinnacles National Monument, 5000 Highway 146, Paicines, CA 95043, 831/389-4485, website: www.nps.gov/pinn.

Directions
From King City on U.S. 101, take the First Street exit and head east. First Street turns into Highway G13/Bitterwater Road. Follow it for 15 miles to Highway 25, where you turn left (north). Follow Highway 25 for 14 miles to Highway 146. Go left on Highway 146 and drive 4.8 miles to the park visitors center, then continue beyond it to the parking lot at the end of the road. If this lot is full, park by the visitors center and walk down the road to the trailhead.

2. LIMEKILN TRAIL

Limekiln State Park, off Highway 1 near Lucia

Total distance: 2.0 miles round-trip   **Hiking time:** 1.0 hour

Type of trail: Mostly flat terrain   **Best season:** Good year-round

Compared to its larger neighbors to the north in Big Sur, Limekiln State Park is a small park, with a relatively quiet campground and only one main hiking trail. Developed facilities are few, but you will find a lovely redwood forest, a perennial creek and waterfall, and an easy hiking trail that leads to a set of 1800s limekilns that were used to make bricks and cement.

Start hiking from the far end of the campground on the signed path through the forest. The route parallels pretty Limekiln Creek, a watercourse that's surrounded by big redwoods, ferns, rocks, and sorrel. Cross a bridge immediately past the campground, and then in another .2 mile, cross a second bridge.

Immediately past the second bridge you'll see a side trail on the right, across the stream. Make note of it for your return trip, then keep heading into the canyon toward the limekilns. You'll cross one more footbridge, then come to the four big kilns, which look like giant smokestacks with mossy, brick bottoms. In 1880, the Rockland Cement Company fired limestone in these metal kilns to make lime,

a limekiln at Limekiln Creek State Park

using this canyon's redwoods for firewood. Coastal cargo ships carried lime, bricks, and cement, as well as redwood lumber, to build the prospering new city of San Francisco. As a result of all this activity, the redwoods you see today in Limekiln Canyon are mostly second-growth. Still, they are large and beautiful.

Beyond the kilns, a sign marks the end of the trail. Turn around here and head back to the trail junction by the second footbridge. If the stream level is low enough, you can rock-hop across the stream (or if you're lucky, a seasonal bridge will be in place), then head up the spur trail toward Limekiln State Park's waterfall. You'll need to cross and re-cross the creek several times, and in winter and spring, you might get your hiking boots wet.

Your scramble ends at the base of the waterfall, where Limekiln Falls pours 100 feet down a nearly vertical sheet of limestone. On one May visit, the falls' flow fanned out to 25 feet wide at the base. In contrast to the dark and shady redwood forest you've been hiking in, the light is surprisingly bright by the waterfall. The falls' limestone cliff prevents any trees from growing nearby and blocking out the light.

Information and Contact
A $5 day-use fee is charged per vehicle. A trail map is available at the entrance kiosk. For more information, contact Limekiln State Park, c/o Big Sur Station, Highway 1, Big Sur, CA 93920, 831/667-2403 or 831/667-2315, website: www.cal-parks.ca.gov.

Directions
From San Luis Obispo, drive north on U.S. 101 for 24 miles to the Highway 46 West exit near Templeton. Turn west on Highway 46 and drive 23 miles to Highway 1. Turn north and drive 50 miles to Limekiln Creek State Park on the east side of the highway. (It's 2.5 miles south of Lucia.) The trailhead is at the far side of the campground.

3. MOONSTONE BEACH TRAIL

San Simeon State Beach, off Highway 1 near Cambria

Total distance: 4.0 miles round-trip   **Hiking time:** 2.0 hours

Type of trail: Rolling terrain   **Best season:** February–May

---

When is the best time to make the trip to Cambria? Without question it's in spring, when the rolling hills alongside Highway 46 are lush and green. February through May is when the advertisers film automobile commercials along this scenic stretch of highway from Templeton to Cambria. The location scouts know what they're doing; the roadside scenery is breathtaking.

If the driving is good, you know the hiking will be even better. So it is on Moonstone Beach Trail at San Simeon State Beach, where you can stroll along the oceanside bluffs and watch the ever-changing spectacle at sea. The blufftop wildflowers are unforgettable in spring, and from December to April whales swim by and blow spouts for the tourists. In summer and fall, you can watch surfers perform their magic tricks on the long, rolling waves.

The best place to start is at Leffingwell Landing at the large state beach parking lot. Leffingwell Landing is in the middle of the trail, so you can walk out and back in both directions, or choose between them. A century ago the landing was a harbor for ships bringing supplies to early settlers along the Central Coast, but today the area is best known for its excellent tidepooling.

Hiking south from the landing, you may have a wet creek crossing in winter at Leffingwell Creek, but you can go around it via a footbridge at the neighboring golf course. Moonstone Beach Trail's southern terminus is at the intersection of Moonstone Beach Drive and Weymouth Street, but you can descend to the beach there and keep walking along the sand, if you wish.

Although the trail parallels Moonstone Beach Drive, the road isn't much of a bother, because the seaward vistas hold all of your attention. In addition to the wide ocean views, you'll have the good companionship of cypress and pine trees, sculpted by the sea breeze. Benches are positioned at high overlooks (accessible via short spurs off the main trail) for hikers who want to cast long, admiring glances at the sea, or each other.

Watch for harbor seals, who frequently pop up from their undersea world to take a peek at the world above. Sea otters also make an appearance; the park lies within the National Sea Otter Refuge.

Heading north from Leffingwell Landing, in .3 mile the trail descends from the bluffs to the sand and follows a wooden staircase to the beach. Keep your eyes peeled for the beach's namesake moonstones and jaspers. You won't need to put these colorful pieces of quartz in your rock polisher and wait for weeks to get smooth stones—the ocean waves have already done the job.

Information and Contact

There is no fee. For more information, contact San Simeon State Beach, San Simeon District, 750 Hearst Castle Road, San Simeon, CA 93452, 805/927-2020 or 805/927-2068, websites: www.cal-parks.ca.gov or www.hearstcastle.org.

Directions

From San Luis Obispo, drive north on U.S. 101 for 24 miles to the Highway 46 West exit near Templeton. Turn west on Highway 46 and drive 23 miles to Highway 1, then continue three miles north on Highway 1, past Cambria, to Moonstone Beach Drive. Turn left on Moonstone Beach Drive and park at Leffingwell Landing.

4. BLUFFS TRAIL

Montaña de Oro State Park, off U.S. 101
near San Luis Obispo

Total distance: 3.0 miles round-trip   **Hiking time:** 1.5 hours

Type of trail: Mostly flat terrain

Best season: Good year-round; the wildflower display is best March–May

The Bluffs Trail at Montaña de Oro State Park is one of the finest coast walks in Central and Southern California, blissfully free of the blight of human development and loaded with classic oceanside beauty. The level trail contours along the top of Montaña de Oro's shale and sediment bluffs, with nonstop views of rocky offshore outcrops, colorful cliffs and

Bluffs Trail, Montaña de Oro State Park

arches, and the big blue Pacific.

Not only that, but the grasslands explode in a brilliant display of orange poppies, coast lupine, and other wildflowers from March to May. This extravagant show is the reason for the park's name—Montaña de Oro, or Mountain of Gold. The combination of flowers, rocky cliffs and outcrops, and surging sea can almost seem like too much beauty to handle in one place.

The bluffs of Bluffs Trail are ancient marine terraces, formed by the coast rising and jolting upward from geological activity. Hundreds of thousands of years ago, as the warmer climate melted glaciers, the sea rose and cut into the land mass, creating beaches and bluffs that grew larger as sand and gravel were washed down. Further geologic action moved the earth's plates, lifting the beaches to form seaside terraces.

New terraces are constantly being formed under water. As the coastline continues to rise, the bluffs will continue to change. The carved rocks and outcrops you see from Bluffs Trail are the result of the most recent erosion of the terrace you are walking on. Wooden railings placed along the trail keep onlookers from leaning too far over the edge of these eroding bluffs.

Bluffs Trail ends without fanfare at a barbed-wire fence marking Pacific Gas & Electric Company property (for emphasis, it's lined with huge cacti). Just follow the tiny loop at its end, then retrace your steps on the trail, enjoying the coastal views from the new perspective.

Options

During low tides, tidepooling can be excellent in Corallina Cove, accessible via a side path off Bluffs Trail. (Look for the cutoff on your right about

.5 mile from where you parked your car.) Another good side trip is an exploration of Spooner's Cove, the beach across from the visitors center turnoff, near where you left your car. Picnic tables and fire grills are in place if you want to have a barbecue lunch after your hike.

Information and Contact

There is no fee. A map of Montaña de Oro State Park is available at the park visitors center, or at nearby Morro Bay State Park. For more information, contact Montaña de Oro State Park, 3550 Pecho Valley Road, Los Osos, CA 93402, 805/528-0513. Or contact Morro Bay State Park at 805/772-7434, or San Luis Obispo Coast State Parks at 805/549-3312, website: www.cal-parks.ca.gov.

Directions

From U.S. 101 in San Luis Obispo, take the Los Osos exit and head west on Los Osos Valley Road. Drive 12 miles on Los Osos Valley Road to the Montaña de Oro entrance, then continue 2.5 miles to the small parking area on the right side of the road, which is 100 yards beyond the left turnoff for the visitors center. The signed Bluffs Trail begins there.

5. LOS OSOS OAKS TRAILS

Los Osos Oaks State Reserve, off U.S. 101
near San Luis Obispo

Total distance: 2.0 miles round-trip   **Hiking time:** 1.0 hour

Type of trail: Mostly flat terrain   **Best season:** Good year-round

---

Few people notice the small sign for Los Osos Oaks State Reserve as they drive by on their way to Montaña de Oro State Park. (We drove past it three times before we found it.) But the lack of fanfare at the trailhead means you'll have a good chance to wander in solitude among the twisted trunks and limbs of Los Osos Oaks.

The reserve's venerable oaks have been around for as long as 800 years. To see these ancients, you can follow any of three short, level trails. Your best bet is to walk a brief stretch on all three. Chumash Loop, Oak View, and Los Osos Creek Trails begin from one trailhead, then split off from one another. If you're short on time and have to choose among them,

Oak View is a short out-and-back and provides the best overview of the reserve's highlights. Chumash Loop is longer and contours around the entire reserve. Los Osos Creek Trail has the least impressive oaks, but follows a marshy stretch of creek.

The oak forest is a mix of very large, old, lichen-covered trees and tiny, dwarfed ones. Some of the oaks' trunks and branches are so twisted and gnarled that they look like a tangled web of elephants' trunks. In many places, the trees have intertwined to create a tunnel of branches, or a walled amphitheater of trunks and limbs. If you're into photography, you'll probably want to shoot images here in black and white.

The lichen hanging from the older oaks is often mistaken for a type of moss or "old man's beard." But this is a true lichen, made up of an alga and a fungus growing in a symbiotic, give-and-take relationship. Lichen has a healthy relationship with the oaks. Unlike mistletoe, it isn't a parasite and doesn't take anything from the trees. Three types of lichen can be found exclusively in Los Osos Oaks Reserve.

Birds also use the reserve's oaks for shelter. The sounds of songbirds will quickly diminish any noise from the nearby road. On one trip, we spotted a beautiful red-shouldered hawk sitting on a low branch on one of the big oaks, less than 20 feet away.

Keep in mind that if the coast is fogged in, hiking in Los Osos Oaks State Reserve is an ideal choice, because all the beauty is right in front of you, close enough to touch.

Los Osos Oaks State Reserve

Options

During monarch butterfly season from November to February, take a short stroll to see the beautiful lepidoptera at nearby Pismo State Beach. The grove is easily accessible off Highway 1, a half mile south of the Pismo Beach city limits. Free parking is available at North Beach Campground.

Information and Contact

There is no fee. For more information, contact Los Osos Oaks State Reserve, c/o Morro Bay State Park, State Park Road, Morro Bay, CA 93442, 805/772-7434. Or San Luis Obispo Coast State Parks at 805/549-3312, website: www.cal-parks.ca.gov.

Directions

From U.S. 101 in San Luis Obispo, take the Los Osos exit and head west on Los Osos Valley Road. Drive 8.5 miles to the Los Osos Oaks State Reserve on the left side of the road, marked by a small sign. (The reserve is located exactly one mile east of 10th Street in Los Osos, and just west of the bear statue on the road.)

6. LITTLE FALLS CANYON

Santa Lucia Wilderness, off U.S. 101 near Arroyo Grande

Total distance: 2–5.0 miles round-trip   **Hiking time:** 1–2.0 hours

Type of trail: Rolling terrain   **Best season:** Good year-round

---

As scenic as Little Falls Canyon is, what people remember most about it is the drive. The trailhead is 17 miles from the freeway on pavement, in which the last several miles are quite narrow and have frequent rockslides. That's the easy part. Then it's another couple miles on a dirt road that crosses Lopez Creek several times, and I don't mean via bridge. The stream crosses the road, and your vehicle must cross the stream. In one stretch the stream simply becomes the road, and you just keep driving. A high-clearance vehicle is more than a good idea in the wet season.

Luckily, the rugged stretch to the trailhead is only 1.6 miles long, so if you fear that your low-slung Ferrari won't make it, just park it and walk.

Once you're at the trailhead, the rest is easy. Little Falls is only a .5-mile walk from the trailhead, tracing along a good trail in the Santa Lucia Wilderness. You stay close to the cool, shady stream, which is teeming with small trout. The path is lined with oaks, sycamores, bays, and maples. Maidenhair and giant woodwardia ferns frame the rocky pools of Little Falls Creek, and wildflowers bloom in patches.

After 15 minutes of hiking, you'll reach an unsigned junction where a spur trail leads left and the main trail heads up and away from the creek. Go left and scramble upstream for a few hundred feet until you reach 50-foot-high Little Falls. The scramble is easily accomplished in about five minutes, but you might get your feet wet.

Little Falls' stream flows down between giant sheets of limestone that look like fresh concrete that suddenly froze in midpour. A maple tree grows about halfway up the fall, and others hang over its lip. The waterfall's pool is about three feet deep, perfect for wading amid the reeds and ferns.

After visiting the fall, head back to the main trail and continue onward, heading farther into the canyon above Little Falls. Here you'll find deeper, water-carved pools, perfect for cooling off. Spring wildflowers become more prolific as you climb higher in the canyon. Look for orange leopard lilies, bush monkeyflower, and purple nightshade. The trail continues for five miles beyond Little Falls, so just choose a turnaround spot wherever you please.

Options
Drive another two miles on the rough dirt road past the Little Falls Trailhead, and you'll reach the trailhead for Big Falls Canyon. Here you'll find another short, easy trail to a waterfall.

Information and Contact
A National Forest Adventure Pass is required; see the Hiking Tips at the front of this book for details. Call the Santa Lucia Ranger District for road conditions in winter and spring. For more information and/or a map of Los Padres National Forest, contact the Santa Lucia Ranger District, 1616 North Carlotti Drive, Santa Maria, CA 93454, 805/925-9538, website: www.fs.fed.us/r5/lospadres.

Directions
From U.S. 101 at Arroyo Grande, take the Highway 227/Lopez Lake exit. Head east on Highway 227, then Lopez Drive, following the signs toward

Lopez Lake for 10.3 miles. Turn right on Hi Mountain Road (before Lopez Lake's entrance station). Drive .8 mile, then turn left on Upper Lopez Canyon Road. Drive 6.3 miles, past a Boy Scout camp, then turn right. In .1 mile, the pavement ends and you pass a Christian camp. Continue for 1.6 miles on the dirt road, crossing the stream several times, to the trailhead for Little Falls. The trail leads from the right side.

7. PAINTED ROCK TRAIL

Carrizo Plain National Monument, off Highway 58 near California Valley

Total distance: 1.5 miles round-trip   **Hiking time:** 1.0 hour

Type of trail: Rolling terrain

Best season: November–February to see sandhill cranes; February–April to see wildflowers

---

At 250,000 acres, Carrizo Plain is considered to be California's largest nature preserve. One of its biggest attractions is the huge number of sandhill cranes that hang around from November to February, passing the mild winter at alkaline Soda Lake and the surrounding plains. The broad, fertile valley is also a resting place for thousands of other migrating and resident birds, but it's the giant cranes that bring the hordes of bird-lovers and photographers to Carrizo Plain.

If you visit in springtime, it is flora, not fauna, that is the main attraction: Carrizo Plain is also home to one of California's most spectacular grassland wildflower displays.

With so many highlights, you'll want to visit Carrizo Plain multiple times, in different seasons. But that takes some planning, because Carrizo Plain is a long, 50-mile drive east of Santa Margarita, where there's a whole lot of . . . well, nothing. Don't expect to find any services out here—there's no gas station, no restaurant, no anything.

Carrizo Plain covers a big chunk of land, but has only a few established hiking trails. One not to be missed is the Painted Rock Interpretive Trail, which leads to a remarkable sandstone amphitheater with walls covered with Native American pictographs. A dirt road leads gently uphill from the trailhead to the 55-foot-tall marine sandstone rock, which juts up

examining the pictographs at Painted Rock

from the middle of the grasslands. From the parking area, it's easy to see where you're heading.

After a brief hike, you'll find the pictographs on the inside walls of the horseshoe-shaped outcrop (walk to your left when you reach the rock). Although some of the drawings have been eroded by time and weather, many are in near-perfect condition. You can't help but wonder at the messages of the 1,000-year-old drawings. Are they rife with meaning, or merely doodles?

Inside the horseshoe, you have a lovely view of the surrounding grasslands. It is clear why Native Americans would choose this unusual natural amphitheater as a sacred ceremonial site. Both Chumash and Yokut Indians hunted and traded in this area as late as the mid-19th century.

While driving and hiking at Carrizo Plain, expect to see some remarkable wildlife. Tule elk and pronghorn antelope have been reintroduced to the area. Before the explorers arrived, these animals roamed the valley in huge herds. The monument is also home to the San Joaquin kit fox, giant kangaroo rat, and burrowing owl.

I stood near the Painted Rock Trailhead and watched a coyote lope across the wide, open plain. It was remarkable how quickly the animal covered a large expanse of land, seemingly without effort. That small scene has probably repeated itself for thousands of years in the Carrizo Plain.

Options
On weekends in April and May, free docent-led hikes visit Painted Rock and also the San Andreas fault site at Wallace Creek. Tours are by reservation only; phone the Goodwin Education Center (805/475-2131) to reserve a spot.

Information and Contact
There is no fee. A Carrizo Plain brochure is available by mail. The Painted Rock Trail may be closed from March 1 to July 15 (except for docent-led tours) to protect nesting falcons; call the visitors center for an update. For more information, contact the Bureau of Land Management, Bakersfield Field Office, 3801 Pegasus Drive, Bakersfield, CA 93308, 661/391-6000, website: www.ca.blm.gov/bakersfield. Or contact the Goodwin Education Center at Carrizo Plain, open Thursday–Sunday, December–May, at 805/475-2131.

Directions
From San Luis Obispo on U.S. 101, drive north for 10 miles and take the Santa Margarita/Highway 58 exit. Drive east on Highway 58 for 48 miles to the Soda Lake Road turnoff. Turn right (south) and drive 13.5 miles to the Painted Rock Trail and visitors center turnoff. Turn right and drive to the visitors center, then turn left and drive two miles to the Painted Rock Trailhead.

8. OSO FLACO LAKE

Oceano Dunes State Vehicular Recreation Area,
off Highway 1 near Santa Maria

Total distance: 2.6 miles round-trip   **Hiking time:** 1.0 hour

Type of trail: Mostly flat terrain   **Best season:** Good year-round

---

Surprise—a 2,000-acre nature preserve is found adjacent to the Oceano Dunes State Vehicular Recreation Area. Usually the two groups make unlikely neighbors, but here a place has been made for the dune buggy and off-roading crowd, and a separate place has been made for the hiking and bird-watching crowd. The twain never meet; everybody's happy.

The preserve was created because of an extensive dune restoration and native plant revegetation project in the mid-1980s. The California Department of Parks and Recreation wanted to protect an area of the dunes' fragile shifting sand, a dynamic ecosystem that is home to tiny plants and animals. These minute sand creatures cannot survive the heavy pressure of big tires and racing engines, or even the gentler pressure of constant human footprints. Today, native plants thrive here, including sand verbena and coreopsis.

The trail to Oso Flaco Lake starts out as a wide path surrounded by thick willows and cottonwoods. Songbirds are ubiquitous here. In .3 mile, the trail cuts off to the left on a wooden boardwalk, opening up to a lovely vista of the two small, reed-filled ponds that make up Oso Flaco Lake, one of the few remaining freshwater dune lakes. A long footbridge leads over the water.

Within minutes of leaving your car, you are in the good company of shorebirds and waterfowl. Ducks, coots, and mergansers play hide-and-seek in the islands of reeds. Birdwatchers should look for the Audubon warbler, long-billed marsh wren, and black-crowned night heron, among others. You won't be in a hurry to cross the footbridge to the far side of the lake; there is too much to see and photograph as you traverse the water. It's a unique perspective—walking "across" a lake instead of around it.

Beyond the lake, the boardwalk extends over a series of low sand dunes. The wooden planks serve the dual purpose of making the trail suitable for wheelchairs and protecting the dunes' fragile plant life.

dunes near Oso Flaco Lake

Where the boardwalk ends, you can continue walking on the dunes, or head to the beach to the right or left. Make some sand angels, or wrestle with your hiking partner in the soft, silky dune sand. The only downer here is the occasional wailing sound of off-road vehicles, but luckily, they have their place, you have yours.

So, what does "Oso Flaco" mean? Skinny bear. But it's been a long time since they've seen any of those around here. The last one disappeared sometime in the late 19th century.

Options

Stroll on the beach as far as you please. Or sign up for a docent-led hike at Oso Flaco Lake; tours are held on occasional weekends. See www.oceano-dunes.com or phone the park for details.

Information and Contact

A $4 day-use fee is charged per vehicle. For more information, contact Oceano Dunes State Vehicular Recreation Area, 928 Pacific Boulevard, Oceano, CA 93445, 805/473-7230 or 805/473-7223, website: www .oceanodunes.com.

Directions

From Santa Maria on U.S. 101, take the Highway 166/Guadalupe exit and drive nine miles west, then turn north on Highway 1 at Guadalupe and drive 3.6 miles. Turn left on Oso Flaco Lake Road and drive three miles to the trailhead.

Coming from the south on U.S. 101, take the Halcyon Road exit and follow it until it dead-ends at Highway 1/Cienaga Avenue. Turn south on Highway 1 and drive 3.5 miles, then turn right on Oso Flaco Lake Road and drive three miles to the trailhead.

9. LAS ZANJAS & EL CAMINO REAL LOOP

La Purisima Mission State Historic Park, off Highway 246
near Buellton

Total distance: 2.5 miles round-trip

Hiking time: 1.5 hours

Type of trail: Rolling terrain

Best season: March–May

You might come to La Purisima Mission anticipating a quiet, meditative afternoon walking around the old mission buildings. And you might get just that, unless it happens to be a school field trip day for a bunch of boisterous kids.

No matter. Despite the common sight of school buses and stacks of lunch boxes at La Purisima Mission, you can still find peaceful sanctuary by setting off on its adjacent hiking trails. Head for the coastal hills, starting with a level loop trail around the mission grounds.

Follow Las Zanjas Trail (also called Las Zonas on some signs), a wide ranch road that leads behind the mission structures. Take the short cutoff on the right (signed as Vista de la Cruz), and after a brief, steep climb, you reach the large cross on the hill. In just a few hundred feet, you are granted a view of the mission below, surrounding grasslands and farmland, and the Pacific Ocean 12 miles to the west.

Continue on Las Zanjas Trail to the park boundary, passing a small pond and evidence of the old mission's aqueduct and irrigation system. Along the way, you'll be accompanied by cool ocean breezes, spring-blooming buckeye trees, and bush monkeyflower. The grasslands are verdant in springtime (wheat and barley are still grown here), and monarch butterflies are often seen flitting among the flowering chaparral. To loop back to the mission, follow El Camino Real, an old paved road.

Be sure to take a tour of the mission before or after your hike. La Purisima is the most completely restored of all of California's 21 Franciscan missions. In addition to the priests' quarters and chapel, you can also see the granary, bakery, and farming structures that helped the mission to thrive, as well as the dormitories where the Spanish soldiers and Chumash Indian workers lived.

Options
Numerous other hiking trails lace the 1,000-acre park. The best of these is a two-mile loop on Huerta Mateo and Mesa Arenosa Trails. You can access this loop from El Camino Real.

Information and Contact
A $5 day-use fee is charged per vehicle. A map of La Purisima Mission State Historic Park is available at the entrance station. For more information, contact La Purisima Mission State Historic Park, 2295 Purisima Road, Lompoc, CA 93436, 805/733-3713, website: www.cal-parks.ca.gov.

Directions
From Buellton on U.S. 101, take the Solvang/Lompoc/Highway 246 exit and drive west for 13.2 miles, then turn right on Purisima Road. Drive one mile and turn right into the park entrance. The trailhead is at the far end of the parking lot, near the visitors center.

10. NOJOQUI FALLS

Nojoqui Falls County Park, off U.S. 101 near Gaviota

Total distance: .5 mile round-trip   **Hiking time:** 20 minutes

Type of trail: Mostly flat terrain   **Best season:** Good year-round

Let's start with the right pronunciation. The park and its namesake waterfall are "Na-Ho-Wee," not "No-Jokey." If you don't say it properly, the locals will mock you without mercy. Get it right, and you're ready to visit the park, which is easily accessed off U.S. 101 heading south from San

Luis Obispo or north from Santa Barbara. It's only a couple of miles off the highway.

The hike to the park's waterfall is short and sweet, requiring a mere 15-minute commitment on a smooth, wide trail through a canopy of 200-year-old California laurels and oaks. Small footbridges carry you over the wet stretches, so you can leave your hiking boots at home. Even Fido is allowed to make the trip, as long as he is on a leash and can appreciate a good waterfall.

Nojoqui Falls is an unusual-looking waterfall, and lovely to see no matter what its flow level. It drops more than 100 feet over a mossy sandstone cliff that is covered with delicate Venus maidenhair ferns. This is one of the

Nojoqui Falls

few places in Santa Barbara County where maidenhairs thrive. They require acidic, calcium-rich soil and plenty of moisture, which are rarities in this arid coastal climate.

A sign at the waterfall explains that Nojoqui Falls is formed where the shale of the lower canyon meets the sandstone of the upper canyon. Rather than being continually eroded by its stream flow like most waterfalls, Nojoqui Falls is continually built up. Calcium deposits from the sandstone of the upper canyon trickle over the face of the waterfall, adding layer upon layer to its cliff.

A stair-stepped rock perch awaits by the fall's pool, where you can sit in the shade of sycamores and have a picnic lunch, or just gaze in admiration at the moss- and fern-covered drop.

Information and Contact

There is no fee. For more information, contact Nojoqui Falls County Park at 805/688-4217 or Santa Barbara County Parks, 300 Goodwin Road,

Santa Maria, CA 93455, 805/934-6123 or 805/568-2461, website: www.sb-parks.com.

Directions

From Santa Barbara, drive 40 miles north on U.S. 101 to the signed turnoff for Nojoqui Falls County Park, north of Gaviota State Beach. Drive one mile on the Old Coast Highway, then turn east on Alisal Road. Drive .8 mile, then turn right into the park entrance. The parking lot and trailhead is .2 mile down the park road.

11. GAVIOTA HOT SPRINGS

Gaviota State Park, off U.S. 101 near Gaviota

Total distance: 1.0 mile round-trip   **Hiking time:** 30 minutes

Type of trail: Some steep terrain   **Best season:** Good year-round

Maybe you've visited Desert Hot Springs, Sycamore Mineral Springs, or the Napa Valley town of Calistoga, and immersed yourself in their warm, natural mineral waters. Although you surely enjoyed the experience, perhaps you wondered what it would be like to soak in an undeveloped hot spring—to bathe alfresco in an earth-made warm-water basin, to be baptized in a pool of mineral water that isn't lined with porcelain or fiberglass.

Gaviota Hot Springs is a great place to have the au naturel hot springs experience. By "au naturel" I don't mean that you should go skinny-dipping; this is a family-style hot spring, where bathing suits are required equipment. In fact, the pools are right alongside the trail, so you won't have much privacy. They're just the right temperature for families with kids—not dangerously hot. This is one place where you won't have a problem convincing your kid to take a bath.

Accessing the pools requires a short but steep climb from the trailhead, mostly on a fire road. A narrow stream lined with sycamores parallels some of the route, but mostly the landscape is composed of grasslands, oaks, mustard, and thistle. When you reach the first trail junction, bear left for the hot springs, then at a second junction, bear right (straight, really). You'll leave the wide fire road and follow a single-track path along Hot Springs Creek for .1 mile to the pools.

The upper pool is the hotter of the two, nearly at bathtub temperature. The smell of sulfur and the sway of the palm tree above may lull you into believing you're at your own private spa. If you look closely, you can see little bubbles coming up from the mud under the pool—geology in action. Clamber in and have a good soak; the water is about two feet deep, better than your average bathtub.

If you want to have the hot springs all to yourself, show up first thing in the morning on weekends or almost anytime during the week. Weekend afternoons, not surprisingly, are the busiest times.

Options
You can continue on the main trail, past the hot springs, on the path to Gaviota Peak. From the hot springs, it's another 2.5 miles to Gaviota Peak, making a six-mile round-trip. The views are tremendous, but the path is steep.

Information and Contact
A $2 day-use fee is charged per vehicle at the hot springs trailhead (it's $5 per vehicle in the main part of Gaviota State Park). For more information, contact Gaviota State Park, c/o Refugio State Beach, 10 Refugio Beach

Gaviota Hot Springs at Gaviota State Park

Road, Goleta, CA 93117, 805/968-1033 or 805/899-1400, website: www.cal-parks.ca.gov.

Directions

From Santa Barbara, drive north on U.S. 101 for 35 miles, go through the tunnel at Gaviota Pass, then take the first exit after the tunnel, signed Highway 1/Lompoc/Vandenburg Air Force Base. At the stop sign, turn right and head south on the frontage road that parallels the freeway. (Don't bear left on Highway 1.) The frontage road ends at the trailhead parking area.

12. KNAPP'S CASTLE

Los Padres National Forest, off U.S. 101 near Santa Barbara

Total distance: 1.0 mile round-trip

Type of trail: Mostly flat terrain

Hiking time: 30 minutes

Best season: Good year-round

Knapp's Castle is one of the historical oddities that give the Santa Ynez Mountains their appealing character. The stone ruins of Knapp's mansion intrigue visitors much in the same manner as Hearst Castle, although more imagination is required. Knapp's Castle also has the capacity to awe; the site's 180-degree views of the Santa Ynez River canyon and Lake Cachuma are downright inspiring.

George Knapp was the chairman of the board of Union Carbide in the early part of the 20th century—a rich man in the days before income taxes. In 1916 he built a five-bedroom sandstone mansion, complete with a pipe organ, on this remote mountain site. Because of the ruggedness of the terrain, and the difficulties of hauling construction supplies on dirt roads, the building took more than five years.

In addition to the main house, Knapp built servants' quarters, a groundskeeper's house, and a road that led to Lewis Canyon below his home, where a cascading waterfall flowed in winter and spring. Not content with the natural seasonal changes of the waterfall, Knapp installed a pumphouse and system of locks in Lewis Creek so he could store water and make the waterfall run at his leisure or for the entertainment of

view of the Santa Ynez Mountains from Knapp's Castle ruins

guests. He installed an observation deck for the falls, a bathhouse, spot-lights for nighttime viewing, and a speaker system so organ music could be piped in from the main house. It may seem obsessive, but the man liked his waterfall.

Knapp's mansion went the way of many extravagant mountain retreats of the early 20th century—it burned in a canyon fire in 1940. The re-maining ruins are quite extensive, and your imagination can easily fill in the missing pieces. Located near the top of Snyder Trail, a well-main-tained pathway that runs from Santa Ynez Canyon six miles uphill to East Camino Cielo, the ruins are actually on private property, but the landowner generously allows hikers to visit the site. (The dirt road to reach the castle ruins is public.) Make sure you mind your manners when you visit, so the landowner will keep the castle ruins open and available for everyone to enjoy.

Start hiking at the gated dirt road on East Camino Cielo that is signed Private Property Ahead. Where the road reaches another gate, walk around it and continue straight ahead to Knapp's Castle. In a few minutes, you'll see the rock chimneys and foundation walls of Knapp's dream house. What captures your attention is the wide-angle view of the Santa Ynez and San Rafael Mountains, and the Santa Ynez River canyon. The rock spires of Knapp's chimneys provide a contrasting geometric foreground for the hazy, distant mountains and valleys. Visit this spot at sunset, and you'll understand what motivated George Knapp to build his dream house here.

Options

After you visit the castle ruins, backtrack to the gate and take the single-track trail that leads downhill and to the right, dropping below Knapp's Castle. This is Snyder Trail, which leads four miles to the Santa Ynez Recreation Area. Views of the Santa Ynez River canyon are excellent along the trail, and in spring, wildflowers bloom in profusion—especially purple nightshade and wild roses.

Information and Contact

A National Forest Adventure Pass is required; see the Hiking Tips at the front of this book for details. For more information and/or a map of Los Padres National Forest, contact the Santa Barbara Ranger District, 3505 Paradise Road, Santa Barbara, CA 93105, 805/967-3481, website: www.fs.fed.us/r5/lospadres.

Directions

From U.S. 101 in Santa Barbara, take the Highway 154/State Street exit and drive north for 10.5 miles. Turn right on East Camino Cielo and drive 2.9 miles to the parking pullout on the right, across from a locked gate and dirt road on the left. The gate is signed Private Property Ahead.

13. INSPIRATION POINT

Los Padres National Forest, off U.S. 101 near
Santa Barbara

Total distance: 4.0 miles round-trip   **Hiking time:** 2.0 hours
Type of trail: Rolling terrain   **Best season:** December–May

A great path for year-round exercise in Santa Barbara, the trail to Inspiration Point is sure to inspire you. It provides lovely views of the Santa Barbara coast and offers spring and early-summer side trips to swimming holes on Mission Creek.

The only problem is that the first part of the route—the Tunnel Trail, one of the most popular paths in Santa Barbara—is poorly signed. Follow these directions carefully or risk wandering around aimlessly on unmarked fire roads.

From the parking area at the end of Tunnel Road, there are three possible roads to follow. You want the middle one, which is the continuation of Tunnel Road. Walk past a water tank and around a gate, then continue uphill on pavement for .7 mile, enjoying spectacular ocean views. On any given day, expect to pass any or all of the following on this road: families coming to splash around in the lower pools of Mission Creek, serious power-walkers on training hikes, and an old guy who leads a three-horse pack train up and down the canyon. It's a busy trail.

At a bridge over Mission Creek, look for seasonal Fern Falls, which in the wet season drops below the bridge. Also look upward at the sandstone peaks ahead; that's where you are heading. Inspiration Point is up there among the tan-colored outcrops. From this bridge, you can sometimes spot hang gliders soaring above the cliffs.

Cross the bridge and continue walking uphill on the deteriorating paved road. Where the pavement ends, a dirt road leads straight ahead and also right. Go straight, walking among red wild fuchsias and peach monkeyflower. In a few hundred yards, you'll see a sign on your left: Jesusita Trail to Inspiration Point and San Roque Road are straight ahead. Walk straight for 100 yards, then bear left on Jesusita Trail, cutting downhill to parallel Mission Creek. Almost immediately, you reach small cascades and rocky pools in the coursing creek; families with small children can stop here for a rest.

To keep on track for Inspiration Point, don't take the streamside trails, but instead keep following the main Jesusita Trail. Cross the creek and prepare for a switchbacking climb to the point, less than one mile away. The trail gets more exposed as you climb, and sandstone outcrops appear along the trail. Colorful sun-loving wildflowers line the trail, including monkeyflower, purple nightshade, and ceanothus.

Inspiration Point, elevation 1,750 feet, is located at the trail's intersection with a dirt road. You are rewarded with views of the Pacific coast, Santa Barbara and Goleta, and the Channel Islands. Feel inspired? It's hard not to. Cross the dirt road, climb on top of a high sandstone boulder, and name each of the Channel Islands in your sight.

Options
Make the pools and waterfalls on Mission Creek your destination. Where Jesusita Trail crosses Mission Creek, head upstream on the unmaintained but obvious trail. A series of waterfalls known as Seven Falls drops over

finely polished granite; the first few cascades are within easy reach. When the creek is high, many clear wading pools are also found.

Information and Contact

There is no fee. For more information and/or a map of Los Padres National Forest, contact the Santa Barbara Ranger District, 3505 Paradise Road, Santa Barbara, CA 93105, 805/967-3481, website: www.fs.fed.us/r5/lospadres.

Directions

From U.S. 101 in Santa Barbara, take the Mission Street exit and follow it east for just over a mile, crossing State Street. Where Mission Street ends, turn left on Laguna Street and drive past the Santa Barbara Mission. Turn right on Los Olivos directly in front of the Mission, then bear left on Mission Canyon Road for .8 mile. Turn right on Foothill Boulevard and drive .1 mile, then turn left on the continuation of Mission Canyon Road. Bear left on Tunnel Road and drive 1.1 miles until it ends. Park alongside the road, on the right.

14. MONTECITO OVERLOOK

Los Padres National Forest, off U.S. 101
near Santa Barbara

Total distance: 3.0 miles round-trip   **Hiking time:** 1.5 hours

Type of trail: Rolling terrain   **Best season:** Good year-round

The East Fork of Cold Springs Trail is a perfect introductory hike to the Santa Barbara front country, with a wide, clear-day view of the Santa Barbara coast and Channel Islands at the trail's Montecito Overlook. In addition to its beautiful scenery, Cold Springs Trail has the distinction of being one of the oldest trails in Santa Barbara, built along its current route around 1899.

The trail starts at a rusty Forest Service signpost on Mountain Drive in an upscale suburban neighborhood. It quickly leads away from the road into shady Cold Springs Canyon. At the trailhead, the creek crosses Mountain Drive on a concrete apron; most people begin hiking from the side of the creek where they parked their car. However you begin, sooner

The east and west forks of Cold Springs Creek converge at a boulder-lined pool.

or later you must get to the main trail on the east (right) side of the creek, then walk with the stream on your left.

For people who think the mountains in Santa Barbara are all dry, chaparral-covered slopes, the East Fork of Cold Springs Trail is an eye-opener to the lush foliage of the mountain canyons. The climb to the overlook is almost entirely under a canopy of leafy alder trees, creating a cool environment even on a warm summer day. Numerous feeder streams and springs keep the ground wet and encourage the wildflowers to bloom. Cold Springs Creek flows year-round, filling its sandstone pools even in most drought years. Ferns and cacti are equally at home alongside the trail.

A quarter mile from the trailhead, the east and west forks of Cold Springs Creek converge at a miniature waterfall. A bench has been placed for viewing the stream's drop over big, rounded boulders. Another trail crosses the creek and leads up the West Fork of Cold Springs; stay on East Fork Trail and continue up the canyon.

After the first mile, the trail leaves the streambanks and begins to switchback uphill, now with a steeper grade. It's only another .5 mile to the overlook, with spring wildflowers accompanying you all the way. When the trail reaches a T-intersection at a wide fire road, you've reached Montecito Overlook, elevation 1,650 feet. Although your coastal view is partially blocked by invading brush at this intersection, follow the fire road a few hundred feet to your right to a high point with a clearer view.

The city of Montecito is spread out below you; you can even see tiny cars driving on U.S. 101. Beyond the city lies the wide blue Pacific, extending out to the horizon as far as the eye can see. On crystal-clear days, you can point out three of the Channel Islands—Santa Cruz, Santa Rosa, and San Miguel.

Options

Beyond Montecito Overlook, the trail continues very steeply to the top of Montecito Peak (elevation 3,214 feet), another two miles away. The view is even better from there, taking in the entire sweep of coast south to the Santa Monica Mountains.

Information and Contact

There is no fee. For more information and/or a map of Los Padres National Forest, contact the Santa Barbara Ranger District, 3505 Paradise Road, Santa Barbara, CA 93105, 805/967-3481, website: www.fs.fed.us/r5/lospadres.

Directions

From Santa Barbara, drive four miles south on U.S. 101 and exit on Hot Springs Road. Turn left on Hot Springs Road and drive 2.5 miles to Mountain Drive. Turn left and drive 1.2 miles to the Cold Springs trailhead. Park off the road near where the creek crosses the road. The trail is marked by a Forest Service sign.

15. SAN YSIDRO TRAIL

Los Padres National Forest, off U.S. 101 near
Santa Barbara

Total distance: 3.6 miles round-trip   **Hiking time:** 2.0 hours
Type of trail: Some steep terrain   **Best season:** December–May

---

If you like running water, San Ysidro Canyon is your chance to see some, even long after the last rain. Other streams in the Santa Barbara area are nearly dry by May, but San Ysidro Creek keeps flowing year-round, creating two lovely waterfalls and many small cascades that can be reached with an easy walk.

Start hiking on the signed San Ysidro Trail by the stables at San Ysidro Ranch, a popular playground of the rich and famous. You'll pass blooming lantana, bougainvillea, and geraniums along this stretch—not exactly wildflowers, but certainly flowers that have gone wild. Don't be disturbed by the "suburbanization" of this part of the trail; the landscape will get more wild as you leave the private property and head deeper into San Ysidro Canyon.

In the first mile, the route goes from single-track to pavement to wide fire road and then back to single-track, roughly following San Ysidro Creek the whole way. You glimpse a continual series of rushing cascades, but the trail keeps its distance from the stream. Almost entirely shaded by oaks and bays, the path stays cool even in summer. Sandstone outcrops rise above the canyon; rock climbers are often seen practicing their craft upon them.

At 1.5 miles, just before the trail ascends a steep slope on a railing-lined series of rocky stairs, take the left cutoff trail, which leads to the stream's edge and a small, five-foot-tall waterfall and sculpted sandstone pool. Often you'll find someone swimming or sunbathing here. Then continue up the trail on the well-constructed rock stairway. (Watch your footing and use the handrail on your downhill return.) You are moving away from the creek, heading for another fork of it.

At 1.75 miles, a stream crosses the trail—sometimes rushing wildly and sometimes seeping slowly. A few hundred feet beyond it, just before the trail curves right and moves away from the creek, take the left cutoff trail for 30 yards to see a sandstone waterfall. Set in the back of a box canyon,

© ANN MARIE BROWN

lower falls at San Ysidro Canyon

the 60-foot-tall cascade displays an incredible array of colors in its cliff face. Lichen, mosses, and ferns appear yellow, green, peach, and gold against the gray sandstone. The waterfall's flow can be thin or wide, depending on when the last rain has come, but the cliff and its fern-filled grotto are impressive anytime.

Options
Beyond this waterfall, the San Ysidro Trail leaves the stream's edge and enters more steep, exposed terrain. It heads for exposed chaparral country and the trail's end at Camino Cielo, a total of 4.2 miles from the trailhead and 3,000 feet above it.

Information and Contact
There is no fee. For more information and/or a map of Los Padres National Forest, contact the Santa Barbara Ranger District, 3505 Paradise Road, Santa Barbara, CA 93105, 805/967-3481, website: www.fs.fed.us/r5/lospadres.

Directions
From U.S. 101 in Montecito, take the San Ysidro Road exit and drive one mile east to East Valley Road/Highway 192. Turn right and drive .9 mile, then turn left on Park Lane. Drive .4 mile, then bear left on East Mountain Drive. Drive .3 mile to the end of East Mountain Drive and park alongside the road. The trailhead is on the right side of the road.

16. PIEDRA BLANCA

Rose Valley Recreation Area, off Highway 33 near Ojai

Total distance: 4.0 miles round-trip

Type of trail: Rolling terrain

Hiking time: 2.0 hours

Best season: Good year-round

Sandstone lovers, this is your spot. Piedra Blanca is a series of huge, rounded sandstone boulders that appear almost otherworldly compared to the surrounding landscape. In a way, they are—the rocks are of marine origin, holdovers from the days when the ocean covered the region that is now Ojai. If you're trying to imagine what this place looks like, think Joshua Tree National Park, and you'll be on the right track. Many of the boulders are larger than your average Volkswagen.

Piedra Blanca is in the Rose Valley Recreation Area of Los Padres National Forest, just a short stretch away from Sespe Creek. The area looks a lot like the desert—plenty of sand and rocks—especially when Sespe Creek is dry. When the creek is running, be sure to bring your waterproof boots, because the trail to Piedra Blanca includes a crossing of its wash.

The trail begins on the closed road to what was once Lion Campground. The camp was closed in 1999 to protect the fragile habitat of endangered toads and frogs. Follow the old road for one mile to the now-closed camp. Cross Sespe Creek (or its dry wash), then pick up the obvious trail on the far side. The rocks of Piedra Blanca are clearly visible from here, so it's easy to see where you're going. The name "Piedra Blanca"—Spanish for "white stone"—tells you all you need to know to identify them.

The trail leads slightly uphill, making a beeline for the sandstone formations. Bear right at a fork, heading toward the big, round, sunbleached rocks.

As you approach and then climb upon the smooth boulders, you see that each rock assumes a different shape depending on your vantage point. A few small scrub oaks manage to eke out a living in the crevices of the rocks, along with some meager grasses that look like dune plants. Go ahead and clamber around at will, exploring the rocks' many curves and crevices, then pick your favorite spot for picnicking or sunbathing. As you might guess, Piedra Blanca is a first-class site for watching sunsets.

Piedra Blanca

Options
Continue hiking beyond Piedra Blanca, following the trail down the back side of the boulders and then along a seasonal creek. The path continues for another five miles, passing several trail camps.

Information and Contact
A National Forest Adventure Pass is required; see the Hiking Tips at the front of this book for details. For more information and/or a map of Los Padres National Forest, contact the Ojai Ranger District, 1190 East Ojai Avenue, Ojai, CA 93023, 805/646-4348, website: www.fs.fed.us/r5/lospadres.

Directions
From Ojai, drive north on Highway 33 for 16 miles to Rose Valley Road and the sign for Rose Valley Recreation Area. Turn right and drive 4.8 miles to the parking area by the gated road.

17. ROSE VALLEY FALLS

Los Padres National Forest, off Highway 33 near Ojai

Total distance: .5 mile round-trip   **Hiking time:** 20 minutes

Type of trail: Mostly flat terrain   **Best season:** December–May

---

Rose Valley Falls is the kind of place where you take your kids when they want to have an adventure, but they're not quite old enough for adventures. The trip to the falls is like a Shirley Temple cocktail—colorful and exciting, but without potential hazards.

Start your hike at the signed trail by campsite 4 in Rose Valley Campground. Head into the woods, cross Rose Creek, then cross it a few more times. From a clearing in the canyon, you get a glimpse of the waterfall far off in the distance—a tall, narrow stream pouring through a notch. If that sight doesn't motivate your five-year-old to keep walking, nothing will.

Bordered on both sides by oaks and fragrant bays, the path is smooth and nearly level, and it parallels the stream all the way. Several side trails head down to small cascades and pools on Rose Creek—good swimming spots on a warm day. You'll continue to get peek-a-boo glances at the falls as you head upcanyon.

In a mere 15 minutes, you're standing at the base of Rose Valley Falls, which, surprisingly, looks nothing like what you saw coming up the canyon. This is only the very bottom of the huge, 300-foot cascade, which drops in two tiers. The upper tier, which you spotted from a distance, is accessible only by climbing (not for novices).

The lower tier is an immense 100-foot slab of sandstone and limestone, bearing a strange molten-rock appearance as if the cliff melted down the hillside in sheets of sand-colored lava. Its entire surface is encased in moss. Water cascades over the limestone and mossy surface in thin, separate streams. Many large boulders are sprawled at the waterfall's base, where you can sit and marvel at this unusual geologic feature.

Information and Contact

A National Forest Adventure Pass is required; see the Hiking Tips at the front of this book for details. For more information and/or a map of Los

Padres National Forest, contact the Ojai Ranger District, 1190 East Ojai Avenue, Ojai, CA 93023, 805/646-4348, website: www.fs.fed.us/r5/lospadres.

Directions
From Ojai, drive north on Highway 33 for 16 miles to Rose Valley Road and the sign for Rose Valley Recreation Area. Turn right, drive three miles, and turn right again at the sign for Rose Valley Camp. Drive .6 mile to the campground. The trail leads from the far end of the camp, near site 4.

18. McGRATH NATURE TRAIL & BEACH WALK
McGrath State Beach, off U.S. 101 near Ventura

Total distance: 3.0 miles round-trip

Type of trail: Mostly flat terrain

Hiking time: 1.5 hours

Best season: April–October

There's a great little nature trail at McGrath State Beach that presents an experience vastly different from a stroll along the long, sandy beach. Conveniently, the nature trail and beach are right next to each other, so there's no need to forsake one for the other. Plan to spend half a day, or all day, and visit both.

McGrath Nature Trail runs along the Santa Clara Estuary, a natural preserve located where the Santa Clara River joins the Pacific Ocean. In that meeting space, freshwater and saltwater plants and animals intermingle, giving visitors the chance to see migrating birds, resident shorebirds, and fish. Jackrabbits, squirrels, and other small critters also make their home here.

The trail starts out in a densely shaded willow thicket, a surprisingly peaceful change from the hustle and bustle of the state beach campground. It parallels the edge of the estuary, where in places the foliage is so dense that it impedes your view. The birds like it this way, however. Watch for the endangered California least tern and Belding's savannah sparrow, as well as more common songbirds, raptors, and shorebirds.

The nature trail follows a rather circuitous route to the beach; you may wonder if you are caught in a labyrinth as you trace the willow-lined path's curves. When you finally reach the sand, walk up and over some low sand

After completing the nature trail at McGrath State Beach, you can wander as far as you like along the sand.

dunes and continue your hike along the shoreline. Head south (left), because the Santa Clara River to the north can be nearly impossible to ford. In a little more than a mile you'll reach small, freshwater McGrath Lake. Keep watching for it on your left, just slightly inland, as you hike along the coast. The lake attracts more than 200 species of birds, including owls, kites, osprey, and herons. Don't forget your bird book and binoculars.

Options
You can continue your walk beyond McGrath Lake for several more miles along the beach.

Information and Contact
A $5 day-use fee is charged per vehicle. For more information, contact McGrath State Beach, 901 South San Pedro, Ventura, CA 93001, 805/654-4744 or 805/899-1400, website: www.cal-parks.ca.gov.

Directions
From U.S. 101 in Ventura, take the Seaward Avenue exit to Harbor Boulevard. Turn south on Harbor Boulevard and drive four miles to the park entrance. The nature trail begins at the day-use parking lot, a quick right turn after the entrance kiosk. (If you are traveling north on U.S. 101, you must take the Victoria Avenue exit to reach Harbor Boulevard.)

Chapter 4

Los Angeles and Vicinity

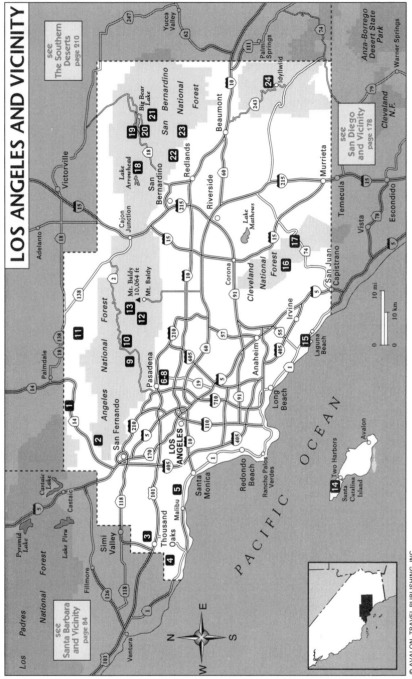

LOS ANGELES AND VICINITY

see The Southern Deserts page 210

see San Diego and Vicinity page 178

see Santa Barbara and Vicinity page 84

PACIFIC OCEAN

© AVALON TRAVEL PUBLISHING, INC.

CHAPTER 4—LOS ANGELES AND VICINITY

I slands, mountains, beaches, lakes, deserts—the Los Angeles region provides all this diversity and more. Most people think of freeway traffic or palm-tree-lined beaches when they think of L.A., but those are only fragments of what this place is all about. Two immense national forests hold most of the mountainous land in the region—Angeles and San Bernardino. The former contains the San Gabriel Mountains, which create a high, impenetrable shield that prevents Los Angeles's smog from dissipating. The mountains, which geologists believe are the most fractured and unstable in California, sustain a network of more than 500 miles of hiking trails. So close to the freeways, high-rises, and smog of Los Angeles, these high mountains and their clean, sweet air are a hiker's paradise. Sick of the freeway rat race? Head for the trails that grace the slopes of Mount Waterman or Vetter Mountain. You can hike away your cares and be back in L.A. in time for dinner.

A few miles to the east, the San Bernardino Mountains in San Bernardino National Forest are one of the highest mountain ranges in California, with peaks that rise to more than 11,000 feet in elevation. The San Bernardinos also contain Southern California's three major recreation lakes: Big Bear, Arrowhead, and Silverwood. A wealth of hiking trails are found in and around these popular recreation areas, including many suited for easy hikes.

Yet another mountain range is found in San Bernardino National Forest: the San Jacintos, topped by Mount San Jacinto at 10,804 feet, which towers over the low desert at Palm Springs. The San Jacintos rise abruptly from the desert floor, completely separated from the other high-elevation ranges of Southern California by low passes and valleys. Most hikers access the San Jacinto range from the resort town of Idyllwild, which is within an hour's drive of most of the Los Angeles Basin.

One more mountain range found in the Los Angeles region is a gentler stretch of sloping peaks rising from the coast: the Santa Monica Mountains. Much of the public land here is part of the Santa Monica Mountains National Recreation Area, but a portion is divided into several state parks and a nonprofit land conservancy. The trails in the Santa Monica Mountains crisscross chaparral- and sage-covered hillsides, oak woodlands, and native grasslands. Rocky sandstone outcrops poke up here and there, adding variety to the landscape.

More surprises wait in the Los Angeles area. If you're a waterfall lover, check out the falls in winter and spring at Placerita Canyon County Park, Monrovia Canyon Park, Wildwood Park, Point Mugu State Park, and Angeles National Forest. If your hiking sensibilities run more toward sunset walks along the beach, hop on a ferry and pay a visit to Catalina Island. Or head to Laguna Beach, where the seaside white sands give way to view-filled coastal hills at Crystal Cove State Park. No matter where you go, try to keep reminding yourself that you're still in L.A. With all this diversity, it can be hard to believe.

1. FOOT TRAIL & GEOLOGY TRAIL

Vasquez Rocks Natural Area, off Highway 14
near Agua Dulce

Total distance: 3.0 miles round-trip   **Hiking time:** 1.5 hours

Type of trail: Rolling terrain   **Best season:** November–April

---

In case you are wondering if there is any "country" left near the city of Los Angeles, the park office at Vasquez Rocks Natural Area should convince you. It's a barn, complete with hay and horses.

But that's just one of many surprises at Vasquez Rocks. Pick up a trail map by the stable, then take a walk on the park's Foot Trail to get a close-up look at the bizarre tilted rock slabs that have made the place famous in television and film productions, including the movie *The Flintstones* and several old Westerns.

Vasquez Rocks was formed around 10 million years ago by earthquake activity on the Elkhorn Fault, an offshoot of the more famous San Andreas Fault. Ancient sedimentary layers were folded, compressed, and tilted upward by the powerful forces of the earth's movement. If you think about it too much, you won't want to stand still for too long in one place.

The result of all this geological activity is the broken, angular landscape you see today. The park's largest sandstone slab is nearly 150 feet high. Some of the slabs are tilted as much as 50 degrees, jutting out at various angles toward the sky. Most of the slabs are yellow and gray, but some are striated with deep hues of reddish brown.

From the parking area, begin hiking on the signed Foot Trail through the colorful sandstone slabs, then loop back on Pacific Crest Trail, which returns to the other side of the parking area. The loop shows off the park's best features, and if you time your trip right, you'll find that the colors in the slabs at Vasquez Rocks make for vivid sunsets.

Aside from the geological history of the park, your visit will also teach you about the human history of Vasquez Rocks. The Tataviam Indians (a band of Serrano Indians) once lived here and used the large rock outcroppings for shelter and shade. They were in the area when the Spanish arrived in the late 1700s, living comfortably in this desertlike environment because of a continual water supply from Agua Dulce Springs.

The Tataviam Indians were not warriors, so they did not fight the Spanish. Many of the Tataviams were taken to local missions; others learned Spanish, intermarried, and adopted Spanish surnames. After only a few generations, the Tataviam language and culture disappeared. Today, archaeologists come to Vasquez Rocks to try to re-create that culture, or at least imagine it, by studying the remaining pictographs, middens, stone tools, and burial grounds.

The park gets its name from Tiburcio Vasquez, a bandit from the mid-1800s, who used the area's caves and rocks as his personal hideaway. He rustled horses, robbed stagecoaches, and did other dastardly deeds, but was considered a local hero because he frequently gave money to poor Mexican families. A major shootout between Vasquez's gang and the local sheriff's posse took place near the tallest rock formation in the park.

Options

Hike the short Geology Trail, which leads from the park entrance. Then spend some time climbing around on the rock formations. If the geology of this park interests you, you should also pay a visit to Devil's Punchbowl Natural Area, which exhibits a different version of the same geologic action (see hike 11 in this chapter).

Information and Contact

There is no fee. A trail map is available at park headquarters. For more information, contact Vasquez Rocks Natural Area, 10700 West Escondido Canyon Road, Agua Dulce, CA 91390, 661/268-0840, website: http://parks .co.la.ca.us.

Directions

From the junction of I-5 and Highway 14, drive northeast on Highway 14 for 15 miles to Agua Dulce. Take the Vasquez Rocks/Escondido Canyon exit and drive north for 2.2 miles to the park entrance. Follow the dirt road to the large parking lot and picnic area and begin hiking on the Foot Trail on the right (south) side of the parking lot.

2. PLACERITA CANYON TRAIL

Placerita Canyon County Park, off Highway 14
near Newhall

Total distance: 5.5 miles round-trip   **Hiking time:** 3.0 hours
Type of trail: Mostly flat terrain   **Best season:** Good year-round

---

Placerita Canyon County Park is a perfect destination for a family outing. With plentiful hiking, picnicking, and horseback riding opportunities, the park is just far enough out of the Los Angeles basin so that going there feels like getting away. And best of all, the park is home to Placerita Creek's waterfall, accessible by an easy hike along the creek.

Start your trip at the park's nature center, where you can learn about the flora and fauna of the area. You'll also find out about the short-lived gold rush that began here in 1842, when a cattleman dug up some wild onions for a snack, and found gold flakes attached to their roots. A half-million dollars' worth of gold was taken from this canyon in the 1840s.

Start hiking on the Canyon Trail, which leads from the southeast side of the nature center parking lot and crosses Placerita Creek. The trail winds through Placerita Canyon, passing shady canyon oaks, sycamores, willows, and blackberry bushes, to the Walker Ranch group camping area. At Walker Ranch, you'll find the stone remains of settlers' cottages that were built in the early 1900s. Walk through the picnic area to its far end, then turn right and pick up the path signed Waterfall Trail. (Ignore the right turn about 30 yards before this one, which is Los Piñetos Trail.)

The trail gets more interesting the farther you go, as it narrows and curves its way deeper into Placerita Canyon. Along the way, you can smell the sulphur from underground springs, and the springtime fragrance of blooming ceanothus. The edible leaves of miner's lettuce grow near the creek. The path crosses the stream a few times, making it advisable to wear waterproof boots in high water, although plenty of visitors wear everyday shoes. In the final 100 yards before the waterfall, the trail ends and you simply hike up the streambed.

Placerita Creek Falls is about 25 feet high, with a narrow stream that cascades down its cliff face. It forms a lovely shaded grotto, with only enough room for a few visitors in its cloister. Did you pack your lunch? Good thinking—the spot clearly suggests a picnic.

Options

If you want to reduce your mileage, you can drive two miles past the park entrance on Placerita Canyon Road to the Walker Ranch gate (a dirt road). Park near the gate, then walk around it and into the Walker Ranch group campground. From there, head straight on Waterfall Trail for a round-trip of 2.4 miles instead of 5.5 miles.

Information and Contact

There is no fee. A park map is available at the nature center. For more information, contact Placerita Canyon County Park, 19152 Placerita Canyon Road, Newhall, CA 91321, 661/259-7721, website: www.placerita.org.

Placerita Canyon's waterfall grotto is a cool and shady spot for a picnic.

Directions

From the San Fernando Valley, drive north on I-5 to Highway 14. Follow Highway 14 northeast for four miles to Newhall, then exit on Placerita Canyon Road. Turn right (east) and drive two miles to the park entrance on the right. Park in the nature center parking lot. (For a shorter hike, drive two miles east of the park entrance on Placerita Canyon Road to the Walker Ranch gate on the right.)

3. WILDWOOD CANYON LOOP

Wildwood Park, off U.S. 101 near Thousand Oaks

Total distance: 4.0 miles round-trip   **Hiking time:** 2.0 hours

Type of trail: Rolling terrain

Best season: Good year-round; wildflowers are excellent February–May

Wildwood Park is one of the best-kept park secrets in Los Angeles, known mostly to the school kids who come here for field trips in the spring. But with its proximity to U.S. 101, it's also the perfect place for harried commuters to take a break from their cars and get back to nature for an hour or so. Trails interweave throughout the park, so you can put together a different loop trip or out-and-back hike every time you visit.

One of the best and easiest hikes leads from the Arboles trailhead in Thousand Oaks. From there, you can walk downhill into Wildwood Canyon and then stroll along its year-round stream, which produces a dramatic waterfall when the water level is high. Even during the dry months, when the waterfall is less than ebullient, the canyon is shady and pleasant.

To see it, hike due west on the Mesa Trail for .5 mile to North Tepee Trail. Turn left and drop down into Wildwood Canyon. After a short descent, you'll enter the hidden canyon, where many signs direct you to Paradise Falls, or sometimes Wildwood Falls, the waterfall's less imaginative name. Of several trail choices, the best approach is from the east on the Wildwood Canyon Trail. This way you can see the stream just before it makes its tremendous hurtle over a basalt lip. The trail parallels the creek downhill to the fall's base. A chain-link fence keeps you from tumbling down the hillside at the steepest dropoffs.

Even in low water, 70-foot-tall Paradise Falls makes a frothy white stream, with a startlingly wide pool at its base. At about 50 yards wide during high water, it is more like a large pond. The presence of year-round water makes this canyon a haven for wildlife; keep on the lookout for mule deer, rabbits, coyotes, and numerous songbirds and raptors. The park's wildlife list includes 60 species of birds, 37 species of mammals, and 22 species of amphibians and reptiles.

If flora interests you more than fauna, watch for interpretive signs along the path that teach you to identify various plants and trees of the park. Spring wildflowers (best seen from February till May) include chocolate lily, goldfields, Indian paintbrush, tidytips, blue-eyed grass, and shooting stars. Two rare plants are found on the cliffs alongside Paradise Falls: Conejo buckwheat and Conejo dudleya.

The basalt of the waterfall's cliff was formed by the same geologic action that created the Montclef Ridge, that strange, plateau-like outcrop you probably noticed at the parking lot. These formations resulted from a series of volcanic eruptions that occurred in this area some 30 million years ago.

From the falls, continue walking downstream, then pick up Lizard Rock Trail at the park's western boundary to loop back. Turn right on Box Canyon Trail to connect to Mesa Trail, then retrace your steps back to the car.

Wildwood Park's waterfall

Information and Contact

There is no fee. For more information and a park map, contact Conejo Recreation and Park District, 403 West Hillcrest Drive, Thousand Oaks, CA 91360, 805/381-2741 or 805/495-6471, website: www.crpd.org.

Directions

From U.S. 101 in Thousand Oaks, take the Lynn Road exit and head north. Drive 2.5 miles to Avenida de los Arboles, then turn left. Drive .9 mile and make a U-turn into the Arboles parking lot on the left side of the road.

4. BIG SYCAMORE CANYON & OLD BONEY TRAILS

Santa Monica Mountains, off U.S. 101 near Newbury Park

Total distance: 5.0 miles round-trip   **Hiking time:** 2.5 hours

Type of trail: Rolling terrain   **Best season:** Good year-round

---

The Santa Monica Mountains National Recreation Area Rancho Sierra Vista/Satwiwa Site is the very long name for the back entrance to Point Mugu State Park. It's a mouthful to say, but all you need to remember is Satwiwa (which means "the bluffs"), the name of the Chumash Indian village that existed here. That's what people call this trailhead, because many come here to visit the park's Native American cultural site.

You can guess your hike will be good when, at the trailhead parking lot, you're greeted by two friendly roadrunners and half a dozen bunnies, the local welcoming committee. (That's what happened on my visit.) Pick up a trail map at the signpost and walk up the gated road from the parking lot. Pass the Satwiwa Culture Center on your left, with its dome-shaped stick dwelling that was re-created to interpret traditional Native American life. The center is open only on Sundays; if you time your visit right, you can turn your hiking trip into a cultural history lesson.

Keep heading uphill, now following a paved road. When you reach a water tank on your right, .5 mile from the parking lot, turn left on a dirt trail (Old Boney Trail) and follow it past two turnoffs for the Satwiwa Loop Trail. Your destination is an obvious signed trail fork. The left fork leads to Hidden Valley Overlook, but you'll take the right fork. Shortly after, you'll cross a stream, which hopefully will be flowing strong on your visit—a sign of good things to come.

Where Old Boney Trail makes a sharp right, switchback uphill and out of the canyon, then take the left fork (signed No Horses) for a few yards to visit a sometimes spectacular waterfall, Sycamore Canyon Falls. The water pours, or trickles if it hasn't rained lately, over a series of sandstone ledges, artfully accented by huge woodwardia ferns, smaller sword ferns, and big-leaf maples. If the stream is running strong, you'll see a half dozen small pools and cascades. The sandstone cliff's total height is more than 100 feet.

After visiting the waterfall, return to the main trail and begin to climb. In .75 mile, where the road forks, bear left. In a few minutes of walking, you'll reach the stone remains of a herdsman's cabin, left from the early 1900s when this area was cattle-grazing land. The cabin burned in a wildfire in the 1950s, and all that remains is a tall chimney and some scattered rocks from foundation walls. It's a good spot for a lunch break before retracing your steps to the trailhead.

Options
Continue hiking from the cabin site, following Old Boney Trail farther south. You can loop back to Satwiwa on several possible trails; make sure you have a park map with you to plan your route.

A waterfall drops over smooth sandstone in Big Sycamore Canyon.

Information and Contact
There is no fee. Maps are available at the trailhead. For more information, contact Santa Monica Mountains National Recreation Area, 401 West Hillcrest Drive, Thousand Oaks, CA 91360, 805/370-2301, website: www.nps.gov/samo.

Directions
From U.S. 101 in Thousand Oaks, exit on Lynn Road and drive south 5.5 miles to Via Goleta. Turn left and drive .75 mile to the last parking lot. Take the trail signed for the Satwiwa Cultural Center.

5. INSPIRATION POINT TRAIL

Will Rogers State Historic Park, off Highway 1 near
Santa Monica

Total distance: 2.0 miles round-trip   **Hiking time:** 1.0 hour

Type of trail: Rolling terrain   **Best season:** Winter and spring

---

Most folks come to Will Rogers State Historic Park to visit the home of the "Cowboy Philosopher" and humorist Will Rogers, or to have a picnic on his massive lawn. Rogers's humble abode was a gigantic 31-room ranch/mansion, built in the 1930s and done up in cowboy decorating style. Rogers's well-rounded life included stints as a steer roper, vaudeville lariat artist, Ziegfield Follies humorist, radio celebrity, and film star, but he was most famous for his common-sense philosophy and humorous observations.

My personal favorite of Rogers's remarks is this one, posted on the main trailhead sign: "If your time is worth anything, travel by air. If not, you might just as well walk." It's a good introduction to the two-mile loop trip to Inspiration Point, which begins by the ranch house. If you can, time your trip for a perfectly clear day, perhaps after a rain or first thing on a winter morning, when the marine layer and smog are gone and the vista is optimal.

To locate the trailhead, walk up the stairs of the ranch house's porch and head right to the porch's far end (away from the visitors center and gift shop). Pick up the dirt trail that leads to your left along the grassy lawn. At the lawn's edge, cross a tiny footbridge and you'll find the trailhead. Go left and uphill.

As you hike, you'll see many single-track paths that lead off the main trail, but just stay on the wide fire road. After a gentle climb, you'll near the highest point in the park at .75 mile and reach a major fork in the road. This is the junction with the Backbone Trail, which leaves Will Rogers State Historic Park and enters Topanga State Park.

Go right for Inspiration Point, leaving the main fire road. In moments you'll be at the point, enjoying superb vistas of Los Angeles to your left, the state park below you, the Santa Monica Mountains to your right, and the Pacific Ocean beyond. There's a horse-hitching post at the top (this being a cowboy's park, of course), and a bench for hikers who wish to enjoy the scene. It's hard to believe that the big city is within view of this tranquil, natural place, but there it is, spread out before you. Considering the expanse of your view, it's also hard to believe that you're only 750 feet up. On the clearest of days, you can see all the way to Catalina Island, 20-plus miles away.

To finish out your hike, backtrack down to the junction with Backbone Trail, then go right and downhill to loop back. You'll come out by the stable area at Will Rogers State Historic Park, where you can say hello to the horses before heading back to your car.

Options
Backtrack to the junction with the Backbone Trail, and hike out and back for any distance into Topanga State Park.

Information and Contact
A $5 day-use fee is charged per vehicle. A park map is available at the entrance station. Polo matches are held at the ranch on weekends April–October; these days are best avoided because of the crowds. For more information, contact Will Rogers State Historic Park, 1501 Will Rogers State Park Road, Pacific Palisades, CA 90272, 310/454-8212 or 818/880-0350, website: www.cal-parks.ca.gov.

Directions
From Santa Monica, drive north on Highway 1 to Sunset Boulevard in Pacific Palisades. Turn right on Sunset Boulevard and drive 4.5 miles to Will Rogers State Park Road, then turn left and drive one mile to the park entrance. The trail begins near Rogers's ranch house.

6. MILLARD CANYON

Angeles National Forest, off I-210 near Pasadena

Total distance: 1.0 mile round-trip   **Hiking time:** 30 minutes

Type of trail: Mostly flat terrain   **Best season:** Winter or spring

---

If you want to guarantee your kids a good time, take them to Millard Campground for the short hike and scramble to Millard Falls. If it's winter or spring, make sure they're outfitted with shoes that can get wet, because the trail follows the creekbed and is often immersed in the water. This trip makes a perfect family adventure that is short enough even for little ones to accomplish, but with scenery to impress hikers of any age.

The only minus to a hike in Millard Canyon is the abundance of carvings found on the smooth-barked alder trees. The carvings desecrate almost every tree as high up as human

Millard Falls

hands can reach. Use this as an opportunity to teach your children never, ever to carve into the trunks of trees. Many people don't realize that over time, this kills the tree. Spread the word.

Start walking at the far edge of the campground, just beyond the camp host's site, where the trail leads to the right past a couple of cabins. After the first few yards, when the stream flow is high, the trail disappears into the creek. Just keep heading upstream, rock-hopping as you go.

The canyon gets progressively narrower as you travel; finally its walls come together at 60-foot-high Millard Falls. The fall drops over a rugged cliff face; its stream splits in two at the top, forced to detour around two boulders that are stuck in the waterfall's notch. (Those boulders won't last forever; another earthquake or two and Millard Falls will have a whole new look.) The two streams rejoin about two-thirds of the way down, creating a tremendous rush of water in springtime. Pull up a rock, have a seat, and enjoy the spectacle.

Options

If you'd like to see Millard Falls from above, drive your car back up the camp road to the top of Sunset Ridge. Park along the road, and walk eastward on the gated, paved Sunset Ridge Fire Road for .2 mile to the left turnoff for Sunset Ridge Trail. Hike about a mile on Sunset Ridge Trail and you'll pass just above the waterfall.

Information and Contact

A National Forest Adventure Pass is required; see the Hiking Tips at the front of this book for details. For more information and/or a map of Angeles National Forest, contact the Los Angeles River Ranger District, 12371 North Little Tujunga Canyon Road, San Fernando, CA 91342, 818/899-1900, website: www.fs.fed.us/r5/angeles.

Directions

From I-210 in Pasadena, exit on Lake Avenue and drive north 3.5 miles to Loma Alta Drive. Turn west (left) on Loma Alta Drive and drive one mile to Chaney Trail at the flashing yellow light. Turn right and drive 1.5 miles on Chaney Trail, keeping left at the fork, to Millard Campground. Park in the lot, then walk down the dirt road on the right (as you drove in) that leads into the campground.

7. STURTEVANT FALLS

Angeles National Forest, off I-210 near Arcadia

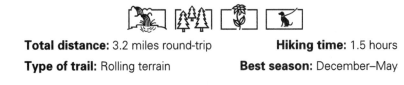

Total distance: 3.2 miles round-trip   **Hiking time:** 1.5 hours

Type of trail: Rolling terrain   **Best season:** December–May

---

Sturtevant Falls is the crown jewel of Big Santa Anita Canyon, a lushly forested, almost magical gulch just a handful of miles from the Pasadena Freeway. Day-hikers in the canyon can't help but covet its small summer cabins, set in the same beautiful ravine where Sturtevant Falls drops. The best kind of life I can imagine in Los Angeles would be to live in one of those cabins and take a daily stroll to the waterfall.

The hike is understandably popular. You leave your car at Chantry Flat and hike downhill into the canyon, following Gabrielino Trail for an easy 3.2-mile round-trip. Since this is a National Recreation Trail, it's open to bikes, horses, and dogs (up to the waterfall cutoff), and you may see some of each on any spring weekend.

The first .6 mile follows a paved road, but once you reach the canyon bottom, you cross Roberts Footbridge over Winter Creek, then head right on a wide dirt path, hiking upstream to Sturtevant Falls. (Don't take the left turnoff for Winter Creek Trail.) A sign near the footbridge details the 1912–1936 period when the confluence of Winter and Big Santa Anita Creeks was the home of Roberts Camp, a popular weekend resort. A stone lodge, dining area, and numerous cabins and tents once stood here— enough buildings to accommodate 180 guests at a time. Some of those old cabins are the ones you see here today.

Gabrielino Trail meanders under the shade of oaks and alders along Big Santa Anita Creek. The stream is tamed somewhat by a series of small check dams, forming oddly pretty artificial waterfalls and glassy pools. At a junction at 1.3 miles, Gabrielino Trail forks left and heads uphill, but you continue straight along the creek for another .3 mile to Sturtevant Falls. You cross the creek, the canyon bends to the left, and then you cross again. Sturtevant Falls suddenly reveals itself, dropping 60 feet over a granite cliff into a perfectly shaped rock bowl.

Like the Grace Kelly of waterfalls, Sturtevant is an elegant act. Set in the back of this shady canyon, it's gracefully framed by alders and has a large pool at its base. When the water level drops, a pebbly beachlike area around the pool is exposed. Sit down and compose a few love sonnets, or spread out a picnic.

Options

Backtrack to the junction where Gabrielino Trail heads uphill, then follow it out and back to Cascade Picnic Area, a shady spot alongside the creek. This adds 2.5 greenery-filled miles to your round-trip.

Information and Contact

A National Forest Adventure Pass is required; see the Hiking Tips at the front of this book for details. For more information and/or a map of Angeles National Forest, contact the Los Angeles

alder trees along Big Santa Anita Creek

River Ranger District, 12371 North Little Tujunga Canyon Road, San Fernando, CA 91342, 818/899-1900, website: www.fs.fed.us/r5/angeles.

Directions

From I-210 in Pasadena, drive seven miles east to Arcadia. Exit on Santa Anita Avenue and drive six miles north to the road's end at Chantry Flat. The trail begins across the road from the first parking area as you drive in.

8. MONROVIA CANYON

Monrovia Canyon Park, off I-210 in Monrovia

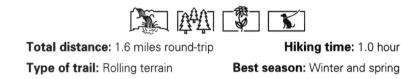

Total distance: 1.6 miles round-trip

Type of trail: Rolling terrain

Hiking time: 1.0 hour

Best season: Winter and spring

Of all the city-owned parks in the Los Angeles area, Monrovia Canyon Park ranks as one of the best. It's clean and well-managed and has beautiful hiking trails. There is nothing to complain about at Monrovia Canyon, except if you try to visit on a Tuesday. That's when the local police use the park for target practice, and they lock the gates and close the whole place down for the day. Time your trip for any other day of the week.

The park's Falls Trail is an ideal easy hike—less than a mile in length, and nearly level the whole way. It starts at the picnic area near the park nature center and museum, located at the far end of the park road.

Walk through the picnic area and look for the signed single-track trail to Monrovia Canyon Falls. At the first junction, head right. Almost immediately, you pass several check dams that make small waterfalls of their own. Keep walking along the creek, heading gently uphill. The canyon is lush and shaded, crowded with alders, oaks, and ferns. This is the kind of place that would be unforgettable in a light rain.

After less than 30 minutes of gentle climbing, you'll reach the 50-foot-high falls, split in the middle by a granite ledge. Monrovia Canyon Falls is fed by a perennial spring, not just by snowmelt and rainfall, so the waterfall flows year-round. Sun-warmed rocks in front of the cataract make perfect seats for gazing in admiration.

Options

You can extend this hike by starting at a lower trailhead by the park entrance kiosk. Following Bill Cull Trail from there, the round-trip to the waterfall is 3.4 miles. Also, the park offers free docent-led hikes every Saturday.

Information and Contact

A $2 day-use fee is charged per vehicle. A park map is available at the nature center. For more information, contact Monrovia Canyon Park, 1200

North Canyon Boulevard, Monrovia, CA 91016, 626/256-8282, website: www.ci.monrovia.ca.us.

Directions

From I-210 in Monrovia, take the Myrtle Avenue exit and drive north to Foothill Boulevard. Turn right, go through two stoplights to Canyon Boulevard, then turn left and drive 1.5 miles to the park (bear right where the road forks). Park at the far end of the park road, near the picnic area and nature center.

9. VETTER MOUNTAIN LOOKOUT

Angeles National Forest, off Highway 2 near
Charlton Flat

Total distance: 2.6 miles round-trip   **Hiking time:** 1.0 hour

Type of trail: Rolling terrain   **Best season:** Good year-round

Vetter Mountain is a San Gabriel Mountains summit that even small children can attain, via a trail that's only 1.3 miles long and gains just 600 feet in elevation. The peak was named for Victor Vetter, a hardworking forest ranger during the 1920s and 1930s. In the last century, Vetter Mountain's summit has been used mostly as a fire lookout station, but during World War II, it served a brief stint as a lookout for spotting enemy aircraft. Today, it functions only for the enjoyment of hikers, who visit its peak for inspiring views of the San Gabriel Mountains.

The trail begins at a turnaround at the end of the Charlton Flat picnic area, on the left side of the road just before an old Forest Service pumphouse. The trail can be tricky to spot and is not always signed. If you don't see it, just start walking up the old road past the pumphouse; the road will connect you to the trail in short order. Make sure you don't take the signed Silver Moccasin Trail, which also connects with the road.

From the trail sign, the path leads along a small ravine, then crosses the pumphouse road in .4 mile. The trail's most notable feature is its plethora of pinecones. They're sugar pinecones, the longest of all the conifers, and great fun for kids to carry around while they hunt for the largest one. Make sure they don't take the cones home, though; if the seeds stay in this forest, more sugar pines can grow.

The trail shortly leaves the forest and enters a more exposed area lined with chaparral. The final .3 mile ascends with greater intensity, then reaches the ridgetop and tops out at a dirt road. Turn left and walk the last 150 yards to the fire lookout tower (elevation 5,908 feet). The short, square building is surrounded on all four sides by a perimeter deck, so you can walk around and enjoy 360-degree views. In summer, the building is open to visitors. Knowledgable guides give tours and answer questions about what it was like to be a lookout person.

Vistas are extraordinary in all directions, with more than 20 named peaks visible, including Mount Baldy, Mount Williamson, Mount Waterman, Twin Peaks, and Mount Wilson. The latter is easy to spot: Mount Wilson is crowned with electronic equipment and the obvious white golf ball of its observatory. Make sure to bring along a good map so you can identify all the peaks and valleys.

Options

The Silver Moccasin Trail travels through this area. A whopping 53 miles long, the trail runs through the San Gabriel Mountains from Clear Creek trailhead to Mount Baden-Powell. A scenic and easy stretch of the trail begins at the nearby Chilao Visitors Center picnic area, five miles northeast of Charlton Flat trailhead on Highway 2. From this trailhead, you can hike to Mount Hillyer for an easy six-mile round-trip. Views from the top are only fair, but the crowds are few and the scenery is sweet.

Information and Contact

A National Forest Adventure Pass is required; see the Hiking Tips at the front of this book for details. For more information and/or a map of Angeles National Forest, contact the Los Angeles River Ranger District, 12371 North Little Tujunga Canyon Road, San Fernando, CA 91342, 818/899-1900, website: www.fs.fed.us/r5/angeles.

Directions

From I-210 in La Cañada, take Highway 2 northeast and drive 23 miles to Charlton Flat. Turn left on the road to Charlton Flat picnic area, then turn right at the fork. Continue through Charlton Flat for .5 mile to a closed gate just before the Forest Service pumphouse. The trail begins on the left side of the road, at the wide turnaround area before the gate.

10. MOUNT WATERMAN

Angeles National Forest, off Highway 2 near
Cloudburst Summit

Total distance: 5.6 miles round-trip   **Hiking time:** 3.0 hours

Type of trail: Rolling terrain   **Best season:** April–October

At 8,038 feet in elevation, the peak of Mount Waterman is a fine destination for an easy-to-moderate hike in the San Gabriel Mountains, and the
view from the summit is one you won't soon forget. If the round-trip
mileage (almost six miles) seems long, relax. This is one of the most well-
graded mountain trails in the San Gabriels. Most of the time, you don't
even notice you're climbing, even though you gain 1,200 feet from the
trailhead to the top.

The trailhead can be a bit tricky to find. It's between Cloudburst Summit and Buckhorn Campground on Highway 2, but you probably won't
see a trail sign. Instead, look for the gated fire road signed Road 3N03.
Follow it uphill for about 50 yards, then look for the single-track trail
leading off to the left. This is Mount Waterman Trail.

The path traces through a shady fir, cedar, and Jeffrey pine forest. A
nice mix of sun and shade makes the trail comfortable in any season. The
first mile lacks any wide-angle views, but has plenty of close-up looks at
the mountain's big trees. With that mile completed, you reach a saddle
on a ridge where the vistas open wide. From here, the views continually
expand, looking toward the western Mojave desert at Lancaster and Palmdale, and over the San Gabriel Wilderness. Once you've gained this ridge,
there are plenty of spots where you can take a break to enjoy the view.

You'll climb through long, well-graded switchbacks to a junction at 2.1
miles, where you turn right for the summit. It's another .7 mile to the
top, with an easy grade. Keep your eyes peeled for bighorn sheep, which
frequent the rocky peak. I spotted a bighorn with massive spiraling horns
just after I passed the trail junction. He crossed the path practically right
in front of me, then dashed off down the mountain with a clattering of
hooves and cascading rocks. It's a sight I'll never forget.

When you reach the U-shaped top of Mount Waterman, you have one
small problem: figuring out which peak is *really* the peak. The top of
Mount Waterman is so wide that there are three summits, and trails lead

to all of them. Head left for .25 mile toward the southwest, and you'll find the highest of the lot. This summit offers the best view out over the magnificent San Gabriel Mountains. Climb to the top of one of the big boulder piles, and you'll see no signs of civilization below, except for the distant towers on top of Mount Wilson. Is there a big city called Los Angeles down there? You just can't believe it.

Options

Follow the Burkhardt Trail from the far end of Buckhorn Campground, across Highway 2 and slightly east of this trailhead. In two miles (turn right at the Pacific Crest Trail junction), you will reach the spot

sugar pine trees on Mount Waterman

where 35-foot-tall Cooper Canyon Falls drops just below the trail. Visit early in the year to see the waterfall flowing at its best.

Information and Contact

A National Forest Adventure Pass is required; see the Hiking Tips at the front of this book for details. For more information and/or a map of Angeles National Forest, contact the Los Angeles River Ranger District, 12371 North Little Tujunga Canyon Road, San Fernando, CA 91342, 818/899-1900, website: www.fs.fed.us/r5/angeles.

Directions

From I-210 in La Cañada, take Highway 2 north and drive 33 miles to the trailhead for Mount Waterman on the right side of the road, one mile east of Cloudburst Summit and just west of Buckhorn Campground. Look for the gated fire road on the right, signed as 3N03, before you reach Buckhorn Camp.

11. LOOP TRAIL

Devil's Punchbowl Natural Area, off Highway 138
near Pearblossom

Total distance: 1.0 mile round-trip

Type of trail: Some steep terrain

Hiking time: 30 minutes

Best season: October–May

Devil's Punchbowl is visual proof that you're in earthquake country, where faulting and erosion have made bizarre shapes out of ancient sedimentary rocks. Before this strange geological phenomena gets swallowed up completely by the perpetual movement of the earth (or eroded away by the forces of entropy), go see it on this easy hike at Devil's Punchbowl Natural Area.

Although the Punchbowl is located on the north slope of the San Gabriel Mountains, this arid land is far different than the high country. It is in the region midway between mountains and desert, an intermediary place where you can see tall mountains nearby (often covered with snow), but it's warm and desertlike where you stand. Elevations in the park range from 4,000 to 6,000 feet.

Devil's Punchbowl was formed along the San Andreas Fault a few dozen million years ago. But, as the old joke goes, it wasn't all San Andreas's fault. We can also blame (or credit) the forces of wind, rain, and erosion. Movement along the fault originally forced sedimentary layers of rock up from the earth and tilted them this way and that, but centuries of stream carving and erosion smoothed and sculpted them. The layers of rock jut out and up at an assortment of angles, creating near-vertical walls as high as 300 feet. Many of the rock slabs look like they're about to topple inward on each other.

Loop Trail begins just to the right of the visitors center. You can walk another short trail first, if you wish: the quarter-mile Piñon Pathway, which begins at the same trailhead. Doing so will help you to identify the plants you see along the Loop Trail—yerba santa, mountain mahogany, manzanita, scrub oak, piñon pines, fremontia, yucca, and basin sage scrub, among others. Then follow the Loop Trail downhill until you reach the bottom of the stream canyon, where riparian plants thrive. Willows grow thick along the stream banks. The leaves of sycamore and alder trees turn bright gold and red in autumn. The switchbacking return uphill is steeper than you might

Devil's Punchbowl Natural Area

expect, so don't be surprised if you're breathing hard on the way back. But you'll want to go slow anyway, to allow plenty of time for gazing in awe at the Punchbowl's strange rock slabs.

Occasionally, snow falls on the Punchbowl in winter, and you shouldn't miss the chance to see the rock slabs dusted in snow. Another must-see event: Park rangers hold full-moon hikes once a month during summer. Check out this place under a full moon, and you might just decide to dedicate your life to the study of geology.

Make sure you stop in at the nature center at Devil's Punchbowl Natural Area. It's a great place to get a wildlife biology lesson. On my trip, the center housed a huge red-tailed hawk, plus a tiny adult screech owl and a collection of snakes. Outside the center, in a large aviary, were two great horned owls. I stared at them and they stared right back at me. I'm quite sure they never blinked.

Options
Take a hike to Devil's Chair, an awesome overlook above the Punchbowl, via Punchbowl Trail. It's 3.5 miles one-way to Devil's Chair from a fork near the end of the Loop Trail, signed To Upper Trail and Burkhardt Trail. Bear left on Burkhardt Trail (a dirt road), then left on Punchbowl Trail. Be sure to carry a map, water, and food for this long hike.

Information and Contact
A $3 day-use fee is charged per vehicle. Park maps are available at the visitors center. For more information, contact Devil's Punchbowl Natural Area, 28000 Devil's Punchbowl Road, Pearblossom, CA 93553, 661/944-2743, website: http://parks.co.la.ca.us.

Directions

From Highway 14 near Palmdale, take the Highway 138 exit east for 16 miles to Pearblossom. Turn right on County Road N-6 (signed as Longview Road) and drive south for eight miles to the Devil's Punchbowl entrance. (The road makes several jogs on the way to the park, but they are all well-signed. You will end up on Devil's Punchbowl Road.) The trail begins behind the park nature center.

12. PINYON RIDGE NATURE TRAIL

Crystal Lake Recreation Area, off Highway 39 near Azusa

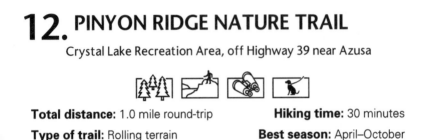

Total distance: 1.0 mile round-trip   **Hiking time:** 30 minutes

Type of trail: Rolling terrain   **Best season:** April–October

---

The Crystal Lake Recreation Area in the mountains above Azusa burned in the wildfires of 2002 and has been closed since then. Scheduled to re-open in the summer of 2004 or 2005, this region will be a great place to witness the processes of fire ecology first-hand, and to see how the landscape heals and regrows after a major burn.

Surprisingly, the Crystal Lake Recreation Area was never very well known, even before it burned. Although many Los Angeles families visited here every year for camping and hiking vacations or to fish in small Crystal Lake, the only natural lake in the San Gabriel Mountains, many others had never heard of it. Even in the nearby towns of Azusa and Glendora, Crystal Lake remained a well-kept secret, despite the allure of its 6,000-foot elevation, dense cedar and pine forests, and clean, fresh air. When the area is reopened to the public, these appealing features will once again be there for the taking, although it may be some time before the forests return to their previous splendor.

A great way to get a taste of the Crystal Lake Recreation Area has always been a stroll on the Pinyon Ridge Nature Trail, beginning alongside the Yerba Santa Amphitheater. Before you begin hiking, stop at the visitors center (you passed it on your way in) and pick up an interpretive brochure. Then walk a short distance on Soldier Creek Trail and bear left at the junction for the start of Pinyon Ridge loop. You can hike the loop in either direction; the interpretive brochure details the loop counterclockwise.

The trail has a gravelly surface, so hiking boots will make your trip easier. As you walk among the piñon pines, you have great views of steep San Gabriel Canyon. A highlight of the trail, Pinyon Ridge Vista Point, is marked by a bench on the ridgetop. Here you can have a seat and listen to the wind rustling in the trees while you enjoy far-reaching views of the valleys below. You can even discern the tip of big San Gabriel Reservoir, which you drove by on your way up Highway 39.

If you hike this trail in the off-season, or any time that the area is quiet, you're almost guaranteed to see wildlife. On our trip, we saw five blacktail deer and dozens of cute chipmunks.

Options
Don't leave the Crystal Lake Recreation Area without paying a visit to Crystal Lake. Drive back down the park road for .5 mile to the lake access road, then turn right and park your car in one of the lots. It's a short walk to the diminutive but pretty lake, where you can fish from shore for stocked rainbow trout. (Don't forget your license.) Or, if you're more ambitious, you can walk back down the park road from the amphitheater, past the visitors center and the Half Knob Trailhead. Look for the Lake Trail sign on your right. Lake Trail leads to the lake in just under a mile.

Information and Contact
A National Forest Adventure Pass is required; see the Hiking Tips at the front of this book for details. For more information and/or a map of Angeles National Forest, contact the San Gabriel River Ranger District, 110 North Wabash Avenue, Glendora, CA 91741, 626/335-1251, website: www.fs.fed.us/r5/angeles.

Directions
From Azusa on I-210, drive north on Highway 39 for 26 miles to the Crystal Lake Recreation Area visitors center and store. Bear right and drive a short distance to the parking area for the Yerba Santa Amphitheater. The Pinyon Ridge/Soldier Creek trailhead is on the left side of the amphitheater.

13. SAN ANTONIO FALLS

Angeles National Forest, off Highway 83 on Mount Baldy

Total distance: 1.5 miles round-trip   **Hiking time:** 1.0 hour

Type of trail: Rolling terrain   **Best season:** February–May

---

When I was a college student in Claremont, wintertime was eagerly awaited, when the Inland Empire air would clear and the first snows would frost the rounded top of 10,064-foot Mount Baldy. From our dormitory rooms in the valley, we could look out our windows and see the wondrous sight of a nearby snowcapped peak—on days when it was 70 degrees and balmy on campus.

Now I look forward to the cold season on Mount Baldy for another reason: winter snows lead to springtime snowmelt, and that makes an impressive show of water in 80-foot-high San Antonio Falls.

The waterfall's season is short because it has a small drainage area and is fed primarily by snowmelt, so you must time your trip for the first warm days after winter, sometimes as early as March. The hike to the falls follows the Mount Baldy ski lift maintenance road, which is paved and has only a slight uphill grade. If the crews are working on the ski lift, you may share the road with a vehicle or two, but this is a rare occurrence.

At .7 mile, you round a sharp curve and see and hear the waterfall. It drops in three tiers; the first is a large freefall drop and the others are curved cascades over steep granite and talus slopes. In a good snow year, white snow patches will frame the waterfall as late as April. The peak of Mount Baldy, high above the falls, can be covered with snow until Memorial Day.

The waterfall's name is derived from its home on the slopes of Mount Baldy, which is really called Mount San Antonio. Few people call the mountain by its formal name; many who live in its shadow aren't even familiar with it. The mountain was named for Saint Anthony of Padua, a Franciscan priest and miracle worker. But the peak's rounded, exposed summit looks more like a Baldy than a saint.

You might see other hikers on the maintenance road carrying ropes and ice axes. They're heading for Baldy's summit, and if there is much snow, they need special equipment to get there. Beyond San Antonio Falls, the maintenance road switchbacks to the right, and most summit

hikers follow it to a trail junction at Baldy Notch. From there, they head left to the top of the ski lift, then hike along the rather treacherous Devil's Backbone to the south side of Mount Harwood and finally the peak of Mount Baldy at 10,064 feet. At a total of six trail miles from San Antonio Falls, this is a destination for the ambitious.

Options

Continue uphill from San Antonio Falls on the ski lift maintenance road. At 2.5 miles from the falls, you reach Mount Baldy Notch, where a restaurant is often open on summer weekends.

San Antonio Falls on Mount Baldy

Information and Contact

A National Forest Adventure Pass is required; see the Hiking Tips at the front of this book for details. For more information and/or a map of Angeles National Forest, contact the San Gabriel River Ranger District, 110 North Wabash Avenue, Glendora, CA 91741, 626/335-1251, website: www.fs.fed.us/r5/angeles.

Directions

From I-10 near Upland and Ontario, exit on Euclid Avenue (Highway 83) and drive north for six miles until Euclid Avenue joins Mount Baldy Road. Drive nine miles north on Mount Baldy Road to Manker Flats Camp, then continue .3 mile to Falls Road on the left. Park in the dirt pullout by Falls Road and begin hiking on the gated, paved road.

14. TWO HARBORS TO CHERRY COVE

Two Harbors, Catalina Island

Total distance: 3.0 miles round-trip   **Hiking time:** 1.5 hours

Type of trail: Mostly flat terrain

Best season: Good year-round; best for wildflowers March–May

When first-timers make the trip to Catalina Island, they usually head for the city of Avalon, Catalina's largest destination. Although Avalon is a fun place—plenty of nightlife, restaurants, hotels, and shops—it's a bit too much like Newport Beach or Balboa Island to feel like a true "getaway." For an out-of-the-ordinary adventure, take the ferry to Catalina's second city (really a small village), Two Harbors. There you'll find a more authentic taste of Catalina Island, as well as a terrific easy hiking trail.

First, a couple of tips: When you make your ferry reservation, make sure you get a direct boat to Two Harbors. The ferry ride becomes interminably long if the boat goes to Avalon first, then stops at multiple private campgrounds around the island.

Next, be aware that you can do this hike as a day trip from the mainland, but you must plan your ferry shuttles carefully to allow enough time. Except for during the summer season, ferries run infrequently to Two Harbors, so if you're visiting in the off-season, you may have to stay overnight to catch the next boat. A few accommodations options exist in Two Harbors, including a campground and a lovely old hotel called the Banning House, both requiring advance reservations. You can also arrange a bus shuttle across the island to Avalon, where there are dozens of hotels.

Your ferry from the mainland will drop you off at Two Harbors' Isthmus Harbor. Stop in at the general store to stock up your daypack, then start hiking on West End Road, a nearly level dirt road that sticks close to the shoreline. You can access West End Road from the pier by walking to your right along the beach. Take the dirt path at the beach's end and make a quick, steep ascent past some tiny shoreline cottages. When you join the dirt road, go right (northwest).

West End Road's wide and smooth path makes it ideal for holding hands with your hiking partner, or gazing at the coastside beauty without worrying about where your feet are going. You are treated to eyefuls of

Two Harbors, Catalina Island

oceanfront scenery, including rocky outcrops, steep headlands, and beckoning coves. Prickly pear cactus is the ubiquitous flora, and a few palm trees wave their fronds above the coastal scrub. Peer down into the emerald waters below your blufftop trail and you'll spot flashes of bright orange: They're garibaldis, California's state saltwater fish.

At 1.25 miles, you reach Cherry Valley and Cherry Cove, named for the native Catalina cherry tree, which erupts into a display of showy white flowers in the spring. The road/trail turns inland to detour around the long, narrow cove. A private camp is located here, and a flotilla of colorful kayaks lines the beach.

Where the trail makes its way back to the coast on the far side of Cherry Cove, follow a short cutoff footpath to a blufftop overlook with a bench and triangular monument. Its engraved memorial is simple: "Dedicated to the memory of Edmund Duboise, a sailor who loved Catalina."

This is a fine spot to pull your lunch out of your daypack and ponder how lucky we are to have this scenic island so close to Los Angeles. If you start to feel homesick for the mainland, just squint. You should be able to make out the Orange County coast, a hazy blur of land some 20-plus miles away.

Options

Continue hiking along West End Road as far as you wish. Approximately four miles from Two Harbors is aptly named Emerald Bay, with an inviting beach that is accessible via a cutoff trail.

Information and Contact

A free Santa Catalina Island hiking permit is required and can be obtained from Two Harbors Visitor Services; phone 310/510-0303 for more information. A free trail map of Catalina Island is available when you pick up your hiking permit. For more information about Catalina Island, visit www.catalina.com or www.catalinaconservancy.org. A fee is charged for the ferry from the mainland to Two Harbors. Phone Catalina Express at the numbers below for current rates and departure information. (Ferry fees are approximately $23 to $36 per adult, less for seniors and children under 12.)

Directions

Catalina Express provides ferry transportation to Two Harbors from San Pedro. Call 310/519-1212 or 800/481-3470 or visit www.catalinaexpress.com for a schedule and reservations.

15. EL MORO CANYON TRAIL

Crystal Cove State Park, off Highway 1 near Corona del Mar

Total distance: 5.0 miles round-trip

Type of trail: Rolling terrain

Hiking time: 2.5 hours

Best season: February–June

Crystal Cove State Park is a miraculous chunk of public land lying smack in the midst of some of the most overdeveloped coastline in California. Considering how much money could be made by turning the park's 2,500 coastal acres into condos and townhouses, it's amazing to see this slice of heaven remaining open and protected in Orange County.

El Moro Canyon is one of the park's many scenic wonders. On average, only 12 inches of rain fall at Crystal Cove each year, but when you see how lush and overgrown the foliage is in El Moro Canyon, you won't believe it. Although El Moro Creek flows only in the wet season, its banks

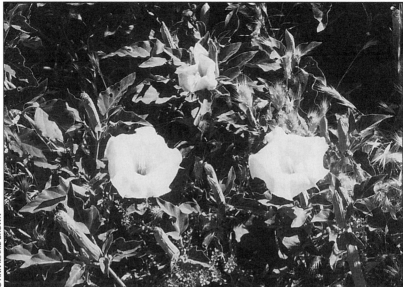

Large white morning glories greet hikers in El Moro Canyon.

are lined with oaks, sycamores, and willows. Birds and butterflies flock to its edges. The trail through El Moro Canyon is a pleasant walk at any time of the year, but best taken after winter and spring rains.

To access the trail, walk from the ranger station parking lot down the road to the entrance kiosk, then turn left on a dirt fire road. The road leads past a trailer park, but the scenery quickly improves as you veer left on El Moro Canyon Trail and head up the shady, tree-lined canyon. Numerous trails cut off to the left and right, but just stay on the main path. The vegetation thickens and thins as you walk, alternately allowing the sun in, then creating a tunnel of cool shade. Scan the rock walls on your right for small, fern-lined sandstone caves.

The most obvious wildlife you are likely to see are dozens of rabbits hopping along the trail in lower El Moro Canyon. Birdwatchers usually fare well, spotting an abundance of songbirds, hawks, quail, and roadrunners. As the trail climbs gradually higher, the riparian habitat gives way to grasslands, which are covered with wildflowers in spring. With the bloom of the flowers come the butterflies. Common varieties include the anise swallowtail (yellow and black) and the red admiral (brown, red, and black).

I suggest a simple out-and-back hike on El Moro Canyon Trail, with a turnaround at about 2.5 miles, before the path climbs significantly.

If you feel like going farther, you'll reach the top of El Moro Ridge at 3.5 miles.

Options

When you've completed your canyon exploration, be sure to pay a visit to Crystal Cove's 3.5 miles of Pacific coastline. Beach access is available at Reef Point, Pelican Point, and Los Trancos. Reef Point is the best spot for swimming and bodysurfing.

Information and Contact

A $6 day-use fee is charged per vehicle. A map of Crystal Cove State Park is available at the visitors center. For more information, contact Crystal Cove State Park, 8471 Pacific Coast Highway, Laguna Beach, CA 92651, 949/494-3539 or 949/492-0802, website: www.cal-parks.ca.gov.

Directions

From Corona del Mar, drive south on Highway 1 for three miles to the entrance to Crystal Cove State Park on the inland side of the highway. Park near the ranger station, then walk downhill to the entrance kiosk and turn left on the dirt road.

16. HOLY JIM FALLS

Cleveland National Forest, off I-5 near Trabuco Canyon

Total distance: 2.5 miles round-trip   **Hiking time:** 1.5 hours

Type of trail: Rolling terrain   **Best season:** Winter and spring

Holy Jim Falls has one of the most intriguing names and interesting histories of any Southern California waterfall. The fall and its canyon were named for James T. Smith, better known as "Cussin' Jim," a beekeeper who lived here in the 1890s. Apparently Smith earned his nickname with his bad temper and colorful way with language. Because honey-loving grizzly bears were plentiful in the area in those days, a beekeeper might have plenty of reasons to be angry.

But conservative mapmakers who plotted Trabuco Canyon in the early 1900s found Smith's moniker in bad taste, so they arbitrarily changed it

© ANN MARIE BROWN

Holy Jim Falls

to "Holy Jim." The sanitized name stuck.

The waterfall has made its own name for itself. A favorite destination of Orange County hikers, Holy Jim Trail is quite busy on winter and spring weekends when the fall is flowing strong. The drive to the trailhead can be a bit of a challenge (five miles on a rocky dirt road, manageable by most passenger cars but high clearance is recommended), but the hike is a breeze. It's a 2.5-mile round-trip stroll through shady oaks, keeping close company with Holy Jim Creek. The only tricky part is that the waterfall isn't right along the main trail; you follow a cutoff trail and then make an easy quarter-mile scramble to reach it. A few hops, skips, and jumps along the streambed, and you're there.

Start by walking down the dirt road that leads to some leased cabins, passing big cactus and succulents, until at .5 mile you reach the official Holy Jim trailhead. Leaving the dirt road for a narrower trail, you're surrounded by a lush canyon filled with oaks, vine maples, spring wildflowers, and even a few ferns, all thriving in the shade alongside Holy Jim Creek. The trail crosses the creek several times, passes several small check dams, and gently gains elevation as it heads upstream.

After nearly 30 minutes of walking, the trail steepens noticeably. As you pass a large, old oak tree on your left, paths branch off in every direction. Stay on the main route by continuing upstream for about 40 yards, then cross the creek again (on your left). Immediately after crossing, follow the trail's right fork, which continues to follow the stream. The left fork switchbacks uphill to the summit of 5,687-foot Santiago Peak, seven miles away.

Now you have only a 10-minute scramble through the rapidly narrowing canyon to reach Holy Jim Falls. A petite but picturesque 20 feet high, the waterfall is set in a small, intimate grotto that forms a nearly circular rock amphitheater. Maidenhair ferns cling to the walls on both sides of the watercourse. You won't want to leave this special place too quickly.

A free brochure describing Holy Jim Trail is available at the Corona Forest Service office (see address below); it corresponds to numbered guideposts along the route and provides interesting facts on the natural and human history of the canyon.

Options
After visiting the falls, backtrack to the junction with Holy Jim Trail to Santiago Peak, and follow that route as far as you like. The summit is a long and arduous seven miles away, but you can always head for Bear Springs instead, only 3.5 miles from the junction.

Information and Contact
A National Forest Adventure Pass is required; see the Hiking Tips at the front of this book for details. For more information and/or a map of Cleveland National Forest, contact the Trabuco Ranger District, 1147 East Sixth Street, Corona, CA 92879, 909/736-1811, website: www.fs.fed.us /r5/cleveland.

Directions
From I-5 at Laguna Hills (north of San Juan Capistrano), exit on El Toro Road and drive six miles east. Turn right on Live Oak Canyon Road and drive about four miles (two miles beyond O'Neill Regional Park). Turn left on Trabuco Canyon Road, a dirt road just past the paved Rose Canyon Road turnoff. (The road is usually suitable for passenger cars, but high clearance is recommended.) Drive five miles to the well-signed parking area for Holy Jim Trail. The trail leads from the parking lot's left side.

17. SAN JUAN LOOP TRAIL

Cleveland National Forest, off Highway 74 near
Ortega Oaks

Total distance: 2.2 miles round-trip

Type of trail: Mostly flat terrain

Hiking time: 1.0 hour

Best season: December–April

Highway 74 from Lake Elsinore to San Juan Capistrano takes visitors through the heart and soul of Orange County. It begins in the lowlands, climbs across the rolling ridgeline of the Santa Ana Mountains, and comes to a scenic denouement at the Pacific Ocean. Most of the country-side through which the road passes is Cleveland National Forest land, but it's some of the least visited public land in Southern California. Why? Be-cause it's hot, that's why. If you visit in summer, you'll bake your boots for sure.

On the other hand, if you time your drive for immedi-ately following a winter rain, or during the spring wild-flower bloom from late Feb-ruary to early May, you'll think you've found paradise right here in Orange County.

You might want a leg-stretching break while driv-ing Highway 74, and you can get it on the San Juan Loop Trail. This easy, in-formative walk is a perfect introduction to the land-scape of the Santa Ana Mountains. Don't be put off by the warning sign at the trailhead, which explains in doomsday style about the dangers of mountain lions,

Tall yuccas bloom in spring along the San Juan Loop Trail.

rattlesnakes, poison oak, and rugged terrain. If you stay on the trail and don't travel alone, it's highly unlikely you'll meet up with any of those hazards. (This sign has surely inspired some would-be hikers to get back in their cars and head for Disneyland instead.)

Begin hiking on San Juan Loop Trail from the north side of the parking lot. The sandy trail is well-maintained and easy to follow. It parallels the highway for its first half-mile, but you'll forget about the road noise as you discover a cornucopia of plant life along the path. In spring, you'll enjoy the blooms of monkeyflower, purple nightshade, and tall yuccas with their silky, milk-white flowers on long spikes. Lizards dart here and there among the foliage. Although dry and exposed, the desertlike terrain is lush and laden with flora.

At .3 mile, the trail passes a railing and overlook above a small seasonal waterfall on San Juan Creek. Scramble down to the water's edge, if you like, to get a better look at the 15-foot-high falls. (A short spur trail leads down to the waterfall from the railing's left side.) The polished, light-gray granite walls of this narrow gorge and the creek's ultraclear pools invite a closer look.

Back on the trail, you'll soon pass the turnoff for Chiquito Trail (a recommended option for those seeking a longer trip). One more highlight awaits on San Juan Loop Trail: a lovely grove of ancient oaks, which provides a cool, shady contrast to the open exposure along the rest of the trail. The oak canopy provides enough shade for ferns to grow. In early spring, they unfurl their new fronds. This is a great place for a picnic.

Beyond the oak grove, the path heads out into the sunshine again and skirts the edge of Upper San Juan Campground. Exposed slopes from here to the trail's finale encourage more spring wildflowers. Your loop finishes out on the opposite side of the parking lot from where you started.

It's worth noting that this trailhead is right across the road from the Country Cottage and General Store, the only game in town for filling your daypack with supplies. The shop is known as "the Candy Store," for two reasons: because that was its original name, but also because, of greater importance to hikers, the woman who runs the place stocks a good supply of handmade chocolates. If you load your pack with them, don't wait too long to indulge. It gets pretty warm around here.

Options
The Bear Canyon Trail begins across the road near the store. Follow that trail out and back through chaparral-covered hillsides. A high point two miles out provides wide views into the San Mateo Canyon Wilderness.

Information and Contact

A National Forest Adventure Pass is required; see the Hiking Tips at the front of this book for details. For more information and/or a map of Cleveland National Forest, contact the Trabuco Ranger District, 1147 East Sixth Street, Corona, CA 92879, 909/736-1811, website: www.fs.fed.us/r5/cleveland.

Directions

From I-5 at San Juan Capistrano, take the Ortega Highway (Highway 74) exit and drive north. In 21 miles, you'll reach the Country Cottage store on the right (.75 mile past Upper San Juan Campground). The trailhead is across the road from the store; turn left and park in the large parking lot. Start hiking from the north side of the parking lot.

18. PACIFIC CREST TRAIL AT DEEP CREEK

San Bernardino National Forest, off Highway 173 near
Lake Arrowhead

Total distance: 3.0 miles round-trip   **Hiking time:** 1.5 hours

Type of trail: Rolling terrain   **Best season:** April–October

---

Just before this book went to press, the Deep Creek canyon near Lake Arrowhead was severely burned in the 2003 wildfires. Because it contains a section of the Pacific Crest Trail, the area should be reopened quickly, but be sure to check with the Mountaintop Ranger District (909/337-2444) before driving to the trailhead.

Deep Creek has many personalities. It's a geologically active creek sporting hot springs and pools, where warm-water lovers flock to bathe. It's a wild trout stream, filled with pockets of moss and algae, the start of a plentiful food chain for the fish. Technically, it's a branch of the Mojave River, which eventually disappears in desert sand.

The section of Deep Creek that is closest to Lake Arrowhead takes on yet another personality: It's a wild waterway that roars through a steep and dramatic gorge. Pacific Crest Trail runs along the gorge's high rim, allowing hikers the opportunity to admire the stream from above while walking on a nearly level stretch of trail.

This section of Pacific Crest Trail is well-signed and easy to follow.

From the trailhead, you head downstream along the creek. Ignore the steep side trails that go to swimming holes (save them for the way back, if you wish), and bypass the footbridge on your right. You want to keep Deep Creek on your right all the way. You'll quickly rise up out of the gorge, paralleling the water but elevated above it.

The Pacific Crest Trail traces above the steep gorge of Deep Creek.

The trail starts in a thick mixed forest of hardwoods and conifers, but shortly opens out to exposed hillsides, including an area that was burned in a forest fire. You gain excellent views of the canyon ahead, and in places, your vista expands to include the Mojave Desert. Being in the cool, conifer-covered San Bernardino Mountains, it's a shock to realize that the Mojave is so close by. This must be a rather grim sight for Pacific Crest Trail through-hikers, who will soon leave the high mountains for the land of no water and little shade.

How far you go is up to you. At 1.5 miles, a rocky outcrop awaits, offering even better views and a suitable turnaround point. On the other hand, if you're really having a good time, you can follow Pacific Crest Trail another 2,000 miles or so all the way to Canada.

Remember that if you choose to fish anywhere along this stretch of Deep Creek, special rules apply. This is a wild trout area, in which only artificial lures or flies with barbless hooks can be used. Rainbow and brown trout, bluegill, and bullhead can be caught.

Options

Just keep on hiking. Approximately 2.5 miles from the trailhead is an area called the Devil's Hole, a dramatic granite gorge where water flows over large boulders, creating rapids and falls.

Information and Contact

A National Forest Adventure Pass is required; see the Hiking Tips at the front of this book for details. For more information and/or a map of San Bernardino National Forest, contact the Mountaintop Ranger District, P.O. Box 350, 28104 Highway 18, Skyforest, CA 92385, 909/337-2444, website: www.fs.fed.us/r5/sanbernardino.

Directions

From Lake Arrowhead on Highway 173, turn east on Hook Creek Road. Follow it, bearing left at a sharp turn, until it turns to dirt and becomes Road 2N26Y. Follow Road 2N26Y for one mile, then bear left at the fork and continue another .2 mile. At the next fork, bear right on Road 3N34F and drive .5 mile to Splinter's Cabin and the Pacific Crest Trail trailhead. (A high-clearance vehicle is recommended.) Head downstream along the trail.

19. WOODLAND INTERPRETIVE TRAIL

San Bernardino National Forest, off Highway 19
near Big Bear Lake

Total distance: 1.5 miles round-trip   **Hiking time:** 45 minutes
Type of trail: Rolling terrain   **Best season:** April–October

---

If you're spending the weekend or the week in Big Bear, you'd be well-advised to pay a visit to the Big Bear Discovery Center in Fawnskin. Rangers there can cheerfully provide you with all the information you want about hiking, fishing, camping, and exploring the Big Bear area. After you have all the facts, you can take this terrific short walk on the nearby Woodland Interpretive Trail.

Pick up an interpretive brochure before your walk so you can learn to identify serviceberry, yerba santa, Jeffrey and ponderosa pines, indigo bush, junipers, and piñon pines. These are some of the characteristic trees and plants of the piñon-juniper woodland, the dominant plant community around Big Bear Lake. This type of foliage thrives at elevations between 5,000 and 8,000 feet, on arid mountain slopes. Although most people think of Big Bear as having heavy precipitation in terms of winter snowfall, the area typically has 330 days of sunshine each year, making it very dry.

Highlights along the trail include a stand of giant Jeffrey pines that are about 400 years old, and several piñon pines. You can examine a pack rat's nest and observe the old tree snag where eagles sometimes perch to do their hunting. Some interesting facts gleaned from the interpretive brochure: A 100-year-old piñon pine will have a trunk diameter of only about six inches. The seeds of serviceberry bushes were ground up and used as food by families during the Great Depression.

eagle's perch, Woodland Interpretive Trail

The trail is almost completely level, so it is manageable for hikers of all abilities. On the loop's return leg, you are treated to great views of the lake, and all the way across it to Big Bear City. Be sure to take the short side path near the trail's end to an obvious rocky overlook—that's where you'll find the best vistas.

Options

If you're looking for a more ambitious hike in the same neighborhood, follow Cougar Crest Trail to 8,200-foot Bertha Peak, a six-mile round-trip. The view from the summit includes Big Bear Lake, Mount San Gorgonio, and the Holcomb Valley. The trailhead is .5 mile west of The Big Bear Discovery Center on Highway 38.

Information and Contact

A National Forest Adventure Pass is required; see the Hiking Tips at the front of this book for details. For more information and/or a map of San Bernardino National Forest, contact the Big Bear Discovery Center, P.O.

Box 66, 41397 North Shore Drive, Fawnskin, CA 92333, 909/866-3437, website: www.fs.fed.us/r5/sanbernardino.

Directions

From the town of Big Bear Lake, drive east on Highway 18 and take the Stanfield cutoff to the north shore of the lake, where it junctions with Highway 38. Turn left on Highway 38 and drive .5 mile to the Woodland Trailhead on the right side of the road. It's directly across the highway from the East Boat Ramp, near the Big Bear Discovery Center.

20. CASTLE ROCK TRAIL

San Bernardino National Forest, off Highway 18 near
Big Bear Lake

Total distance: 2.0 miles round-trip   **Hiking time:** 1.0 hour

Type of trail: Some steep terrain   **Best season:** October

Hiking the Castle Rock Trail is a great way to break from the masses at Big Bear Lake, and get a close-up look at a series of giant, weather-carved granite boulders. On this trail, you'll climb enough to get your heart working hard and see Big Bear's big patch of blue water as a bird would see it—from up high, in wide perspective, and far away from the crowds.

A couple of tricky features of this trail: There's not much of a parking area at the trailhead, just a small pullout large enough for about eight cars. It's easy to drive right by it; follow the directions below exactly. Once you start hiking, you find that the trail climbs steeply right away—there's no warm-up. Although the path to Castle Rock has a mere 700-foot elevation gain, it's compressed into one mile. Given the 6,700-foot elevation at Big Bear Lake, lowlanders can plan on breathing hard and fast during the ascent. But since the trail to Castle Rock is short, you can take it as slowly as you want.

The trail is located by the area of Big Bear Lake called Boulder Bay, a perfectly descriptive name for this rocky landscape. The trail surface is smooth sand, surrounded by manzanita, big conifers, and tons of rocks. A stand of large ponderosa and Jeffrey pines is made more impressive by an abundance of fallen ones that have lost their lives to lightning or the extremities of winter. Years of decay have worn them down so they look like odd-shaped wooden sculptures among the rocks.

As you hike upward, you gain tremendous views of the lake, but you'll miss them completely unless you turn around. (A tip: Shouting "Hey, look at the view!" provides a perfect excuse to stop and catch your breath.) You may also find yourself in the company of some very loud stellar's jays, who will allow you to intrude on their territory only if you will be audience to their squawking.

In a little under a mile, you'll reach a rocky overlook, where many hikers stop to catch their breath on a granite boulder. Here

Hikers head up the steep slope to Castle Rock.

the main trail becomes a spiderweb of trails. Continue uphill on the most defined path, and shortly you'll reach a saddle. Castle Rock, easily distinguishable by its shape, is just to the east and slightly off the trail, just before the grade descends. Climbing to the top of Castle Rock requires some skill; it's not for the inexperienced. No need to bother—the view is excellent from its base.

While you are here, consider the Indian legend surrounding Castle Rock. Supposedly, when the wind is just right, you can hear the cry of the Indian princess who waits for her lover on Castle Rock.

Options

Don't hike all the way to Castle Rock; instead make your destination the first set of large granite boulders you reach (.8 mile from the trailhead). Those on the right side of the trail have the best view of the lake. Climb on top, pull your lunch out of your daypack, and enjoy the scene.

Information and Contact

A National Forest Adventure Pass is required; see the Hiking Tips at the front of this book for details. For more information and/or a map of San Bernardino National Forest, contact the Big Bear Discovery Center, P.O. Box 66, 41397 North Shore Drive, Fawnskin, CA 92333, 909/866-3437, website: www.fs.fed.us/r5/sanbernardino.

Directions

From the dam on the west end of Big Bear Lake, drive one mile east on Highway 18 (Big Bear Boulevard) to the signed Castle Rock Trailhead on the right, by the Big Bear City Limit sign. Drive 50 yards farther east to the turnout on the lake side of Highway 18. Walk across the road to the trailhead. (If you are driving to the trailhead from the town of Big Bear Lake, look for the pullout on your right, immediately after you pass Papoose Bay Estates.)

21. CHAMPION LODGEPOLE PINE

San Bernardino National Forest, off Highway 18
near Big Bear Lake

Total distance: 1.0 mile round-trip

Hiking time: 30 minutes

Type of trail: Mostly flat terrain

Best season: April–October

Let's see now. The biggest giant sequoia tree is the General Sherman Tree in Sequoia National Park. The biggest coast redwood tree is the Mendocino Tree in Montgomery Woods State Reserve. The biggest Joshua tree is the Champion Joshua near Granite Peak in San Bernardino National Forest. So which is the biggest lodgepole pine tree? It's the Champion Lodgepole, just a few miles from Big Bear Lake.

The Champion Lodgepole is growing in a grove of world-champion trees, the largest lodgepole pines around. The Champion is about 400 years old, stands 112 feet tall, and has a circumference of 20 feet. Since most lodgepole pines grow to only 70 feet tall, the Champion has them beat by a mile. The other lodgepoles near the Champion Lodgepole are no slackers in the size department, either—many of them are more than 80 feet tall.

What's strange is that these big trees are growing at 7,500 feet in elevation, when usually in Southern California lodgepole pines won't grow at less than 8,000 feet. Lodgepoles traditionally like high elevations and cool air. They are favored as lumber because they grow dependably straight and have few knots and twists in their wood. You can easily identify the lodgepole pine by its paired needles—two needles per bundle, as opposed to other pines, which typically have three or five needles per bundle.

The trail to reach the big tree is easy and level, following a small stream for .4 mile to a junction. Look for corn lilies and wildflowers along the streambanks in spring and early summer. Turn right at the junction and walk about 50 yards to the Champion Lodgepole, which is situated at the edge of a pretty meadow. It is easy to spot not only because of its immense size, but also because it has a split-rail fence around it to protect its root system. Pay homage to the giant tree, then turn around and head back the way you came.

Options
If you wish to hike farther, you can retrace your steps to the intersection where you turned off for the Champion Lodgepole, then follow the opposite fork, Siberia Creek Trail. The trail continues for another mile to the Gunsight, an interesting rock formation.

Information and Contact
A National Forest Adventure Pass is required; see the Hiking Tips at the front of this book for details. For more information and/or a map of San Bernardino National Forest, contact the Big Bear Discovery Center, P.O. Box 66, 41397 North Shore Drive, Fawnskin, CA 92333, 909/866-3437, website: www.fs.fed.us/r5/sanbernardino.

Directions
From the dam on the west end of Big Bear Lake, drive 3.5 miles east on Highway 18/Big Bear Boulevard to Mill Creek Road. Turn right (south) on Mill Creek Road (Forest Service Road 2N10) and follow it five miles, through several junctions. (The road turns to dirt.) At Forest Service Road 2N11, turn right and drive one mile to the parking area. The route is well-signed for the Champion Lodgepole Pine trailhead.

22. PONDEROSA VISTA & WHISPERING PINES NATURE TRAILS

San Bernardino National Forest, off Highway 38 near
Angelus Oaks

Total distance: 2.0 miles round-trip **Hiking time:** 1.0 hour
Type of trail: Rolling terrain **Best season:** April–October

---

Everybody knows that if you take a drive along the Rim of the World Highway between Angelus Oaks and Big Bear Lake, you have nonstop views of gorgeous mountain scenery through your windshield. But plenty of people miss out on an easy stop along that highway, where you can park your car in one place and access two short hiking trails on opposite sides of the road. Make the stop, and the scenery is not just outside your windshield, it's at your feet, your fingertips, and all around you.

Both trails are loops of about one mile in length. Here's what you'll find on each: Ponderosa Vista Nature Trail is a great introduction to the flora and fauna of San Bernardino National Forest. You can choose between the short loop (.3 mile) and the long loop (.6 mile), or you can hike both. The interpretive plaques along the way are a bit corny—somebody got carried away with flowery prose—but they do provide good information on local birds (acorn woodpeckers, redbreasted sapsuckers, and yellow-rumped warblers) and native trees. We learn that the ponderosa pine, with a lifespan of about 300 years, is the most common conifer in San Bernardino National Forest. Incense cedars, black oaks, white firs, and piñon pines also grow in the area.

The highlight of Ponderosa Vista Nature Trail is its vista—an overlook point with a view across the Santa Ana River canyon. An old photograph at the overlook shows what the canyon looked like in the early 20th century, and the accompanying text describes the building of the Rim of the World Highway in 1935. That was the same year that black bears were introduced to the area. No wonder—with the new highway, the bears could just get in their RVs and drive in.

Right across the road from Ponderosa Vista Nature Trail is Whispering Pines Nature Trail, another short, easy interpretive trail. Time to play Trivial Pursuit: This trail appeared on what television show, filmed in 1969, about a blind girl and a furry dog? If you guessed *Lassie,* you win.

In summer, you can purchase an interpretive booklet for the trail, sold at Barton Flats Visitors Center or the Mill Creek Ranger Station.

Whispering Pines Nature Trail has less of a grade than Ponderosa Vista Nature Trail, so it's easier, but somewhat less scenic. It also suffers slightly from road noise drifting up from the nearby highway. The most impressive sight on the trail is its many ponderosa pines that have been drilled with millions of holes—the handiwork of industrious acorn woodpeckers. See if you can spot the woodpecker's black and white stripes, high up in a tree.

view of Mount San Gorgonio from the Ponderosa Vista Nature Trail

Options

Hike only Ponderosa Vista Nature Trail, and then take a drive over to nearby Jenks Lake, a small but scenic lake with a picnic area. You can walk around the lake's edge, or fish for stocked trout in springtime. (See the driving directions below.)

Information and Contact

A National Forest Adventure Pass is required; see the Hiking Tips at the front of this book for details. For more information and/or a map of San Bernardino National Forest, contact the Mill Creek Ranger Station, 34701 Mill Creek Road, Mentone, CA 92359, 909/794-1123, website: www.fs.fed.us/r5/sanbernardino.

Directions

From I-10 at Redlands, take the Alabama Avenue exit and drive north to Lugonia Avenue. Turn east on Lugonia, which becomes Mentone Boulevard, Mill Creek Road, and then Highway 38. It is 25 miles from the intersection of Alabama and Lugonia Avenues to the Ponderosa Vista Nature Trail on the left side of the road. (If you reach the Jenks Lake turnoff, you've passed it.) Park in the well-signed parking lot by the trailhead. The Whispering Pines Nature Trail begins across the road.

23. ASPEN GROVE TRAIL

San Gorgonio Wilderness, off Highway 38 near
Angelus Oaks

Total distance: 4.0 miles round-trip   **Hiking time:** 2.0 hours

Type of trail: Rolling terrain   **Best season:** April–November

---

Aspen Grove Trail in the San Gorgonio Wilderness has two things you won't commonly find around Big Bear Lake: beavers and quaking aspens. If that doesn't inspire you to take a hike, try this: The scenic drive to reach the Aspen Grove trailhead is worth the trip by itself. From anywhere along Forest Service Road 1N05, you get truly remarkable views of the high peaks of the San Gorgonio Wilderness. Bring your camera and plenty of film.

You must start by making a decision: Do you just want to enjoy the scenic drive, make a quick visit to the aspen grove, and then be on your way, or do you want to take a longer hike of a couple of miles or more? If you choose the latter, you must get a day-hiking permit for the San Gorgonio Wilderness before you drive to the trailhead. Permits are free; just show up at the ranger station at Barton Flats or Mill Creek and sign the proper documents. Without a permit, you must confine your hiking to the first .25 mile of trail, which is just far enough to get you down to Fish Creek to see the aspens.

Make your choice, get your permit or don't, then take the drive to the trailhead. Try to keep your hands on the wheel as you head uphill on the smooth dirt road. Compelling views await at every turn—of the steep, dramatic canyon alongside you, a dry lakebed below, and towering mountains high above.

From the trailhead, a short walk down a closed dirt road leads you into the cool and shady grove of aspens. If you're accustomed to the aspen trees of the southern Sierra, you'll notice that these have smaller leaves—

snowy walk along Fish Creek, near the aspen grove

an adaptation to the dry climate. However, with the slightest breeze, they put on the same tremulous display as their northern cousins.

During the Ice Age, aspens ranged from the Sierra Nevada to Baja, Mexico, but as the planet warmed up, the trees couldn't take the heat, and their range became smaller. Now the only remaining aspen groves in San Bernardino National Forest are this one along Fish Creek and another along Arastre Creek. These two groves are 200 miles south of the next grove of their kind.

The Fish Creek grove is small, and to make matters worse, it is constantly threatened by nonnative beavers that chew down the trees to build dams on Fish Creek. The Department of Fish and Game introduced the beavers in the 1940s, thinking they would be good for the ecosystem. Now Fish and Game is trying to remove the beavers, but the little guys with big teeth are hard to catch.

If you obtained a wilderness permit and want to hike farther than the aspen grove, you can cross Fish Creek and enter the San Gorgonio Wilderness. The trail to the right leads only 20 yards to a few more aspens, then peters out. Follow the trail to your left (uphill), heading slightly away from the creek. A pretty walk of less than two miles through a fir and pine forest will deliver you to two meadows, first tiny Monkeyflower Flat and then, after crossing Fish Creek again, Lower Fish Creek Meadow. The latter is a fine place to lay out a picnic and count the wildflowers in springtime.

Here's an important tip: Remember that aspens are deciduous and don't releaf until early May. They stay bright green, shimmering in the breeze, until fall. October, when the leaves turn a brilliant gold, is unquestionably the best time to see them.

Information and Contact

A National Forest Adventure Pass is required; see the Hiking Tips at the front of this book for details. A free wilderness permit is required for both day-hiking and backpacking; they are available from the Mill Creek Ranger Station, the Barton Flats Visitors Center, or the Big Bear Discovery Center. For more information and/or a map of San Bernardino National Forest, contact the Mill Creek Ranger Station, 34701 Mill Creek Road, Mentone, CA 92359, 909/794-1123, website: www.fs.fed.us/r5/sanbernardino.

Directions

From I-10 at Redlands, take the Alabama Avenue exit and drive north to Lugonia Avenue. Turn east on Lugonia, which becomes Mentone Boulevard, Mill Creek Road, and then Highway 38. Drive northeast for 32 miles to Forest Service Road 1N02, signed for Heart Bar Campground, Coon Creek, and Fish Creek. Turn right (south) and drive 1.2 miles to Road 1N05, then bear right. Drive 1.5 miles to the Aspen Grove Trailhead, on the right at a turnout in the road.

24. ERNIE MAXWELL SCENIC TRAIL

San Bernardino National Forest, off Highway 243
near Idyllwild

Total distance: 5.0 miles round-trip   **Hiking time:** 2.5 hours

Type of trail: Rolling terrain   **Best season:** May–October

If you like tall mountains, granite rock formations, giant-sized conifers, and the clean air of high elevation, you'll like the resort town of Idyllwild. It's a taste of the Sierra Nevada in Southern California.

And if you like to hike, dozens of trails await exploration. The only hitch is that because of the mountainous terrain, most paths trace a steady uphill route, and the ascent is made more difficult by high elevation and thin air. But there's one exception: Ernie Maxwell Scenic Trail. With only a 600-foot elevation change on a gently undulating pathway, this is the perfect route for hikers who don't want to do a lot of heavy breathing.

Because the trail is set in a dense conifer forest, you won't enjoy many far-reaching views. Instead, the beauty is close at hand. The path leads downhill at the start, contouring through a forest of mostly Jeffrey, ponderosa, and coulter pines, with firs and incense cedars scattered among them. Practice your tree identification as you hike. Jeffrey pines are noted by their sweet scent, which is reminiscent of vanilla or butterscotch. Incense cedars have shaggy bark and smell like pencils.

Strawberry Creek, a seasonal stream, keeps the area near the start of the trail fertile and wet. At your feet, you'll find ceanothus, manzanita, and bush lupine. Where the trees thin out somewhat, raise your eyes toward the sky—you'll get peekaboo views of Lily Rock (a big white dome at 7,500 feet in elevation) and Tahquitz Peak (a steeplelike granite summit at 8,828 feet in elevation).

There's no destination along Ernie Maxwell Scenic Trail; the path just comes to an end where it reaches a dirt road. You simply turn around and hike back, enjoying the forest all over again. And in case you find yourself wondering, the trail was named for a local Idyllwild citizen who had the vision and persistence to see it built. A local conservationist, Ernie Maxwell was also the editor of the Idyllwild newspaper.

Options
Idyllwild's most famous hiking trail begins from this same trailhead at Humber Park. It's the Devils Slide Trail to 8,828-foot Tahquitz Peak, an 8.4-mile round-trip. You need to get a free wilderness permit from the ranger station in Idyllwild to hike the trail. Because the path is so popular, it's best to wait until after Labor Day (or before Memorial Day) to make the trip. And be prepared for a challenging, though visually rewarding, hike.

Information and Contact
A National Forest Adventure Pass is required; see the Hiking Tips at the front of this book for details. For more information and/or a map of San Bernardino National Forest, contact the San Jacinto Ranger District, P.O.

Box 518, 54270 Pinecrest, Idyllwild, CA 92549, 909/659-2117, website: www.fs.fed.us/r5/sanbernardino.

Directions

From I-10 at Banning, turn south on Highway 243 and drive 27 winding miles to the town of Idyllwild. Turn east on North Circle Drive, which becomes South Circle Drive and then Fern Valley Road. Follow Fern Valley Road to Humber Park. (You will drive a total of two miles from downtown.) The trailhead is at the lower end of the parking lot.

© ANN MARIE BROWN

Chapter 5

San Diego and Vicinity

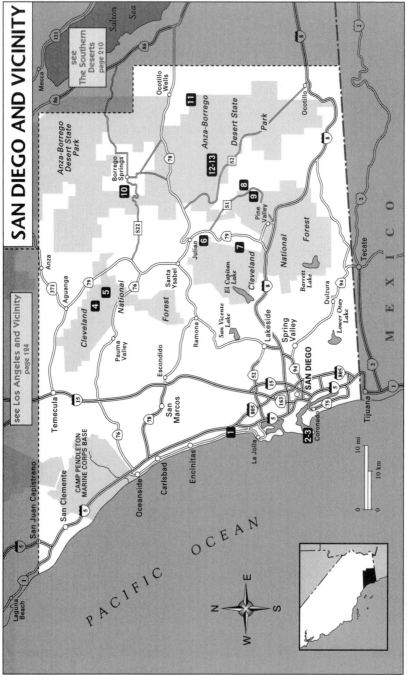

SAN DIEGO AND VICINITY

see The Southern Deserts page 210

see Los Angeles and Vicinity page 124

Anza-Borrego Desert State Park

Anza-Borrego Desert State Park

Cleveland National Forest

Cleveland National Forest

PACIFIC OCEAN

MEXICO

© AVALON TRAVEL PUBLISHING, INC.

CHAPTER 5—SAN DIEGO AND VICINITY

San Diego is a sun-drenched region with 75 miles of beaches, two distinct mountain ranges, and one giant-sized desert, Anza-Borrego. Blessed with a nearly perfect year-round climate and stunning natural beauty, San Diego is an ideal place for easy hikers to lace up their boots. After all, in few other places of the world can you walk on the beach, hike to a 5,700-foot summit, and admire the stillness of a desert palm grove—all in the same day.

Let's begin with the desert. Anza-Borrego Desert State Park encompasses 600,000 acres of palm groves, year-round creeks, slot canyons, and badlands. It is California's largest state park and nearly four times the size of Zion National Park. Desert flora runs the gamut from the expected, like barrel cactus and mesquite, to the rare, like stands of jumping cholla cactus and aptly named elephant trees. Majestic and endangered bighorn sheep are commonly seen. Hiking trails lead to leafy fan palm groves, cholla cactus gardens, and old homesteading sites. Hikers who show up in spring are treated to an array of desert wildflowers, including the distinctive flaming-red plumes of ocotillos.

Just to the west of this giant desert lie the Laguna and Cuyamaca Mountains. The Cuyamacas are mostly contained within Cuyamaca Rancho State Park, where 110 miles of trails await hikers. The 4,000- to 6,500-foot elevations here host mixed forests of ponderosa and Jeffrey pine, fir, incense cedar, and live and black oak. Alongside the Cuyamacas are the Lagunas, which are managed as part of Cleveland National Forest. With a dramatic setting that overlooks the desert thousands of feet below, the Laguna Mountains are easily explored on foot.

Situated to the north of the Laguna-Cuyamaca range is the smaller Palomar range, which is well-known for its Sierra-like landscape. The entire range extends only 25 miles along the northern border of San Diego County, but what it lacks in size it makes up for in beauty. Its 6,000-foot elevation gives rise to dense stands of fir, cedar, spruce, and black oak. Most of the land in the Palomar Mountains is part of Palomar Mountain State Park or Cleveland National Forest.

If your idea of hiking in San Diego isn't climbing mountains, wandering through conifer forests, or exploring deserts, but rather traipsing alongside the ocean, head for the coastside parks of Torrey Pines State Reserve or Cabrillo National Monument. In addition to providing wide vistas of San Diego's spectacular coastline, both parks offer a close-up look at the meeting place of sand and sea. Explore the wildlife-rich tidepools at Cabrillo or hike through Torrey Pines' sandstone badlands to the beach.

Adding up the sum of all these parts begs the question: For hikers who want it all, does San Diego have it all? The answer: Unquestionably yes.

1. RAZOR POINT & BEACH TRAIL LOOP

Torrey Pines State Reserve, off I-5 in Del Mar

Total distance: 2.0 miles round-trip

Type of trail: Rolling terrain

Hiking time: 1.0 hour

Best season: March–May

On weekend afternoons, consider yourself lucky if you can get a parking spot at Torrey Pines State Reserve. This coastal park is so beautiful that it's deservedly popular, but that means it's wise to confine your visits to weekdays, or get there early in the morning on weekends.

Windswept Torrey pines, the park's namesake tree, grace the coastal bluffs. Torrey pines grow only two places in the world: here and on Santa Rosa Island in Channel Islands National Park. It is estimated that there are fewer than 10,000 of these trees in existence. Adding to the coastal scenery, wildflowers bloom in the sandy soil in springtime. If you time it right, you may see white morning glories, blue dicks, red Indian paintbrush, tiny white popcorn flowers, and purple nightshade.

From the visitors center parking lot, begin hiking on the Razor Point Trail, which provides dramatic views of the reserve's eroded coastal badlands. They look like they're straight out of Death Valley—colorful hills that are creased and wrinkled with narrow canyons and caverns—except that there's a big ocean beyond them.

A spiderweb of paths, only some of which are signed, weaves along the coastal bluffs. Be sure to stay on formalized paths and don't make your own—the soil is already eroded, and the flora is slow to recover. Razor Point Trail visits several overlooks, including Razor Point, a narrow backbone of sandstone that provides a view straight down to the surging sea. Yucca Point is a similar overlook a few yards off the main trail, also worth a visit.

Wander roughly south from Razor Point (paralleling the ocean) until you hook up with Beach Trail, then turn right and squeeze through the steep, narrow, sandstone-lined entrance to the beach. When the tide is low, you can hike along the sand.

For your return trip, you can follow Beach Trail all the way back to the parking lot to make a semi-loop, or take Beach Trail back to the Razor Point Trail and retrace your steps from there. Beach Trail is the shortest, most direct route between the visitors center and the ocean, but it's also the steepest—downhill to the beach and uphill on the way back.

Options

Take a walk on the .5-mile Parry Grove Trail, which leads to some of the oldest Torrey pines in the reserve. Or hike Guy Fleming Loop Trail, a .75-mile trail featuring Torrey pines, ocean views, great spring wildflowers, and sandstone formations.

Information and Contact

A $4 day-use fee is charged per vehicle. A map of Torrey Pines State Reserve is available at the park visitors center. For more information, contact Torrey Pines State Reserve, c/o San Diego Coast State Parks, 9609 Waples Street, San Diego, CA 92121, 858/755-2063, websites: www.torreypine.org or www.cal-parks.ca.gov.

Torrey Pines State Reserve

© ANN MARIE BROWN

Directions

From I-5 in Del Mar, take the Carmel Valley Road exit and drive west for 1.5 miles. Turn south on Camino del Mar and drive .75 mile to the reserve entrance. Drive up the hill one mile and park by the visitors center. The trailhead is across the park road from the visitors center.

2. BAYSIDE TRAIL

Cabrillo National Monument, off I-5 in San Diego

Total distance: 2.0 miles round-trip   **Hiking time:** 1.0 hour

Type of trail: Rolling terrain   **Best season:** Good year-round

While everybody else at Cabrillo National Monument is visiting the Old Point Loma lighthouse, taking photographs by the statue of Señor Cabrillo, or enjoying the wonderful view of San Diego Harbor from the visitors center, you can sneak off for a hike on the Bayside Trail and find a surprising amount of solitude.

The solitude comes with plenty of sparkling coastal vistas, plus an interesting lesson in native coastal vegetation. But first, start with a couple of side trips: Take the paved trail from the main parking lot to the Old Point Loma lighthouse, then climb up the narrow stairway and peer inside the rooms filled with period furniture. Imagine what life was like for the lighthouse keeper and his family living in these tiny rooms in the late 1800s.

The Old Point Loma lighthouse's beacon was first lit in 1855, and it served as the southernmost Pacific Coast lighthouse in the United States until 1891. Its light could be seen 20 miles out to sea, and was first fueled by whale oil, then lard oil, and finally kerosene. The lighthouse sat idle for 40 years until it was restored in the 1930s to become part of the national monument.

After visiting the lighthouse, check out the ocean views from the overlook area on its far side. At 420 feet above sea level, you are in an excellent spot for gray-whale-watching.

Having completed your side trips, get on with the main attraction. Pick up the paved road on the east side of the lighthouse, signed Bayside Trail. Take the left fork, a gravel trail, and wind gently downhill around Point Loma. On every step of the trail, the whole of San Diego Bay and the Pacific Ocean are yours to survey. Huge Navy ships sail out to sea, flocks of gulls follow the fishing boats into the harbor, and large offshore kelp beds sway near the ocean's surface. This is one of the two largest kelp forests in the world.

Try to tear your eyes away from the coastal goings-on so you can read the interpretive signs. If you do, you'll learn about coastal sage scrub, including California sage-brush, black sage, chamise, cliff spurge, San Diego barrel cactus, and manzanita. These plants thrive in this seaside environment despite the fact that Point Loma gets only about nine inches of rain a year.

If you're hiking in winter, you may see local birds such as California quail, American kestrels, and mourning doves. In spring, the migrating birds show up, including seven kinds of hummingbirds, warblers, bushtits, and wrentits. The birds like the bluffs along this trail because they are protected from the wind. The headlands on the east side of Point Loma protect San Diego Bay from the strong gale you probably experienced on the west side, by the lighthouse.

A statue of explorer Juan Rodriguez Cabrillo stands sentinel at Cabrillo National Monument.

The trail ends directly below the statue of Cabrillo. The marble monument is about 300 feet above you on the bluffs; the voices of visitors snapping photos drift down from on high. A rather abrupt sign reads, "Trail ends. Return by the same route." Darn. You probably won't feel like leaving.

Information and Contact

A $5 day-use fee is charged per vehicle, good for seven days. A map/brochure of Cabrillo National Monument is available at the entrance kiosk or visitors center. For more information, contact Cabrillo National Monument, 1800 Cabrillo Memorial Drive, San Diego, CA 92106, 619/557-5450, website: www.nps.gov/cabr.

Directions

From I-5 South (or I-8 East or West) in San Diego, take the Rosecrans

Street exit (Highway 209) and drive south. Staying on Highway 209, you will turn right on Cañon Street, then left on Catalina Boulevard. The road ends at Cabrillo National Monument. The Bayside Trail begins by the old lighthouse.

3. CABRILLO TIDEPOOLS

Cabrillo National Monument, off I-5 in San Diego

Total distance: 1.0 mile round-trip   **Hiking time:** 1.0 hour

Type of trail: Mostly flat terrain   **Best season:** Good year-round

---

Everybody loves tidepools, and the ones at Cabrillo National Monument are some of the best in Southern California. There are two things you must do to optimize your trip: First, check the tide chart in the local newspaper so that you plan your visit during low tide. Second, stop in at the Cabrillo National Monument visitors center to pick up brochures on how to explore the tidepools and identify what you see.

There are two low tides and two high tides each day, one lower than the other, so do your homework and then show up at the time of the lowest tide if you can, so you can walk the farthest and see the most sea critters.

The tidepools are a one-mile drive from the main part of Cabrillo National Monument, where the visitors center and lighthouse are. From the parking lot, a fenced trail takes you along the blufftops for a few hundred feet, then you descend to the rocky beach and start to meander. The southernmost tidepools, below the Coast Guard station, are closed for restoration and monitoring (watch for the closure sign on the cliffs). The remaining pools are yours to explore. You'll get a peek at mussels, crabs, abalones, barnacles, starfish, anemones, snails, and limpets. If you're lucky, you might see an octopus or a sea urchin.

The park's brochures explain about the four central zones of a tidepool area. The first is the low intertidal zone, which is underwater 90 percent of the time, so you see its inhabitants only during the lowest tides of the year. This is where the most elusive creatures are: eels, octopus, purple sea urchins, sea hares, brittle stars, giant keyhole limpets, sculpins, and bat stars. The second area is the middle intertidal zone, which is underwater

Cabrillo National Monument's tidepools

only 50 percent of the time, so it's in between the low and high tide line. This area has the creatures we usually associate with tidepools: sea stars, urchins, sea anemones, gooseneck barnacles, red algae, and mussels.

In the high intertidal zone (underwater only 10 percent of the time), you see the common acorn barnacles, shore crabs, black tegulas, and hermit crabs. These creatures can live out of water for long periods of time. The final area of a tidepool region is the splash zone, where you see rough limpets, snails, and periwinkles.

Armed with all this knowledge and your tidepool identification brochures, start wandering among the rocks and pools. If you have children with you, remember to tell them that they may look at and gently touch the sea creatures, but they may not pick them up or take them out of their environment. Because this is a national monument, every rock, plant, shell, and marine animal is protected by law.

Information and Contact

A $5 day-use fee is charged per vehicle, good for seven days. A map/brochure of Cabrillo National Monument is available at the entrance kiosk or visitors center. For more information, contact Cabrillo National Monument, 1800 Cabrillo Memorial Drive, San Diego, CA 92106, 619/557-5450, website: www.nps.gov/cabr.

Directions

From I-5 South (or I-8 East or West) in San Diego, take the Rosecrans Street exit (Highway 209) and drive south. Staying on Highway 209, you will turn right on Cañon Street, then turn left on Catalina Boulevard, and continue to the monument entrance. After paying the entrance fee at the kiosk, take the right fork (immediately following the kiosk) that is signed Tidepools Parking Area. Continue down the hill to the parking area.

4. WEIR & LOWER DOANE VALLEY LOOP

Palomar Mountain State Park, off Highway 76 near
Santa Ysabel

Total distance: 3.0 miles round-trip   **Hiking time:** 1.5 hours

Type of trail: Rolling terrain   **Best season:** Good year-round

---

You're hankering for a trip to the Sierra, but you only have the afternoon off. What to do? If you live anywhere in the San Diego area, put on your hiking boots and head for Palomar Mountain State Park.

Palomar Mountain is set at 5,500 feet in elevation, where the air is cool, the conifers form a dense and shady canopy, and suburban sprawl seems far, far away. The first time I visited, I felt disoriented, but pleasantly so. I kept shaking my head in disbelief at the Sierra Nevada–like feel of the place. Is this really San Diego County? You bet.

A good introduction to the park is this loop hike on three trails: Doane Valley Nature Trail, Weir Trail, and Lower Doane Valley Trail. After entering the park, follow the signs to the parking area at Doane Pond. If you are hiking with children, they can bring their fishing rods and start or end their trip by dropping a line in the small, three-acre pond, which is stocked with trout and catfish. Even if you don't catch fish, the little pond makes a very picturesque stop. Local schoolchildren have planted a butterfly garden nearby, so you may enjoy the good company of flitting, colorful lepidoptera.

For your hike, head away from Doane Pond on the Doane Valley Nature Trail, which begins by following Doane Creek. Pick up an interpretive brochure at the trailhead so you can practice your tree identification as you walk. The wide variety of species you'll see includes incense cedars, western dogwoods, red firs, and pines.

The nature trail crosses the park road and heads downhill into the forest. At the first fork after the road crossing, veer left on Weir Trail (signed Weir Lookout), which traces along the west side of Doane Creek. You'll saunter past mountain meadows and under the spreading canopy of big trees. The conifers in this park are large and old, with many fallen branches littering the forest. Watch for mushrooms growing on their trunks, including distinctively shaped shelf mushrooms.

You'll meander along the stream for about a mile until you come to a left fork for Baptist Trail. Don't take that fork, but shortly beyond it, cross the creek on your right. This puts you on Lower Doane Valley Trail, which makes a loop around a lovely meadow. Bird sightings are common here. You may see mountain quail, easily identified by their distinct head-dresses that look like a single, long, tufted feather. Note the handiwork of resident woodpeckers in the tree trunks. Other common birds in the park are mountain chickadees, nuthatches, jays, dark-eyed juncos, and band-tailed pigeons.

When the trail nears Doane Valley Campground, pause to admire the giant, spreading oak that grows there, then cross the creek again and make a sharp switchback to the right on Doane Valley Nature Trail. The

The incense cedars at Palomar Mountain State Park are easy to identify by their lacelike foliage.

nature trail will close out your trip, bringing you back to the trailhead in .7 mile. Pay close attention to the trees between interpretive posts 10 and 14. They're giants among giants.

So, who was this Doane fellow whose name appears throughout the park? George Doane settled on Palomar Mountain in the early 1880s to raise cattle and hogs. He was famous for his huge beard, which reportedly flowed from his eyebrows to his waist. He was equally famous for pursuing, with little success, the women of Palomar Mountain. Here's the quote by which he is immortalized: "Though I like donuts and clams, still better I like schoolmarms."

They weren't too fond of him, however. Eventually, Doane went out and got himself a mail-order bride.

Options
From Doane Pond, you can add on another short loop in the opposite direction. Follow Thunder Spring Trail from the southeast end of Doane Pond along Doane Creek, then loop back on Upper Doane Valley Trail.

Information and Contact
A $5 day-use fee is charged per vehicle. A map of Palomar Mountain State Park is available for $1 at the entrance station or park headquarters. For more information, contact Palomar Mountain State Park, P.O. Box 175, Palomar Mountain, CA 92060, 760/742-3462 or 760/767-5311, website: www.palomar.statepark.org.

Directions
From I-15 north of Escondido, drive east on Highway 76 for 21 miles. Turn left (north) on Road S6 (South Grade Road) and drive 6.5 miles to its junction with Road S7. Turn left on Road S7 and drive three miles into the park. Drive past park headquarters, then turn right and park in the lot by Doane Pond. The trail begins from the right side of the parking lot.

5. OBSERVATORY TRAIL

Cleveland National Forest, off Highway 76 on
Palomar Mountain

Total distance: 4.4 miles round-trip   **Hiking time:** 3.0 hours

Type of trail: Rolling terrain   **Best season:** Good year-round

---

There's nothing quite as effective as a visit to the Palomar Observatory for changing your perspective on things. On a typical trip, you'll learn all kinds of mind-expanding facts, like this one: More than 100 billion galaxies like ours are within spotting range of the observatory's Hale telescope. Kind of makes you feel small, doesn't it?

Although you can drive to the Palomar Observatory, it's much more fun to hike the National Recreation Trail from the Forest Service's Observatory Campground on Palomar Mountain. It's an aerobic climb to reach the observatory, 2.2 miles away and with only a 600-foot elevation gain.

From the start, the trail is densely shaded with oaks and pines. You'll find many giant-sized pinecones along the trail, tossed off by the prolific coulter pines, as well as wildflowers clustered around your feet from March through May. If you've visited nearby Palomar Mountain State Park a mile down the road, you'll see that this north slope of Palomar Mountain is remarkably different. The flora here—oaks, manzanita, and coulter pines—are those that thrive in more arid areas.

At .5 mile along the path, you'll come to an overlook platform with a lovely view of green Mendenhall Valley, marred only by a few scattered buildings and reservoir tanks. Beyond it the trail heads back into the forest to climb some more. The final stretch deposits you at the observatory parking lot. Turn right, walk through the lot and past the museum, and head straight for the big white golf ball that is the 200-inch Hale telescope.

The trail may have been peaceful, but you'll have plenty of company at the observatory, especially on weekends or when school field trips are in progress. Walk up the few flights of stairs to the telescope viewing area, where you can see and learn about the giant telescope and the man who invented it, George Ellery Hale.

Times are hard for the people from Cal Tech who operate the Hale telescope. Back in the 1930s, when they built the telescope on Palomar Mountain, it was isolated and dark at night. Now, with the increasing use of high-pressure sodium lights on city streets, and with so many people using outdoor lights in their yards, the Hale telescope's power is weakened by light pollution. Today, the telescope can work only with the power of a 140-inch telescope, which is only half as good as a 200-inch telescope. If you live in the San Diego area, you can do your part by turning off outside lights at night, and encouraging your neighbors to do so.

Information and Contact

A National Forest Adventure Pass is required; see the Hiking Tips at the front of this book for details. For more information and/or a map of Cleveland National Forest, contact the Palomar Ranger District, 1634 Black Canyon Road, Ramona, CA 92065, 760/788-0250, website: www.fs.fed.us/r5/cleveland.

little hiker on the Observatory Trail

© ANN MARIE BROWN

Directions

From I-15 north of Escondido, drive east on Highway 76 for 21 miles. Turn left (north) on Road S6 (South Grade Road) and drive 6.5 miles to where it junctions with Road S7, then continue north on Road S6 for three more miles to Observatory Campground on the right. Drive through the camp to the signed parking area for the amphitheater and trailhead.

6. CANYON OAK & DESERT VIEW LOOP

William Heise County Park, off Highway 78/79 near Julian

Total distance: 3.5 miles round-trip   **Hiking time:** 2.0 hours

Type of trail: Some steep terrain   **Best season:** Good year-round

---

The folks who built the trails at William Heise County Park must have loved roller coasters. The trails go up, down, and curve every which way, as if the trail builders were just having fun. You will, too, when you hike this loop on Canyon Oak and Desert View Trails.

William Heise County Park is located near the town of Julian at 4,000 feet in elevation. The terrain is shady oak woodland mixed with a few conifers—the transition zone between valley and mountains. If you're lucky enough to visit in autumn, you'll see the black oaks display their autumn coats. In any season, the park is usually pleasantly cool for hiking, except perhaps at midday on summer afternoons.

If you're camping in the park, start hiking from the Canyon Oak trailhead at the entrance to the Area 1 group camp (also called the Youth Area). If you're just driving in for a day hike, park your car above campsite 64 in the group camp, then walk back down to the trailhead, signed Nature Trail/Canyon Oak Trail.

In .25 mile, you'll veer left and head northeast to join Canyon Oak Trail. As you climb upward and circle around a lovely grove of oaks, you might try to imagine the daily routine of the Kumeyaay Indians who lived here and used the oaks' acorns for food. Many of these oaks are hundreds of years old, so they've seen people of vastly different cultures pass under their branches.

At a signed junction with Desert View Trail, bear left. (Canyon Oak Trail loops back downhill to your starting point.) The trail is steep, but in only .1 mile you reach an overlook, complete with a bench to rest on while you admire the surrounding vista. Is this the desert view of Desert View Trail? No. It's a sea of conifers, the forested slopes of the Cuyamaca Mountains. The desert view comes later.

From the bench, prepare to do some serious climbing for the final .75 mile to a higher, more dramatic overlook at Glen's View. You're out of the shade now and on sunny slopes lined with sage, manzanita, and scrub oak. The trail keeps ascending steadily to Glen's View at 4,939 feet in elevation. Watch for a spur trail on the left; the viewpoint is about 100 yards off the main trail (and still uphill!).

At Glen's View, you'll find a simplified viewing scope on top of a stone monument. Encroaching brush obscures some of the vista, so climb around on the rocks to get up as high as you can, and voilà! There's the low desert and the Salton Sea to the east and the Pacific Ocean to the west. A marker on the monument shows you which way to look for North Peak, Coronado Bridge (40 miles away), Oceanside, Palomar Observatory, Toro Peak (37 miles away), and the Salton Sea (45 miles away). What you see the most of are pine-covered slopes, especially to the south, and the green-gray Cuyamaca and Laguna Mountains.

When you've seen enough, head back down the spur trail, then turn left to finish out your loop on Desert View Trail. It's all downhill from here. Where your trail meets up with the self-guided nature trail by the group camp, follow the nature trail back to the pavement. Walk through the campground and down the park road, keeping to the right, to return to your car.

Options
For a shorter walk, just hike the Canyon Oak Trail loop; don't combine it with the Desert View Trail loop. At the junction with Desert View Trail, hike uphill on Desert View for a few more yards to the bench and overlook, then turn around and loop back downhill (turn left) on Canyon Oak Trail. This makes a 1.3-mile loop.

Information and Contact
A $2 day-use fee is charged per vehicle. A free map of William Heise County Park is available at the entrance station. For more information, contact San Diego County Parks and Recreation Department, 2454 Heritage Park Row, San Diego, CA 92110, 858/694-3049, website: www.sdparks.org.

Directions
From Julian, drive two miles west on Highway 78/79, then turn left (south) on Pine Hills Road. Drive two miles, then turn left on Frisius Drive and drive two more miles. Frisius Drive turns into Heise Park Road and enters the park. From the entrance kiosk, continue straight on the park road to near its end at the Area 1 group camping area on the left (also called the Youth Area). Park your car above campsite 64, then walk back down to the trailhead, signed Nature Trail/Canyon Oak Trail.

7. STONEWALL PEAK TRAIL

Cuyamaca Rancho State Park, off Highway 79 near Julian

Total distance: 4.0 miles round-trip   **Hiking time:** 2.0 hours

Type of trail: Rolling terrain   **Best season:** Good year-round

---

For years, I avoided hiking Stonewall Peak at Cuyamaca Rancho State Park because I feared that the trail was too popular, and hence, too crowded. The line of cars at the day-use parking area in Paso Picacho Campground always scared me away. But finally, on a clear-blue Saturday morning one January, I got to the Stonewall Peak trailhead by 8 A.M. and hiked to the summit in blissful solitude.

Two hours later, the trail was a parade of people—mostly parents with children of all ages—curving through a myriad of switchbacks to what is probably San Diego County's most visited summit.

Why is Stonewall Peak so popular? Because its views are terrific, its trailhead is close to a large state park camp, and its summit is easy enough for small children to attain. The trail that ascends Stonewall Peak

Protective railings line the summit of Stonewall Peak.

is well-graded and just plain pleasant every step of the way, with a 900-foot elevation gain spread out over two miles.

Although somewhat dwarfed by neighboring Cuyamaca Peak, Stonewall Peak is no slouch in the summit department at 5,730 feet in elevation. (Cuyamaca Peak is almost 800 feet higher.) Stonewall Peak overlooks the site of the Stonewall Mine, which yielded over two million dollars' worth of gold in the 1880s. The peak also overlooks a large chunk of the Cuyamaca Mountains, including close-up landmarks like Cuyamaca Peak, Lake Cuyamaca, the white golf ball of the Palomar Observatory, and the Anza-Borrego Desert. If you squint a bit, you can make out the snowy peaks of Mount San Jacinto and Mount San Gorgonio.

Dozens of switchbacks whisk you to the summit, making the climb go almost unnoticed. The trail is mostly shaded by black oaks and incense cedars, but there are a few exposed stretches, so don't forget your sun protection. The final 50 yards of trail are cut into an exposed stone ridge, with granite stairsteps and a handrail to keep you from going over the edge. The rocky summit seems to jut into open space. It, too, is lined with a metal handrail. Young hikers will feel like they've climbed Yosemite's Half Dome.

Stonewall Peak and the Stonewall Mine were named after Civil War general Thomas Stonewall Jackson, but not everyone approved of this appellation. Those who weren't fond of Jackson insisted that the peak was named for its "stone wall" or exposed granite crown at the top. Stonewall Peak's granite wall can be easily seen and identified from many points in the park.

Options

Another great easy hike from Paso Picacho Campground is Azalea Glen Loop Trail, best hiked in springtime when the azaleas are in bloom. The trailhead is by the entrance kiosk.

Information and Contact

A $4 day-use fee is charged per vehicle. Maps of Cuyamaca Rancho State Park are available at Paso Picacho Campground. For more information, contact Cuyamaca Rancho State Park, 12551 Highway 79, Descanso, CA 91916, 760/765-0755, website: www.cuyamaca.statepark.org.

Directions

From San Diego, drive east on I-8 for 40 miles to the Highway 79 exit. Drive north 11 miles on Highway 79, then turn left into Paso Picacho Campground. After passing the kiosk, bear right and park in the picnic area lot. Walk across the highway to the trailhead, which is directly opposite the campground entrance.

8. GARNET PEAK

Cleveland National Forest, off Highway 79 near Julian

Total distance: 4.2 miles round-trip   **Hiking time:** 2.5 hours
Type of trail: Some steep terrain   **Best season:** Good year-round

---

If Stonewall Peak is the most visited summit in San Diego County (see the preceding hike), Garnet Peak must be in the top five. On a winter Saturday, we passed more than 100 hikers, plus dozens of happy dogs on leashes, on the trail to Garnet's rocky summit.

Garnet Peak's main attraction is its dramatic desert and mountain views. In winter, the vistas are the most spectacular, mostly because of clear visibility but also because the high Southland mountains it overlooks are often crowned in snow. You can see Southern California's frosty white trio of mammoth peaks: Mount San Gorgonio (the highest in Southern California at 11,490 feet), Mount San Jacinto (the second highest at 10,804 feet), and even Mount Baldy (in the top 10 at 10,064 feet). Mount Baldy is nearly 100 miles away, far to the northwest, so you can't discern it on a merely average visibility day.

From Garnet Peak, these 10,000-foot-plus mountains appear as three distant white mounds floating on the horizon. In the foreground is something even more dramatic: a huge expanse of Anza-Borrego Desert, including red- and gold-colored Storm Canyon, a few thousand feet downhill.

The route to Garnet Peak begins on Pacific Crest Trail at the Penny Pines trailhead, where you'll see a list of the names of people who have donated funds to California's national forests for reforestation. Follow the well-graded Pacific Crest Trail to the north (left), hiking along the edge of the pine grove. Because you're on the desert side of the mountain, only chaparral grows alongside the trail; there's nothing tall enough to block your view. Wide desert vistas open up almost immediately, and they keep getting wider as you hike along the edge of the Laguna Mountain rim.

canine hikers and their human companions on Garnet Peak

Two cutoff trails on the right, at about 1.5 miles, lead to rocky view-points, but neither is as spectacular as Garnet Peak's summit. The second cutoff trail provides good views of Garnet Peak itself, a big hunk of granite off to your left. The third right-hand turnoff is the real thing—Garnet Peak's summit trail (it may not be signed). The path is rocky, but in less than a mile you reach the jagged, 5,900-foot summit, where you're rewarded with extraordinary clear-day views of the Anza-Borrego Desert, Salton Sea, Plaster City, Palomar Observatory, Mount San Jacinto, Mount San Gorgonio, Mount Baldy, the Laguna and Cuyamaca Mountains, and more.

The view, which seems to go on forever, is equally good in every direction. The peak holds a completely exposed position on the ridgeline of the Laguna Mountains, with no other high peaks nearby to block your line of vision. Another reason for the view's impact is the extremity of Garnet Peak's vertical rise. From on top of Garnet Peak looking east, the desert floor is 5,000 feet below—a vertical mile—and it appears to be straight down.

While you're at the top, look for an unofficial summit register, which is usually stuffed into a coffee can and buried under a rock. The piles of ragged notebooks and torn clippings make interesting reading.

Be sure to add a few pithy or piquant words of your own before heading back downhill.

Options
Hike only as far as one of the first overlook points, then turn around and head back.

Information and Contact
A National Forest Adventure Pass is required; see the Hiking Tips at the front of this book for details. For more information and/or a map of Cleveland National Forest, contact the Descanso Ranger District, 3348 Alpine Boulevard, Alpine, CA 91901, 619/445-6235, website: www.fs.fed .us/r5/cleveland. A map of the Laguna Mountain Recreation Area is available from the Descanso Ranger District or the Laguna Mountain Visitors Center.

Directions
From Julian, drive south on Highway 79 to the left fork for Road S1/Sunrise Scenic Byway. Bear left and drive south for approximately 12 miles to the Penny Pines Plantation, between mile markers 27.5 and 27.0. The trail begins here.

9. LIGHTNING RIDGE TRAIL
Cleveland National Forest, off Highway 79 near Julian

Total distance: 1.5 miles round-trip   **Hiking time:** 1.0 hour
Type of trail: Rolling terrain   **Best season:** December–April

Timing is everything on Lightning Ridge Trail. Sure, the route is pleasant enough to hike any day of the year, because the 5,500-foot elevation and the pine-needle-lined trail make pleasant walking. But if you play your cards right, you can hike Lightning Ridge Trail on one of the few days of the year when a lake magically appears in Laguna Meadow, and wildflowers bloom in profusion at its edges. From the top of Lightning Ridge, you'll look down at the grassy, watery spectacle below and know that you've witnessed a sight rarely seen.

One of several pleasant and easy hiking trails in the Laguna Mountain Recreation Area, Lightning Ridge Trail is suitable for hikers of any ability, with a smooth surface and only 250 feet of elevation gain. Following this pathway, you gain a clear understanding of how beautiful and unusual this high, cool mountain on the edge of the desert really is.

The trail begins at a stone monument by the amphitheater at Laguna Campground. It follows along the edge of a meadow for the first few hundred yards, then heads into the trees and makes several long, sweeping switchbacks uphill. This trail is a surprising contrast to the nearby trails on the east side of the Laguna Mountains. Here on the west side, the slopes are wetter and cooler. Instead of chaparral growing in profusion, you'll find tall pines and oaks, and woodland shrubs like manzanita. As you climb higher, tall trees show evidence of lightning strikes.

The path reaches its high point where it crosses a dirt road by a water reservoir on top of Lightning Ridge. Although this cistern is not particularly scenic, Laguna Meadow lies directly below, gracefully framed by pine trees. With luck, you'll be able to catch sight of ephemeral Little Laguna Lake. Even if the lake is nonexistent, the meadow is a beautiful sight, especially after winter and spring rains when it is filled with wildflowers. By Memorial Day the meadow grasses are often dry and brown.

If you miss the seldom-seen meadow lake, you have another special occasion to shoot for: Walk this trail on a winter day when it's covered with a few inches of snow.

Options

You can make a loop out of this trip by connecting with the trail to Horse Heaven Group Camp at the top of the ridge.

Information and Contact

A National Forest Adventure Pass is required; see the Hiking Tips at the front of this book for details. For more information and/or a map of Cleveland National Forest, contact the Descanso Ranger District, 3348 Alpine Boulevard, Alpine, CA 91901, 619/445-6235, website: www.fs. fed.us/r5/cleveland. A map of the Laguna Mountain Recreation Area is available from the Descanso Ranger District or the Laguna Mountain Visitors Center.

Directions

From Julian, drive south on Highway 79 to the left fork for Road S1/Sunrise Scenic Byway. Bear left and drive south for approximately 13 miles to Laguna Campground on the right, between mile markers 26.5 and 26.0.

Turn onto the camp road and drive .75 mile, staying straight and following the signs for the amphitheater. Park in the amphitheater lot, then look for the small stone monument just beyond the restrooms, on the northeast side of the parking lot. The trail begins here.

10. BORREGO PALM CANYON

Anza-Borrego Desert State Park, off Highway S22 near
Borrego Springs

Total distance: 3.0 miles round-trip   **Hiking time:** 1.5 hours

Type of trail: Mostly flat terrain   **Best season:** November–May

---

The walk from the Anza-Borrego Desert State Park campground to Borrego Palm Canyon is only 1.5 miles long, but it feels like a trip from the desert to the tropics. You start out in a rocky, sandy, open plain, sweating it out with the cacti and ocotillo plants, and you end up in a shady oasis of fan palms, dipping your feet in the pool of a fern-covered waterfall.

It's incredible but true; water flows from springs most of the year in this part of Anza-Borrego, forming a cool stream and a 15-foot waterfall that drops over big boulders in the back of Borrego Palm Canyon. A large grove of palm trees thrives alongside the life-giving spring, providing shade and an ideal destination for hikers. Even families with small children can walk the nearly level route to the palm oasis and desert waterfall. Just don't try it during the summer months, when the air temperature is unbearably hot and the stream becomes a mere mirage.

The trip begins on the signed Borrego Palm Canyon Trail from the campground of the same name. The sandy route is marked clearly, so if your water bottles are filled, just start walking. Make sure you bring along an interpretive brochure from the park visitors center so you can identify the array of desert plants growing along the trail, including cheesebush, brittlebush, catclaw (ouch!), and chuparosa. All these bushes mean one thing—there's no shade anywhere.

In a half mile, after passing interpretive post 20, you're suddenly rewarded with the refreshing sight of hundreds of bright green, leafy palm trees ahead. After walking amid brown bushes, brown sand, and brown rocks, the sight of these palms is more exciting than you might expect.

in the pool at Borrego Palm Canyon's oasis

© ANN MARIE BROWN

Borrego Palm Canyon has more than 800 mature native palms. It's the largest of the more than 25 groves in the park, and one of the largest oases in the United States.

Head toward the palms, and in a few minutes you're nestled in their shade, listening to the desert wind rustle their fronds. Keep heading farther back in the canyon, amid more palms and over and around a few boulders. Another 10 minutes of walking brings you to the waterfall, which streams down over giant boulders framed by palm trees.

Some of the palms are ringed by split-rail fences; this is to protect their delicate seedlings and aid their propagation. Too many heavy footsteps could kill the palm seedlings.

At the fall's base is a marvelously clear pool with a sandy bottom, where you can wade in and cool off your feet. Tiny maidenhair ferns grow around the water's edge. On our trip, a bright green hummingbird flitted about the scene. Sit for a while and listen to the croaking of frogs and the wind in the palms.

Options
Experienced desert hikers can travel farther back in Borrego Palm Canyon, but this requires skill in climbing over boulders and dry waterfalls.

Information and Contact
A $4 day-use fee is charged per vehicle. A map of Anza-Borrego Desert State Park is available at the park visitors center. For more information, contact Anza-Borrego Desert State Park, 200 Palm Canyon Drive, Borrego

Springs, CA 92004, 760/767-5311 or 760/767-4205, website: www
.anzaborrego.statepark.org.

Directions

From Julian, drive east on Highway 78 for 19 miles to Highway S3/Yaqui
Pass Road. Turn left (north) on Highway S3/Yaqui Pass Road and drive for
12 miles to Borrego Springs. Turn left on Highway S22/Palm Canyon
Drive, and drive one mile to the signed junction just before the park visitors center. Turn right and drive one mile to Borrego Palm Canyon Campground. The trailhead is at the west end.

11. ELEPHANT TREE TRAIL

Anza-Borrego Desert State Park, off Highway 78 near
Ocotillo Wells

Total distance: 1.2 miles round-trip   **Hiking time:** 1.0 hour

Type of trail: Rolling terrain   **Best season:** November–May

Elephant Tree Trail is one of the feature trails of Anza-Borrego Desert State
Park. It's not just its intriguing name that makes it popular; it's also its location in the geologically spectacular Fish Creek area, and the unusual
desert foliage you can see and identify along its route.

But don't expect to see a herd of elephants, or even a herd of elephant trees, on this desert path. You'll see only one of the wrinkly trees,
Bursera microphylla, and it doesn't look much like an elephant. But take
this walk anyway, not only to see a rare botanical specimen, but also for
a pleasant stroll among creosote bush, burroweed, indigo bush, barrel
cactus, ocotillo, catclaw, cholla, and smoke tree. There's enough desert-
plant identification to keep you thumbing through your cactus encyclo-
pedia all day.

But what about the elephant tree? Miners and prospectors in the late
1800s told stories of the strange-looking trees in this desert, but botanists
didn't locate them in Anza-Borrego until 1937. In Alma Wash, the trees
numbered in the hundreds, scattered along steep cliffs. The Native Americans believed the trees were powerful; they used their sap for medication
and as a good-luck charm.

an elephant tree in Anza-Borrego Desert State Park

In some areas of Mexico the elephant tree is a common desert plant, called *torote,* but here in the United States it is quite rare. And in Anza-Borrego, it is becoming more rare: this trail used to feature a half-dozen elephant trees, but an unknown ailment has killed all but one of them. The dead remains of the trees are known as the "elephant graveyard."

Named because of its wrinkled trunk, the elephant tree can grow to be 10 feet tall—huge by desert standards. It is an odd patchwork of colors: creamy white bark, blue berries, and orange twigs. Its bark is ragged looking, like skin peeling from a bad sunburn. It emits an evocative odor, something like a spicy air freshener.

If you're lucky enough to visit in the spring, after a good rainy winter, you'll probably see pink sand verbena in bloom along this trail, and ocotillos sprouting brilliant red flower plumes. If you are here only a day or so after a rain, you'll find that the tall, spiky ocotillos bear green leaves, although the rest of the time they look like dormant sticks. The ocotillos produce leaves only during rainfall; the leaves fall off shortly after the rain stops. Rain also makes desert lavender produce a heady scent, and causes the barrel cactus to expand into fat little waterlogged balls.

Options

Depending on the road conditions when you visit and what type of vehicle you're driving, you can continue your exploration by heading farther south on Split Mountain Road to hike Wind Caves Trail, which shows off carved sandstone formations. Drive two miles past the Elephant Trees turnoff to the Fish Creek Wash turnoff. Turn right and drive four miles on dirt to the Wind Caves trailhead. Four-wheel drive is sometimes required for the sandy road.

Information and Contact

There is no fee at this trailhead. A map of Anza-Borrego Desert State Park is available at the park visitors center. For more information, contact Anza-Borrego Desert State Park, 200 Palm Canyon Drive, Borrego Springs, CA 92004, 760/767-5311 or 760/767-4205, website: www.anzaborrego.statepark.org.

Directions

From Julian, drive east on Highway 78 for 35 miles to Ocotillo Wells. Turn south on Split Mountain Road and drive 5.8 miles to the right turnoff that is signed for Elephant Trees. Turn right and drive .8 mile on a dirt road to the trailhead. (If the road is too sandy for your vehicle, just park and walk; it's a very short distance.)

If you are coming from Borrego Springs, take Borrego Springs Road southeast to Highway 78, then turn east (left) and drive 6.5 miles to Ocotillo Wells and Split Mountain Road.

12. GHOST MOUNTAIN/MARSHAL SOUTH HOME

Anza-Borrego Desert State Park, off Road S2 near
Blair Valley

Total distance: 2.0 miles round-trip   **Hiking time:** 1.0 hour

Type of trail: Some steep terrain   **Best season:** November–May

---

When most people imagine living off the land and getting back to nature, they picture themselves doing so in a forest, in the mountains, or maybe near the sea. Almost instinctively, they choose a place where water is plentiful.

When Marshal South had the same idea in the 1930s, he decided to live off the land in Anza-Borrego Desert. Not only that, but he decided to bring his wife with him, and raise a family of five children.

South was a writer and his wife, Tanya, was a poet. They built an adobe home on top of Ghost Mountain, where they lived with their children for more than 16 years. Eventually, Tanya grew tired of her husband's odd behaviors and idealism, and the family split up. One by one, they departed the South homestead, and Marshal South's dream was left to return to the desert sand.

The meager remains of the South home, now just a few crumbling adobe walls and bent mattress frames, can still be seen on top of Ghost Mountain. Marshal South Trail is the well-graded path that takes you there, with a 400-foot elevation gain. Even though the trail has an easy to moderate grade, remember that this route is uphill and has no shade, so hike it only when the desert air is cool.

The trail is located in the Blair Valley region of Anza-Borrego, which is higher in elevation than other parts of the park, and usually a few degrees cooler. Blair Valley displays more foliage than many other parts of the park, especially tall stands of ocotillo, yucca, and cholla. The 2,800-foot elevation is hospitable to a wide variety of high desert plants. In spring, Blair Valley has some of the best wildflowers in the park.

South called Ghost Mountain "Yaquitepec," although no one is quite sure what that meant. Life in the desert was difficult for the South family, but they lived simply, trying to survive in the spartan style of early Native

Marshal South's homestead remains on the top of Ghost Mountain.

Americans. They raised vegetables and gathered native plants. South wrote magazine articles about desert life to make money for needed supplies.

Obtaining water was a major difficulty. The issue was compounded by the fact that the South homestead was atop a mountain, rather than on the desert floor where they might have been able to dig a well. South's solution was to construct an elaborate series of cisterns and troughs to store water. Supplies were brought in from Julian by Model T, then carried uphill on foot. The family captured as much rainwater as they could, then stored and rationed it carefully.

Upon your arrival at the top of Ghost Mountain, you can walk around its summit and see the decaying remains of South's water storage system. A few partial foundation walls still stand, as well as the remains of what appears to have been a terraced garden. Despite the impracticality of this hilltop location, you begin to understand why South chose this spot, out of all the possible desert sites. Ghost Mountain is truly lovely, with 360-degree desert views. Hawks fly overhead, and butterflies flit about the desert flora. It's strangely moving to view the rusting remains of South's dream. Seeing this place really sparks your imagination.

Information and Contact

There is no fee at this trailhead. A map of Anza-Borrego Desert State Park is available at the park visitors center. For more information, contact Anza-Borrego Desert State Park, 200 Palm Canyon Drive, Borrego Springs, CA 92004, 760/767-5311 or 760/767-4205, website: www.anzaborrego.statepark.org.

Directions

From Julian, drive east on Highway 78 for 12 miles to Road S2, then turn south and drive six miles to the left turnoff for Blair Valley Camp. Turn left (east) and drive 1.4 miles on a dirt road, then bear right at the fork. Drive another 1.6 miles, then bear right again and drive .5 mile to the Ghost Mountain/Marshal South Home trailhead.

13. PICTOGRAPH TRAIL TO OVERLOOK

Anza-Borrego Desert State Park, off Road S2 near
Blair Valley

Total distance: 3.2 miles round-trip   **Hiking time:** 2.0 hours

Type of trail: Rolling terrain

Best season: November–May; best for wildflowers March–April

Although a Native American pictograph site is the destination on this excursion in Anza-Borrego Desert State Park, Pictograph Trail comes with a bonus: an inspiring overlook of the Vallecito Mountains from the brink of a dry waterfall. It's a desert view that's hard to forget.

The trail leads from the Pictograph trailhead in Blair Valley, elevation 2,600 feet. An immediate surprise is that you'll see a fair amount of grass and tall shrubs here, as well as plentiful cactus. Mojave yucca, junipers, and thistle sage grow tall, while goldfields and filaree carpet the ground in springtime. In contrast to the rest of Anza-Borrego Desert, Blair Valley looks like a veritable jungle of foliage. This area is usually somewhat cooler than the rest of the desert, and plants (and people) love it here.

When you reach the trailhead, follow the trail as it leads among huge granite boulders. It heads through a dry wash and then ascends a ridge for .5 mile, then begins to descend. Before the trail starts to drop, turn around and take a look at the view from whence you came. From the ridgeline, you can see toward Julian and the Laguna and Cuyamaca Mountains. On my trip, ominous rain clouds were stacked up over the distant green hills, but the sun was shining and the breeze was blowing pleasantly in the Blair Valley desert.

At just under one mile from the trailhead, you'll find some pictographs on the side of a boulder on your right. Painted in red and yellow by the nomadic Kumeyaay Indians, the slightly faded designs were made with natural pigments and are probably as much as 2,000 years old. No one really knows what these painted symbols mean, but it is believed that high priests or shamans performed rituals in areas where the rock art is found. Such rituals might include adolescent rites, solstice ceremonies, or vision quests. This is considered to be one of the best preserved of more than 50 Native American rock art sites in Anza-Borrego.

After pondering the pictographs, continue 1.3 miles farther on the trail. The canyon narrows dramatically until its walls come together at the lip of a dry waterfall, more than 150 feet tall. From its edge, the vista is stunning, both of the steep dropoff and the far-off Vallecito Mountains and valley to the south. The perpendicular dropoff makes you feel like you're on a high peak, even though the walk you took to get here was almost level.

Options

Don't miss the .25-mile Morteros Trail in Blair Valley. You passed the trailhead on your drive in to the Pictograph trailhead; on your drive back out, you'll reach the trailhead in 1.5 miles. The Morteros Trail leads to the site of a Kumeyaay Indian village, used seasonally for almost 1,000 years. Several boulders bear deep, round indentations from Native American women grinding acorns to make meal.

Information and Contact

There is no fee at this trailhead. A map of Anza-Borrego Desert State Park is available at the park visitors center. For more information, contact Anza-Borrego Desert State Park, 200 Palm Canyon Drive, Borrego Springs, CA 92004, 760/767-5311 or 760/767-4205, website: www.anzaborrego.statepark.org.

Directions

From Julian, drive east on Highway 78 for 12 miles to Road S2, then turn south and drive six miles to the left turnoff for Blair Valley Camp. Turn left (east) and drive 1.4 miles on a dirt road, then bear right at the fork. Drive another 1.6 miles, then bear left at the next fork. In another .25 mile, bear left again. Continue two more miles to the end of the road at the Pictograph trailhead. (Total mileage from the turnoff at Blair Valley Camp is 5.2 miles, all on well-graded dirt.)

© ANN MARIE BROWN

Chapter 6

The Southern Deserts

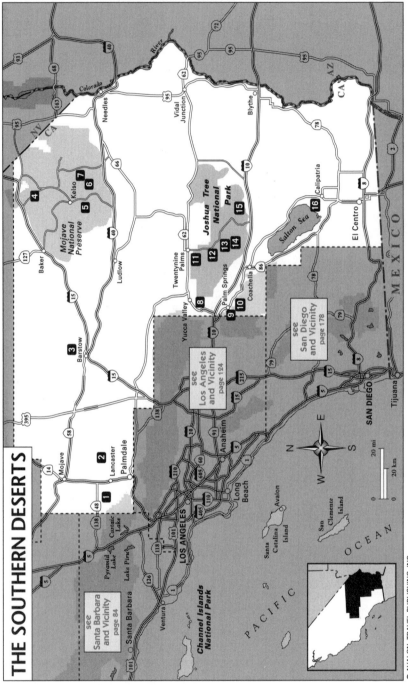

THE SOUTHERN DESERTS

© AVALON TRAVEL PUBLISHING, INC.

CHAPTER 6—THE SOUTHERN DESERTS

The Southern Deserts region contains two of California's most spectacular national parks, Joshua Tree and Mojave, a series of state and regional parks in the western Mojave, plus the world-famous oasis of Palm Springs and its surrounding desert canyons. Connoisseurs of barrel cactus, Joshua trees, palm groves, and other desert flora will find those treasures here. Come armed with a big hat and a plentiful supply of water, and you can help yourself to an abundance of easy desert trails.

Although both Joshua Tree National Park and Mojave National Preserve are considered desert parks, each is distinctly different. Joshua Tree is best known for its wide desert plains covered with strange-looking Joshua trees, amazing rock formations and boulder piles, rugged mountains, and gold mining ruins. Much of the park is higher than 4,000 feet in elevation. The most comfortable weather usually occurs from October to May; summer temperatures frequently soar past 100 degrees. Hiking trails in Joshua Tree are plentiful and varied; destinations include gold mine stamp mills, old homesteads, mountain summits, and fan palm oases.

Only 50 miles to the north, Mojave National Preserve is located where the Mojave, Great Basin, and Sonoran Deserts join. As a result of this convergence, Mojave contains a wide diversity of plant and animal life, as well as interesting geological features. Hiking trails lead to the summit of Cima Dome, a granite batholith covered with a dense forest of Joshua trees, and through the volcanic rock cliffs of Hole-in-the-Wall. The 500-foot-tall Kelso Dunes, second highest in California, are another of the preserve's attractions. Like Joshua Tree, Mojave National Preserve is mostly high desert terrain, with elevations ranging from 2,000 feet to 5,000 feet. Although summers can be hot, December to February is frequently windy and cold. Higher elevations of the park are sometimes dusted in snow.

The desert's most famous city, Palm Springs, was originally the home of the Agua Caliente band of the Cahuilla Indians, who still own major portions of the town's land. Not unlike today's Palm Springs visitors, the Agua Caliente worshipped the pure water flowing down the desert canyons, the natural hot springs, and the wind-sheltering curve of the San Jacinto Mountains. For a real taste of the Palm Springs desert, pay a visit to the Agua Caliente Indian Canyons. You won't find manicured golf courses or trendy nightclubs there, but you will find lush stands of palms, mesquite, and creosote, and the magical silence of the desert.

If the heat in Palm Springs starts to wear you down, you can always buy a ticket for the Aerial Tramway and be whisked from the desert floor to Mount San Jacinto State Park and Wilderness at 8,516 feet in elevation. In a few short minutes, you'll travel from palms to pines, where the air temperature is usually 30 degrees cooler. One trip on this amazing contraption, and you'll never think of Palm Springs the same way again. Hike in the morning among cactus and creosote bushes, then hike in the afternoon among conifers and corn lilies. In one trip to the Southern Deserts, a hiker can enjoy the best of both worlds.

1. SOUTH & NORTH POPPY LOOP

Antelope Valley California Poppy Reserve,
off Highway 14 near Lancaster

Total distance: 2.6 miles round-trip   **Hiking time:** 1.5 hours

Type of trail: Rolling terrain   **Best season:** February–May

---

Our first trip to the Antelope Valley California Poppy Reserve was a bit disappointing. We showed up in late March, expecting to see the hillsides completely covered in bright orange poppies, but only a few straggler flowers remained, dry and shriveled from the Mojave Desert wind.

We were victims of poor planning, with no one to blame but ourselves. If you want to see the magic poppy show at Antelope Valley California Poppy Reserve, you must get up-to-date information and time your trip perfectly.

Here's how to do it: Phone the park's "poppy hotline" frequently starting in mid-February (661/724-1180). A recording will tell you when the wildflower bloom is at its best in the Lancaster area. Occurring any time from late February to May, the peak bloom varies every year depending on rain, wind, sun, and temperature. When the poppy hotline says that it's time, come immediately; don't wait two weeks.

Several possible loop hikes are possible in the reserve, but the best for poppy-watching is a combined loop that leads from the west side of the visitors center, a futuristic-looking structure built into the hillside. Alongside the building sits the windmill that generates electricity to power it. Take a look inside the visitors center at the interpretive exhibits and the lovely watercolor paintings by Jane Pinheiro, then pick up South Loop Poppy Trail on the left side of the building. You probably got a good look at the poppies as you drove in—if they're in bloom, they're self-evident on the undulating grass hillsides. But nothing prepares you for the colorful miracle of seeing them close up.

Antelope Valley California Poppy Reserve

Many other wildflowers bloom at the reserve in and among our California state flower. From a distance, all you see are orange poppies, *Eschscholzia californica,* but up close, you'll notice variation. You'll see owl's clover (tubular yellow flowers on bright red spikes), lupine (pea-like blue or purple flowers), goldfields (white or yellow daisylike flowers with branching stems), and cream cups (creamy gold flowers on long, hairy stems).

The South Loop connects to the North Loop; you can hike both trails if you wish or take the cutoff in between for Tehachapi Vista Point. It's worth climbing the short hill to the point, where you can get up high and look around at miles of poppies and grasslands.

Weather plays a huge factor in this giant poppy extravaganza. The dry desert wind that blows almost constantly is what ultimately puts an end to the poppy show. Cloudy or overcast days can also affect the impact of the display. When it's gray, the flowers won't open, even in their peak bloom time. The moral of the story: Check on conditions before you drive to the park.

Options
Just walk the South Loop of the poppy reserve and return via Tehachapi Vista Point, which is only 1.4 miles round-trip.

Information and Contact

A $4 day-use fee is charged per vehicle. Phone the Poppy Hotline at 661/724-1180 each spring for the best bloom time. For more information, contact Antelope Valley California Poppy Reserve, 15101 West Lancaster Road, Lancaster, CA 93536, 661/724-1180 or 661/942-0662, websites: www.calparksmojave.com or www.cal-parks.ca.gov.

Directions

From Lancaster on Highway 14, take the Avenue I exit and turn west on Avenue I, which becomes Lancaster Road. Drive 14 miles to the entrance to Antelope Valley California Poppy Reserve on the right. The trail begins by the visitors center.

2. SADDLEBACK BUTTE TRAIL

Saddleback Butte State Park, off Highway 14
near Lancaster

Total distance: 3.2 miles round-trip

Hiking time: 2.0 hours

Type of trail: Some steep terrain

Best season: November–May

Saddleback Butte State Park is located on the western edge of the Mojave Desert, a place that doesn't seem exactly like the desert, but doesn't seem like any other familiar landscape, either. From Saddleback Butte, you can see the high mountains of the San Gabriels, jauntily snow-capped in winter, while you're standing in a native Joshua tree woodland. The park is within a short drive of the heavily developed cities of Lancaster and Palmdale, but it's set in a vast land of nothingness in the alluvial bottomland of the Antelope Valley. This land in the western Mojave seems to be neither here nor there.

The park's signature hike is a tromp through a forest of Joshua trees for 1.6 miles to the top of Saddleback Butte, a granite summit at 3,652 feet in elevation. Although that altitude may not sound impressive, consider that the butte's peak is 1,000 feet above the broad alluvial plain that surrounds it. It's the only really tall thing around, so you can see for many miles from its top.

The park contains some fascinating desert flora and fauna. Prevalent foliage includes Joshua trees and creosote plants, both of which are a delight for photographers, especially with a backdrop of blue desert sky. The Joshua tree grows only in the Mojave Desert, which is why it is protected here and at Joshua Tree National Park. Although common in many desert areas, creosote is one of the oldest living plants on earth—up to 10,000 years old.

Start hiking from the park campground through sand and Joshua trees, heading directly for the clearly visible peak. With luck, you picked a cool day, because there is little shade anywhere. At one mile out, a trail leads left to Little Butte; you continue straight for the rocky peak of Saddleback Butte. The last half-mile is very steep, especially compared to the first mile, which is nearly level. You leave all the Joshua trees behind and climb up, up, and up the rocky trail. Just when it starts to get uncomfortably steep, the trail veers sharply right and brings you to a saddle in the middle of the butte. The vista opens wide at the saddle, which will inspire you to continue your ascent along the butte's granite backbone. If you have small children with you, hold on to them beyond the saddle, because the trail gets extremely rocky.

At the tip-top of Saddleback Butte, you are rewarded with sweeping vistas of Antelope Valley, the San Gabriel Mountains, the Tehachapi Mountains, and the Mojave Desert. Looking over the back side of the butte,

Joshua tree in Saddleback Butte State Park

there is only a wide, level plain between you and the San Gabriels, with a few miniature granite buttes jutting upward from it. Nothing compares in size to the one you're standing on.

If you are lucky, you may see a coyote, jackrabbit, or kit fox as you hike, and if you are extremely lucky, you may see a desert tortoise. Springtime is the best season for tortoise sightings, when the giant reptiles leave their deep underground burrows to get some fresh air and chomp on the wildflowers. They are extremely shy and fragile creatures. If you see one, please only look at it—don't touch it or pick it up.

Information and Contact
A $5 day-use fee is charged per vehicle. For more information, contact Saddleback Butte State Park, 17102 East Avenue J, Lancaster, CA 93535, 661/727-9899 or 661/942-0662, websites: www.calparksmojave.com or www.cal-parks.ca.gov.

Directions
From Lancaster on Highway 14, take the 20th Street exit. Drive north for .4 mile, then turn right (east) on Avenue J. Drive 19 miles on Avenue J to 170th Street East. Turn right, drive one mile, then turn left on Avenue K at the sign for the state park campground.

3. OWL CANYON TRAIL

Bureau of Land Management Lands, off I-15 near Barstow

Total distance: 4.0 miles round-trip   **Hiking time:** 2.0 hours

Type of trail: Some steep terrain   **Best season:** November–May

There's a secret cave in the desert north of Barstow, and flashlight-carrying hikers can tunnel through it to enter a hidden canyon with tall, sheer, wind-sculpted walls.

That's just one of the many delights of the Owl Canyon Trail, located in the Bureau of Land Management's Rainbow Basin. The area is only a few miles away from millions of drivers on I-15, yet you will usually find only a few other hikers joining you on the trail.

Owl Canyon

Got your flashlight? Good. The trail begins at the BLM's Owl Canyon Campground, near campsite 11, at an ordinary-looking dirt-and-gravel wash. Within minutes, your surroundings get more interesting as you walk into colorful Owl Canyon. The canyon gets progressively narrower and rockier, and the sedimentary substances that make up its walls change inch by inch. You'll see sandstone, siltstone, shale, and white volcanic rock. There's so much to look at and photograph, and so many boulders and obstacles to climb over, you won't be traveling very fast.

The canyon is part of the larger Rainbow Basin, named for its cornucopia of colorful sediments—deposits that were formed in lakebeds 20 million years ago. Although the most colorful portions of the basin can be viewed only by taking the auto tour through the canyon, hikers get their fair share of the rainbow here in Owl Canyon. Not only that, but if you visit early in the morning or at sunset, you may be fortunate enough to spot one of the barn owls that reside here and give Owl Canyon its name.

At .6 mile (about 15 minutes from your car), you'll see the cave entrance on your right. Turn on your flashlight, watch your head, and start exploring. You'll find that you can tunnel right through the cave into a small side canyon, equally colorful and intriguing as the one you came from. The cave tunnel is about 75 feet long.

Retrace your steps through the tunnel to the main canyon, then continue up the pathway. Small dry waterfalls may cause difficulties for some hikers, but most can clamber over them. The trail ends near the base of Velvet Peak (really a granite ridge, not a summit), at the back of a wide and colorful rock amphitheater. You'll find a few Joshua trees growing here and a fine view of the surrounding desert. Retrace your steps whenever you're ready.

Information and Contact
There is no fee. For more information, contact Bureau of Land Management, Barstow Field Office, 2601 Barstow Road, Barstow, CA 92311, 760/252-6000, website: www.ca.blm.gov/barstow.

Directions
From I-15 at Barstow, take the East Main Street exit and drive 1.7 miles. Turn north on First Street and drive .9 mile. Turn left (north) on Irwin Road and drive 5.6 miles. Turn left on Fossil Beds Road (a gravel road) and drive 2.9 miles to the access road for Owl Canyon Campground. Turn right on the camp access road, drive .3 mile, then turn right again and drive 1.6 miles to the family campground (beyond the group camp). The trail begins by campsite number 11.

4. TEUTONIA PEAK TRAIL

Mojave National Preserve, off I-15 near Baker

Total distance: 4.0 miles round-trip

Hiking time: 2.0 hours

Type of trail: Some steep terrain

Best season: November–May

Cima Dome is a summit for geometry and geology enthusiasts. The granite dome's claim to fame is that it is the most symmetrical dome of its type in the country. And what type is that? It's a batholith—a molten mass of igneous rock that, while rising from the earth's core, stopped far below the surface.

The dome sits 1,500 feet above the surrounding landscape and covers almost 70 square miles. It's so big that when you're on top of it, you really can't tell that you're on top of it. It seems like you're standing on a broad, level plain—just like so much of the desert.

In contrast to Cima Dome is Teutonia Peak at elevation 5,767 feet. When you're on top of Teutonia Peak, you know it for sure—the desert vistas are head-swiveling, and the wind usually blows fiercely.

The hike to Teutonia Peak is one of the best walks in Mojave National Preserve. The trailhead elevation is 5,018 feet, unusually high for the desert. The first mile of walking is level and pleasant, leading through piñon pines and cholla cactus.

As you walk across the broad, flat surface of the dome, you can clearly see your destination, Teutonia Peak, as well as the rugged-looking New York and Ivan-

roadside tortoise warning sign in the Mojave

pah Mountains in the distance. Although Cima Dome was once covered with volcanic debris, it is now covered with Joshua trees, some as tall as 25 feet. They're a different variety from the kind found in Joshua Tree National Park. So much vegetation grows on Cima Dome that it looks completely unlike the western side of Mojave National Preserve. At times, it's hard to believe this is still the same park.

The Joshua forest is inviting to animals and birds, too. The yellow songbird you may see is the Scott's oriole, which makes its nest in the Joshua tree's foliage. Ladder-backed woodpeckers can also be spotted, usually drilling holes in dead piñon pines and Joshua trees.

After passing through a couple of cattle gates, the trail gets progressively steeper, but only in the last half mile do you really climb. At 1.9 miles you reach a saddle just shy of Teutonia's summit, which reveals panoramic desert views. The rocks all around you are quartz monzonite. From here, you can scramble the last short stretch to the boulder-covered summit, or simply stay at the saddle and enjoy the vistas. As you gaze at the flatlands below, try to keep it straight: You're overlooking massive Cima Dome. But because it's so large and you never see its edges, you'd just never know it.

Information and Contact
There is no fee. For more information and a map, contact Mojave National Preserve, P.O. Box 241, Baker, CA 92309, 760/733-4040, website: www.nps.gov/moja.

Directions
From Barstow, take I-15 east for approximately 85 miles to Cima Road (about 25 miles east of Baker). Turn right (south) on Cima Road and drive 12 miles to the sign for the trailhead, on the right (west) side of the road.

5. KELSO DUNES

Mojave National Preserve, off I-40 near Baker

Total distance: 3.0 miles round-trip   **Hiking time:** 1.5 hours

Type of trail: Some steep terrain   **Best season:** November–May

What's the most popular place in Mojave National Preserve to watch the sun set? Unquestionably, it's Kelso Dunes.

Kelso Dunes are the second highest sand dunes in California, and probably the most frequently visited of the tall desert dunes. (Eureka Dunes in Death Valley National Park are the tallest dunes, but they require an arduous drive; see hike 1 in the Death Valley chapter.) The entire Kelso Dunes complex is 45 miles square, and the dunes reach a height of 700 feet.

Before you start walking, read the interpretive signs at the Kelso Dunes trailhead so you learn all about these wind-shaped land forms and how they are created. Then follow the obvious trail toward the dunes. When it diminishes, just set out any which way toward the closest dune. (Constantly shifting sand makes a formal trail impossible.)

The Kelso Dunes exhibit a wide variety of plant life. More than 100 different plants live here, including grasses, shrubs, and wildflowers. In a wet spring, desert wildflowers bloom on and around the dunes. Sand verbena and desert primrose are the major springtime flowers. Year-round you can see creosote bush, dune grass, burrowbush, sand mat, and galleta grass.

The dunes themselves are gold in color, which you can plainly see from the trail-head parking area. When you examine them closely, you see they also have traces of black and pink, and they appear more pink by the glow of the setting sun. The sand grains that cause the dunes' colors include rose quartz, feldspar, and black magnetite.

If you climb high enough in the dunes, you are re-warded with views of the surrounding desert peaks, including the Granite and

Treasures such as this desert tortoise shell can be found around the Kelso Dunes.

Providence Mountains. Most people don't bother to go all the way to the top, though; they just plop themselves down and make sand angels, or roll around on the dunes' silky surface. Another popular activity is push-ing the sand with your feet to create miniature sand avalanches, which will sometimes result in a harmonic booming sound. Some desert-lovers swear by the healing power of these vibrating noises. Most geologists agree that the sound is caused by the extreme dryness of the East Mojave air, combined with the movement of the wind-polished, ultra-smooth sand grains.

Early in the morning (right around sunrise) or close to sunset are the best times to visit Kelso Dunes, because of the incredible show of color and light. Full-moon evenings are also popular, and it's easy to imagine why: They'll have you dreaming of Arabian nights.

Information and Contact

There is no fee. For more information and a free map, contact Mojave National Preserve, P.O. Box 241, Baker, CA 92309, 760/733-4040, website: www.nps.gov/moja.

Directions

From Barstow, take I-15 east for approximately 60 miles to Baker, then turn south on Kelbaker Road and drive 42 miles, past Kelso, to the signed road on the right for Kelso Dunes. Turn right (west) and drive three miles to the dunes parking area.

If you are coming from the south on I-40, take the Kelso/Amboy exit and drive 14 miles north on Kelbaker Road to the signed road on the left for Kelso Dunes. Turn left (west) and drive three miles to the dunes parking area.

6. MITCHELL CAVERNS & CRYSTAL SPRINGS

Providence Mountains State Recreation Area,
off I-40 near Essex

Total distance: 3.5 miles round-trip   **Hiking time:** 2.0 hours

Type of trail: Rolling terrain   **Best season:** November–May

It doesn't matter how big you are, it's what's inside that counts.

That was the moral of our walking tour of Mitchell Caverns in Providence Mountains State Recreation Area. The featured attraction at Providence Mountains is one of the smallest limestone caverns in the United States that is open to the public on a commercial basis. For its size, it boasts an extra-large helping of rare and unique cavern features.

We didn't know anything about caverns before we visited, but after a few minutes on the walking tour we could identify stalagmites, stalactites, helictites, draperies, cavern coral, and flowstone, or at least admire them when our guide pointed them out. In every chamber of Mitchell Caverns, our park ranger guide was telling us something akin to this: "Such-and-such a formation is so rare, and so unique, that it's one of only two such formations in all of the United States' 10,000 limestone caverns." (Cavern people take their statistics seriously, and are very enthusiastic about their field.)

If you've made the long drive to Providence Mountains State Recreation Area—a major haul from almost everywhere—you should plan to spend the day, or camp overnight in the campground, so you can do more on your visit than just tour the fascinating caverns. The tour itself involves a 1.5-mile walk, but the park also has an excellent two-mile trail to Crystal Springs, which can easily fill the time before or after your cavern exploration.

It's an uphill trek on Crystal Springs Trail, which leads from the park visitors center to a spectacular rocky overlook in the Providence Mountains. Along the way, you'll see a wide variety of desert flora, including more types of cactus than you can shake a stick at. Remember, this is the high desert at 4,300 feet in elevation, so the climate is not as inhospitable to plant and animal life as it is in Death Valley or the lowlands of Anza-Borrego Desert. The terrain here seems almost lush in comparison to many desert areas; we were amazed at the wide variety of plants, including barrel cactus, chollas, mormon tea, creosote, cliff rose, catclaw, and blue sage.

The trail feels unusually remote for a state park. Rocky outcrops shoot up from both sides of the path as you walk between piñon pines and junipers. Trailside cacti sometimes attempt to reach out and grab you, but watch where you put your hands and feet, and you'll be fine. The trail leads up Crystal Canyon, where bighorn sheep are sometimes seen by lucky hikers. Every once in a blue moon, someone spots a wild burro high up on the canyon walls, but the burros are even more elusive than the bighorns.

The trail ends without fanfare near Crystal Springs, but you can scramble off-trail a few feet to a jumble of boulders where you can lay in the sun and admire the lovely view over the Marble Mountains and Clipper Valley. On a clear day, you can see all the way to Arizona.

Options

Two other trails lead from near the visitors center at Providence Mountains: Niña Mora Overlook Trail travels from the park campground to a ridgecrest overlook a quarter mile away. The equally short Mary Beale Nature Trail provides a chance to brush up on your desert plant identification.

Information and Contact

A $4 day-use fee is charged per vehicle at Providence Mountains State Recreation Area. In addition, a $4 fee is charged per adult ($2 per child ages 6–16) for the tour of Mitchell Caverns. Tours are held daily at 1:30

P.M. September 1–May 31, and also at 10 A.M. and 3 P.M. on weekends during this period. In summer, tours are scheduled only on weekends at 1:30 P.M. Reservations are recommended for tours. For more information, contact Providence Mountains State Recreation Area, P.O. Box 1, Essex, CA 92332, 760/928-2586 or 760/389-2281, website: www.calparksmojave.com or www.cal-parks.ca.gov.

Directions
From Barstow, take I-40 east for approximately 100 miles to the exit for Essex Road, Mitchell Caverns, and Providence Mountains State Recreation Area. Turn north on Essex Road and drive 15.5 miles to the Providence Mountains visitors center. Park in the lot signed Tour Center.

7. RINGS TRAIL

Mojave National Preserve, off I-40 near Essex

Total distance: 2.0 miles round-trip	**Hiking time:** 1.0 hour
Type of trail: Some steep terrain	**Best season:** November–May

This hike is just for fun. The Rings Trail at Mojave National Preserve isn't much of a hike, per se, but it's a fun and easy outdoor adventure that kids and kids-at-heart will remember as the highlight of their trip to the Mojave.

The adventure begins at Hole-in-the-Wall Campground, one of the two "developed" campgrounds in Mojave National Preserve, which means it has pit toilets and a limited supply of water. Head for the picnic area, where you'll find a trail sign for the Rings Climb and Overlook. Go left to the overlook first, so you can see down into the rocky abyss into which you'll descend. Then backtrack and follow the Rings Trail for a few hundred feet to the Rings Climb.

You can leave your ropes, pitons, and carabiners at home for the Rings Climb. Although it may be too difficult for very inflexible or overweight hikers, most people make it easily down (and then back up) the steep and narrow passage. Rings climbers' smiles are predictably wide. We watched several people go up and down a few extra times, just for grins.

Here's how the "climb" works: Large iron hooks, connected to circular rings, have been drilled into the cliff face. You put your hands and feet through the rings, one at a time, and make your way up or down the rock. Most people find that the upward direction is easier because you can see where you are going. Your first passage is downward, however, as you leave the Rings Trail and descend into Wildhorse and Banshee Canyons.

At the bottom of the Rings Climb, you wander through a cathedral-like wonderland of rock cliffs. If you're into photography, this place will slow you down because you'll be shooting everything in sight. Too soon the path leaves the rock cathedral, then connects to the trail leading between Hole-in-the-Wall and Mid Hills Campground. This eight-mile-long trail is a scenic route through the Mojave Desert, crossing dense fields of sage and other high-desert brush. Hike on it for as long or as short as you wish. Or what the heck—just turn around and climb back up the rings again.

Hole-in-the-Wall cliffs by the Rings Trail

The story of the fascinating rocks at Hole-in-the-Wall is a tale of volcanism. About 15 million years ago, volcanic eruptions coated this area with lava, ash, and rocky debris. Gases captured during the eruption were trapped in the rock, and as they cooled unevenly, they formed holes in the rock. The action of wind and rain over millions of years enlarged these holes, creating the formations and caverns that exist today. The extraordinary color you see (a mix of red and maroon on gray) is the result of iron compounds slowly rusting.

Options

Put in some miles on the trail between Hole-in-the-Wall and Mid Hills Campground. Carry plenty of water; there is no shade.

Information and Contact

There is no fee. For more information and a free map, contact Mojave National Preserve, P.O. Box 241, Baker, CA 92309, 760/733-4040, website: www.nps.gov/moja.

Directions

From Barstow, take I-40 east for approximately 100 miles to the exit for Essex Road, Mitchell Caverns, and Providence Mountains State Recreation Area. Turn north on Essex Road and drive about 10 miles to the fork in the road for Providence Mountains. Bear right at the fork (now on Black Canyon Road) and drive eight miles north to the Hole-in-the-Wall Campground turnoff. Turn left at the sign for the visitors center and follow the dirt road past the visitors center to the picnic area. The trailhead is at the Hole-in-the-Wall picnic area; it is signed as Rings Climb and Overlook.

8. BIG MORONGO CANYON LOOP

Big Morongo Canyon Preserve, off Highway 62 near
Palm Springs

Total distance: 1.5 miles round-trip   **Hiking time:** 1.0 hour

Type of trail: Mostly flat terrain

Best season: Late fall, winter, or spring

Big Morongo Canyon Preserve is a birder's paradise, plain and simple. More than 235 bird species have been identified in the preserve, including several rare and endangered species. If you aren't carrying binoculars and a field book when you visit, you'll feel like a real outsider.

Luckily, you don't have to know anything about birds to have a good time. We studied the interpretive exhibit at the trailhead kiosk, and a few minutes later we were able to spot and identify a pair of western tanagers. (And usually we can't tell a blue jay from a blue grouse.) It made us feel like first-class ornithologists.

Pick up the checklist of Morongo Valley birds at the trailhead. You will most likely encounter Gambel's quail, mourning doves, Virginia rails, hummingbirds, woodpeckers, and tyrant flycatchers. Rare birds to watch for are the least Bell's vireo and the vermilion flycatcher, both of which sometimes nest in the canyon.

Start this loop trip from the trailhead kiosk by bearing left to connect to Desert Willow Trail, an exposed pathway through a desert wash. Then in .4 mile, turn left on Yucca Ridge Trail. As you climb Yucca Ridge, you'll gain panoramic views of Big Morongo Canyon, Mount San Jacinto, and Mount San Gorgonio. Note the gneiss and schist rock formations along the trail; they are some of the oldest rocks in California at one to two billion years old.

After following Yucca Ridge for .7 mile, connect to the shadier Mesquite Trail and enjoy a streamside walk under a canopy of Fremont cottonwoods and red willows. You may smell the distinct odor of sulfur from underground springs. Finally you'll join Marsh Trail for the last stint back to the trailhead, walking along a boardwalk made of recycled milk containers. If you haven't added a few bird species to your life list by this point in the hike, you will now. More than 1,400 pairs of birds per square kilometer nest in this marsh annually.

The canyon and its creek attract mammals as well as birds: We saw a mule deer on our visit, but occasionally visitors will spot a desert bighorn sheep, bobcat, fox, or mountain lion.

Big Morongo Canyon got its name from the Morongo Indians, a clan of the Serrano Indians, who once lived here. These nomadic people used the canyon as a travel route between the high and low deserts. The canyon had water year-round from Big Morongo Creek, and plenty of food and game. Although average annual rainfall in the area is only about eight inches, Big Morongo Creek originates in the less arid mountains northwest of the valley. Plentiful precipitation in the mountains keeps the creek water flowing, although it diminishes to a trickle in summer.

Information and Contact
There is no fee. For more information, contact Big Morongo Canyon Preserve, P.O. Box 780, Morongo Valley, CA 92256, 760/363-7190, website: www.bigmorongo.org.

Directions
From Banning, drive east on I-10 for 16 miles to the Highway 62 exit. Turn north on Highway 62 and drive 11 miles to Morongo Valley. Look for a sign on the right for the Big Morongo Canyon Preserve (at East Drive); turn right and drive 200 yards to the preserve entrance on the left. Trails begin at the information kiosk.

9. DESERT VIEW TRAIL

Mount San Jacinto State Park, via Palm Springs Aerial Tramway

Total distance: 1.6 miles round-trip

Type of trail: Mostly flat terrain

Hiking time: 1.0 hour

Best season: Good year-round

The first time you ride the Palm Springs Aerial Tramway, you realize that human beings are capable of making miracles. In just a few minutes, you are *whooshed* from Palm Springs' desert floor at 2,643 feet in elevation to San Jacinto State Park and Wilderness at 8,516 feet. The vehicle responsible for this transformation is a circular tram car about 18 feet in diameter, hooked to thin cables and attached to three long-legged towers. Its passengers ride from cactus to clouds, from palms to pines, and sometimes from desert heat to snow flurries.

The tramway is beyond thrilling. On the 15-minute ride, you get a close-up view of the mountainside as you quickly ascend, plus long-

Palm Springs Aerial Tramway

distance perspective on the desert you just departed. Views extend all the way to the Salton Sea, 50 miles to the south. The vistas are so incredible in every direction that it's hard to know which way to look.

As if the tram ride alone weren't worth the price of admission, there's more to look forward to. When your car reaches the upper station, you disembark, walk past the gift shop and down the stairs, and head out of the building to the beautiful land of Mount San Jacinto State Park. This transition can be a shock to your senses—the air is usually 30 to 40 degrees cooler than the desert below. You're in a forest of big conifers, interspersed with meadows full of wildflowers and an intermittent creek.

Several possible hikes begin from the top of the tramway, but the easiest is the Desert View Trail. Follow the paved path downhill from the back of the tram station, then pick up the trail on your left signed Nature Trail; it joins Desert View Trail. As you walk through dense stands of conifers, the route seems more like "Forest View Trail" than "Desert View Trail," until you reach an overlook with a mind-boggling view of Palm Springs and the Indian Canyons, 6,000 feet below. Where else, for so little effort, can you get such expansive views of the desert while breathing high mountain air?

It's not uncommon to spot wildlife on this short loop hike. Birdwatchers should be on the lookout for Cooper's hawks, yellow-rumped warblers, nuthatches, and woodpeckers. One of the most unusual inhabitants of Mount San Jacinto is the ring-tail, which looks something like a raccoon crossed with a house cat. But because the ring-tail is nocturnal, you're unlikely to see one.

One of the best seasons to hike Desert View Trail is in wintertime. Even though Mount San Jacinto may be snow-covered anytime from late November to April, the tramway stays open and a concessionaire rents cross-country skis and snowshoes. Crowned in a layer of white stuff, the park becomes a winter wonderland.

Whenever you visit, stop in at the park's nature center on the bottom floor of the tramway building. It is filled with exhibits on the flora and fauna of the mountain. Two videos are shown in a small screening room: One details the conception and building of the aerial tramway; the other describes the wilderness region of the state park.

Options

For a longer walk, from the bottom of the paved walkway go right toward the ranger station. Self-register for a free wilderness permit (the registration box is on the building's front porch), then follow the signs to Round Valley, two miles distant. Continue another mile to Willow Creek, then at the next junction loop back to the tramway station.

Information and Contact

The Palm Springs Aerial Tramway charges $20.80 per adult and $13.80 per child under 12 for a round-trip ticket. Phone 760/325-1391 or visit www.pstramway.com online for more information about schedules, fees, and special programs. A hiking trail map of the San Jacinto State Park and Wilderness is available for $1 at the visitors center. For more information, contact Mount San Jacinto State Park and Wilderness, P.O. Box 308, 25905 Highway 243, Idyllwild, CA 92549, 909/659-2607, website: www.sanjac.statepark.org.

Directions

From Banning, drive 12 miles east on I-10 and take the Highway 111/Palm Springs exit. Drive nine miles south on Highway 111 to Tramway Road, then turn right and drive 3.8 miles to the tramway parking area. Buy your ticket at the tramway station and ride the tram to its end at Mountain Station. Walk out the back side of the station, follow the paved path downhill, then head left for the Nature Trail and Desert View Trail.

10. MURRAY CANYON TRAIL

Agua Caliente Indian Reservation, off Highway 111
near Palm Springs

Total distance: 4.0 miles round-trip   **Hiking time:** 2.0 hours

Type of trail: Mostly flat terrain

Best season: November–May (closed weekdays June–September)

If you want to see the "real" Palm Springs, leave the shopping malls and swimming pools behind and head for Murray Canyon. Located on the Agua Caliente Indian Reservation, Murray Canyon is a vestige of what Palm Springs used to be—wide-open vistas of red rock, an oasis of fan palms, a life-giving stream, and an abundance of barrel cactus and other desert flora. You won't find any tennis courts, golf courses, or beauty salons here.

Your hike begins from the east side of the picnic grounds between Murray and Andreas Canyons, at a sign reading, "Murray Canyon, 20 minutes." It's accurate, sort of. Twenty minutes won't get you to the good stuff, merely to the start of the canyon and the first cluster of palm trees.

hikers on Murray Canyon Trail

We passed a guy who had traveled only this far and was clearly disappointed. He told us, "Nothing much down there. Not even much water." Don't make his mistake. Have faith and keep hiking.

After an initial stretch through open desert terrain, you enter Murray Canyon, which narrows and twists and turns so that you never see where you're going until you come around the next bend. This keeps the anticipation high. Gradually the stream you've been following begins to show a greater flow of water, and accordingly, the streamside reeds, willows, palms, and wild grape intensify their growth. The palms are *Washingtonias;* nearly 1,000 of them thrive in Murray Canyon. If you're a fan of red rock, you'll love the 100-foot-tall slanted outcrops that jut out from the earth. They're a photographer's delight.

At 1.5 miles, you'll pass the turnoff for Kaufmann Trail on the left, then climb up and over a jumble of boulders. Continue for another 10 to 15 minutes until you suddenly come upon a delicate waterfall, sculpted out of fine, polished granite. The fall has two cascades, each with a mirrorlike pool at its base, set about 50 yards apart. If the day is warm, you'll feel compelled to wade in. A half-dozen more cascades await farther back in this canyon, earning these falls the name Seven Sisters.

Upon our return to the trailhead, my hiking partner asked me what I liked best about our trip to Murray Canyon. Was it the waterfall? The colors of the desert? The magnificent fan palms? No, none of the above. What I liked best were the hundreds of foot-high barrel cacti that cling to every available spot on the canyon walls. They look like cute little spiny creatures peeking out at you.

Options

If you've enjoyed Murray Canyon, sign up for an easy guided hike in equally spectacular Tahquitz Canyon, also located on the Agua Caliente Indian Reservation. (You may not hike in Tahquitz Canyon without a guide.) For reservations and information, phone 760/416-7044 or visit the website, www.tahquitzcanyon.com.

Information and Contact

A $6 day-use fee is charged per adult; $2 for children 6–12. A free map/brochure is available at the entrance kiosk. For more information, contact Agua Caliente Band of Cahuilla Indians, Indian Canyons Visitors Center, 2777 North Palm Canyon Drive, Palm Springs, CA 92256, 760/325-3400 or 760/323-6018, website: www.indian-canyons.com.

Directions

From Palm Springs, drive south through the center of town on Highway 111/Palm Canyon Drive, and take the right fork signed for South Palm Canyon Drive. Drive 2.8 miles on South Palm Canyon Drive, bearing right at the sign for Palm Canyon/Andreas Canyon. Stop at the entrance kiosk, then drive about 200 yards and turn right for Murray Canyon. Drive past the Andreas Canyon trailhead and continue to the Murray Canyon picnic area, one mile from the entrance kiosk.

11. FORTYNINE PALMS OASIS

Joshua Tree National Park, off Highway 62 near
Twentynine Palms

Total distance: 3.0 miles round-trip   **Hiking time:** 1.5 hours

Type of trail: Rolling terrain   **Best season:** November–April

---

The biggest surprise on Fortynine Palms Oasis Trail is not the large and lovely grove of fan palms at the trail's end. It's that there are no Joshua trees to be found anywhere along the trail. What? No Joshua trees? If you've spent a few days in Joshua Tree National Park, you get accustomed to seeing the tall yuccalike plants everywhere you look.

But you won't find them here. Fortynine Palms Oasis Trail is located at the far northern edge of the park, where the elevation is just low enough to be outside of the Joshua trees' reign. Your trailside companions include a multitude of rotund, reddish-colored barrel cacti, which bloom in profusion in April and May; and brittlebush, a shrub with silvery green leaves and a yellow, daisylike flower.

The Fortynine Palms Oasis Trail is built on an old Indian pathway, and it's well-maintained and easy to follow. It carves a few curves, then undulates up and over a small ridge, so you're never sure exactly where you're heading. A strange contradiction on this seemingly remote trail is that you can still see and hear far-off Highway 62 and the town of Twentynine Palms. The road noise travels right up the canyon, and from the trail's high plateau, you can look out over the suburban desert sprawl.

This odd mix of the wild and the civilized ends when you reach the rocky palm grove. There, civilization is forgotten as you are cloistered in a small, hidden valley filled with fan palms. A group of 10 palm trees appears first, and then a larger cluster about 50 yards away. Many have blackened trunks from occasional natural fires in the canyon. Fire is beneficial to mature palm trees, because it increases seed production and opens up space for the seeds to germinate.

You may hear water trickling among the palms, but rarely does much appear above ground, except for a few stagnant-looking pools. These pools are a rare and precious drinking-water source for bighorn sheep, coyotes, and myriad other wildlife. Every once in a while, a lucky hiker will spot a bighorn ram on the rocky ridges above the oasis, warily await-

You won't be in a hurry to leave the peaceful oasis at Fortynine Palms.

ing his or her turn at the watering hole. Bighorns look more like big goats than sheep; they are almost white in color and can weigh up to 200 pounds. Bighorns once ranged over a large expanse of Southern California, the Southwest, and Mexico, but in the last century, their numbers have decreased substantially.

If you have kids or kids-at-heart with you, they'll want to clamber around on the large boulders surrounding the palms. The rocks are covered with colored lichens and make a fine seat for a picnic, or for listening to the wind in the palms. Look for wildflowers, including a species of desert orchid, which bloom near the pools in spring. Birdwatchers will want to sit and wait for the appearance of an oriole, finch, or hummingbird, all of which are commonly seen.

The only negative at the oasis is that many of the palm trees have been carved with people's initials. Take this opportunity to teach your children about the harm that is done, both to the tree and the scenic beauty, with this type of graffiti.

Options

Drive two miles farther west on Highway 62 and take the signed turnoff for Indian Cove Campground. Two trails lead from the camp area: a .5-mile interpretive trail and the longer Boy Scout Trail.

Information and Contact
There is no fee at the Fortynine Palms Oasis trailhead, but there is a $10 entrance fee per vehicle at the rest of Joshua Tree National Park, good for seven days. Park maps are available at park entrance stations. For more information, contact Joshua Tree National Park, 74485 National Park Drive, Twentynine Palms, CA 92277, 760/367-5500, website: www.nps.gov/jotr.

Directions
From Banning, drive east on I-10 for 16 miles to the Highway 62 exit. Turn north on Highway 62 and drive 29 miles to the town of Joshua Tree. Continue east on Highway 62 for 10 miles, to just west of the town of Twentynine Palms. Turn right (south) on Canyon Road, located by the High Desert Animal Hospital. Drive 1.7 miles on Canyon Road; bear left where the road forks. The pavement ends at the Fortynine Palms Oasis trailhead.

12. BARKER DAM LOOP

Joshua Tree National Park, off Highway 62 near
Twentynine Palms

Total distance: 1.5 miles round-trip   **Hiking time:** 1.0 hour

Type of trail: Mostly flat terrain   **Best season:** November–April

---

There's a lake in the desert in Joshua Tree National Park, and it's hidden in a magical place called the Wonderland of Rocks. You can't water-ski or fish there, but you can birdwatch and photograph the reflections of odd-shaped boulders in the water's surface.

Okay, a caveat is in order: Sometimes there is a lake in this desert, but it's completely dependent on annual rainfall. The first few years of the 21st century brought an extreme drought to Joshua Tree, and the lake dried up and vanished. The lake, when it exists, is formed by Barker Dam, which was built around 1900 to improve upon a natural boulder dam. The original dam captured rain runoff and contained it in a large, rock-lined basin, to the delight of desert animals and birds. When rancher C. O. Barker of the Barker and Shay Cattle Company traveled through the area and found the natural dam and its tiny lake, he

© ANN MARIE BROWN

high water in the lake at Barker Dam

thought he might be able to turn this part of the desert into ranchland. After all, it had the magic ingredients for survival—water, and a way to store it.

Barker built a bigger, stronger dam, then brought his cattle in to graze. After several years, Barker moved on, and a decade later the dam was enlarged by William Keys, owner of the nearby Desert Queen Ranch. With Keys's development in the 1950s, the lake attained its largest size, about 20 acres.

Eventually, this desert site became a part of Joshua Tree National Park, and now in years of normal rainfall, Barker Dam's lake is once again a watering hole for native animals, such as bighorn sheep and coyotes. It is also visited by resident and migratory birds; lucky visitors may spot American coots, grebes, ducks, and even an occasional shorebird. Every now and then a green-backed heron, great blue heron, or night heron will show up, as it takes a break during its long migration.

The drive to the Barker Dam trailhead alone is worth the trip, because you get a close-up look at some of Joshua Tree National Park's best granite formations in an area called the Wonderland of Rocks. The rocks are fantastic both in shape and configuration. Huge pieces of granite are piled on top of each other in odd jumbles. Kids of all ages can spend hours imagining what creatures the rocks resemble.

From the Barker Dam parking area, head straight on the trail. This is fun hiking—you must walk over and around a collection of rocks and boulders as you proceed along the sandy path. You'll reach the lake (or the place where the lake should be!) in a half mile. Willows, cattails, and saltbrush grow near its edges.

The trail loops back past some petroglyphs (take the short signed spur trail) and Indian grinding holes. If the petroglyphs seem remarkably visible and clear to you, it's because years ago a movie crew painted over them to make them more visible to the camera. For this tragic reason, the park calls these paintings the "Disney petroglyphs." Still, they are worth seeing, and you can muse over their intended meanings.

Options

Across the road from Hidden Valley Campground is the trailhead for Hidden Valley Trail (you passed it as you drove to the Barker Dam trailhead). This one-mile trail is a fascinating walk through giant boulders to the valley hideout of an 1880s cattle rustler.

Information and Contact

There is a $10 entrance fee per vehicle at Joshua Tree National Park, good for seven days. Park maps are available at park entrance stations. For more information, contact Joshua Tree National Park, 74485 National Park Drive, Twentynine Palms, CA 92277, 760/367-5500, website: www.nps.gov/jotr.

Directions

From Banning, drive east on I-10 for 16 miles to the Highway 62 exit. Turn north on Highway 62 and drive 29 miles to the town of Joshua Tree, and Park Boulevard. Turn right (south) on Park Boulevard and drive 14 miles to Hidden Valley Campground on the left. Turn left and drive 1.7 miles to the signed trailhead for Barker Dam.

13. RYAN MOUNTAIN TRAIL

Joshua Tree National Park, off Highway 62 near
Twentynine Palms

Total distance: 3.0 miles round-trip   **Hiking time:** 2.0 hours

Type of trail: Some steep terrain   **Best season:** November–April

---

The view from Ryan Mountain's summit is one of the finest in all of
Joshua Tree National Park.
Not only that, but the trail
to reach it is one of the best
maintained, and easiest to
follow, of all the park's
trails. This hike should be
on everybody's itinerary.

Our first visit to Ryan
Mountain was on a cool day
in December, when the
wind was blowing hard. By
the time we reached the
5,460-foot summit, we could
barely keep our balance in
the howling gale. Still, the
panorama was so transfixing
that we stayed on the peak
for as long as we could. The
summit vista includes
Queen Valley, the Wonder-
land of Rocks, Pinto Basin,
Lost Horse Valley, and Pleasant Valley, as well as the
high peaks of far-off Mount
San Gorgonio and Mount
San Jacinto. (In winter,

on the windy summit of Ryan Mountain

these two peaks are usually covered in snow, so they are easy to identify.)

The weather isn't always cold and blustery on Ryan Mountain. In summer it can be hot, still, and extremely uncomfortable for making the

short climb to the mountaintop. If your trip is between May and September, make sure you get an early-morning start to beat the heat.

Ryan Mountain Trail begins at a roadside parking area, then travels through boulders and Joshua trees—no surprises here. The ascent may seem a bit steep, even though it's only a 1,000-foot elevation gain, but it's over quickly. Just sweat it out. You'll want to stop every few minutes to look around at the ever-widening desert views, your reward as you climb.

When you reach the summit, have a seat on one of the rocks of Ryan Mountain and enjoy the show. The peak's boulders are estimated to be several hundred million years old, which is much older than most of the rocks in Joshua Tree National Park. If you pace around a few yards on the peak's surface, you get a full 360-degree panorama: mountains on one horizon, miles of desert on the other.

Look around for the summit register; it's usually buried in a pile of rocks. The register may be a coffee can filled with tiny notebooks and scraps of paper, or it may be something more formal; it depends on who has been on the summit recently. Spend a few minutes reading the comments of other hikers, then add a few acute observations of your own.

Options
Take the nearby hike to Lost Horse Mine. Drive west to Park Boulevard, then turn south, as if heading for Keys View. In two miles you'll see the turnoff for the Lost Horse Mine trailhead. The four-mile round-trip trail leads to a historic gold mining site.

Information and Contact
There is a $10 entrance fee per vehicle at Joshua Tree National Park, good for seven days. Park maps are available at park entrance stations. For more information, contact Joshua Tree National Park, 74485 National Park Drive, Twentynine Palms, CA 92277, 760/367-5500, website: www.nps.gov/jotr.

Directions
From Banning, drive east on I-10 for 16 miles to the Highway 62 exit. Turn north on Highway 62 and drive 45 miles to Twentynine Palms and the park visitors center. Turn right on Utah Trail Road and drive eight miles to a Y junction. Bear right and drive nine miles, past Sheep Pass Campground, to the trailhead parking area on the south side of the road. (Or, from the town of Joshua Tree, follow Park Boulevard south for 16 miles. Turn left at Cap Rock Junction, then drive 2.5 miles to the trailhead on the right.)

14. SKULL ROCK TRAIL

Joshua Tree National Park, off Highway 62 near
Twentynine Palms

Total distance: 1.7 miles round-trip   **Hiking time:** 1.0 hour

Type of trail: Mostly flat terrain   **Best season:** November–April

---

Joshua Tree National Park is probably as famous for rock formations as it is for Joshua trees. If you've been admiring the park's weird and wonderful hunks of quartz monzogranite from your car window, a walk on Skull Rock Nature Trail will provide you with a closer look.

The "official" trail, which is only .25 mile long, begins right along the road near Jumbo Rocks Campground. If you're not staying in the camp, park your car along the road and start hiking on the northwest side at the signed trailhead. You'll head counterclockwise, and after completing the official interpretive trail, you'll follow an obvious use trail that leads to Skull Rock and its many odd-shaped companions. With your first few footsteps, you'll squeeze past some weathered boulders, but you won't rub elbows with the best of them until the end of the trail.

Skull Rock Trail is highly recommended not just for its fine examples of Joshua Tree National Park geology, but also for its excellent interpretation of desert flora. Signs along the pathway point out paperbag bush, which has many inflated seed pods that look like white paper bags; dwarf-sized Mueller's oak, which has tiny, oaklike leaves; and cholla cactus, which has sharp, barbed spines. You get a complete high-desert botany lesson along Skull Rock Trail. Soon you can quiz your hiking partner on the identifying characteristics of peachthorn, creosote, buckwheat, and catclaw acacia. The most interesting fact we learned was that the park's plentiful Joshua trees got their name from the Mormons, who said that the Joshua's uplifted branches reminded them of the Biblical Joshua in prayerful supplication.

What about the big rocks? That's why we're here, after all. The trail winds among the giant, rounded formations, which look a lot like sandstone but are actually monzonite. Although they were first formed in larger, solid pieces, the rock was segmented by joints or cracks. Erosion, rain, and alternating cold and hot air went to work on these cracks, eventually splitting the rocks into smaller, odd shapes. More years of natural forces

Skull Rock Trail

and erosion rounded off their rough edges, as if they were ice cubes being held under a faucet. Flash floods have piled them up in the strange jumbles you see now.

The informal trail reaches the park road, crosses it, then heads into the Jumbo Rocks Campground. In most camps, this would make for a boring stretch of trail, but at Jumbo Rocks, there's much to see, including some wind-sculpted rock caves and campsites made private by nature's positioning of the boulders.

Just beyond the entrance to the camp's Loop E, pick up the use trail again, heading for Skull Rock, which looks eerily like the top half of a human skull. When you near it, the path deteriorates into a spiderweb of paths, with footprints leading in all directions. This is where everybody sets out on their own, climbing around on Skull Rock and the many interesting formations surrounding it. If you get confused about which way to go, just scramble to the top of any high rock and you'll spot the nearby road where you parked your car.

Information and Contact

There is a $10 entrance fee per vehicle at Joshua Tree National Park, good for seven days. Park maps are available at park entrance stations. For more information, contact Joshua Tree National Park, 74485 National Park

Drive, Twentynine Palms, CA 92277, 760/367-5500, website: www.nps.gov/jotr.

Directions

From Banning, drive east on I-10 for 16 miles to the Highway 62 exit. Turn north on Highway 62 and drive 45 miles to Twentynine Palms and the park visitors center. Turn right on Utah Trail Road and drive 8.5 miles to a Y junction. Bear right and drive four miles to the trailhead parking area alongside the road, shortly before the entrance to Jumbo Rocks Campground. Begin hiking on the right (northwest) side of the road. (Or, from the town of Joshua Tree, follow Park Boulevard south for 16 miles. Turn left at Cap Rock Junction, then continue seven miles to the trailhead.)

15. MASTODON PEAK LOOP

Joshua Tree National Park, off I-10 near Indio

Total distance: 3.0 miles round-trip   **Hiking time:** 1.5 hours

Type of trail: Rolling terrain   **Best season:** November–April

---

The loop trail to Mastodon Peak is an excellent trip for families, combining elements of human and natural history on a pleasant excursion in the southern part of Joshua Tree National Park. The trail begins at Cottonwood Spring Oasis, a trickling spring surrounded by a few fan palms and native cottonwoods. Although the spring was created by an earthquake, it's not a completely natural paradise. The spring was improved upon in the late 1800s in order to make it a rest stop for prospectors and miners traveling to and from the desert mines.

Near Cottonwood Spring, you can find evidence of the Native Americans who lived here, in the form of bedrock mortars (grinding holes) in the granite. Early Serrano, Cahuilla, and Chemehuevi Indians once camped in this area in mud-plastered shelters and rock caves. They carefully guarded the locations of desert springs such as Cottonwood, which were critical to their survival.

You'll also find the remains of an arrastra near the spring. A time-worn, decaying wheel made of wood and stone, the arrastra was used by prospectors in the early 20th century as a primitive gold mill.

Walk past the oasis, following the trail signed for Lost Palms Oasis and Mastodon Peak. The path is a smooth, easy stroll, curving around tall ocotillo plants, yucca, and many small cacti. At a junction at .6 mile, take the left fork for Mastodon Peak, .5 mile farther. (The right fork leads to Los Palms Oasis; see Options for this hike.) When you reach Mastodon's base, you see that the peak does resemble its prehistoric namesake. Size up the rocky summit, then make a decision: to scramble to the top, or be content with the views from below? If you choose the former, head to

fractured rock along the trail to Mastodon Peak

your right, toward the back (east) side of the peak, then scale the large boulders to reach the summit. This short, fun scramble is worth the effort, but it may be too risky for small children or acrophobes.

Mastodon's summit view extends all the way to the Salton Sea, shimmering in the distance some 30 miles away. The Eagle Mountains are visible to the east, plus Mount San Jacinto to the west, Monument Mountain to the northwest, and the Cottonwood Spring area immediately north.

After getting an eyeful of the panorama, climb back down from the summit, then continue on the loop. Your return trip leads past the Mastodon Gold Mine, which was worked from 1919 to 1932 with a modicum of success; and the Winona Mill Site, where a small town was built for miners and ore-processing workers. Little remains of the town besides some planted cottonwood and eucalyptus trees and a few concrete house foundations. The trees provide welcome shade for wildlife and weary hikers.

From the mill site, continue a short distance to a fork in the trail. The right fork continues to Cottonwood Spring Campground; the left fork leads you back to your car at Cottonwood Spring Oasis.

Options
Take the right fork in the trail for Lost Palms Oasis, one of the largest palm oases in the park. Just be certain to pick a cool day and bring plenty of water for the 7.5-mile round-trip.

Information and Contact
There is a $10 entrance fee per vehicle at Joshua Tree National Park, good for seven days. Park maps are available at park entrance stations. For more information, contact Joshua Tree National Park, 74485 National Park Drive, Twentynine Palms, CA 92277, 760/367-5500, website: www.nps.gov/jotr.

Directions
From Indio, drive east on I-10 for 25 miles. Turn north on Cottonwood Spring Road and drive eight miles to Cottonwood Spring Visitors Center. Turn right and drive 1.2 miles, past the campground entrance, to the day-use parking area at Cottonwood Spring Oasis.

16. ROCK HILL TRAIL

Sonny Bono Salton Sea National Wildlife Refuge, off Highway 111 near Calipatria

Total distance: 2.0 miles round-trip   **Hiking time:** 1.5 hours

Type of trail: Some steep terrain   **Best season:** October–April

---

The Salton Sea ranks as one of the strangest natural wonders of Southern California. It's a vast inland sea that was created by an accident, then altered further by human hands. It's also an important haven for migratory birds and waterfowl of all shapes and sizes, and one of the Southland's best bird-watching sites. More than 400 bird species have been spotted here. Pack your binoculars before you make the long drive.

This 380-acre water body is set in the huge Imperial Valley, a desert basin that is 200 feet below sea level. Long ago, that basin was a giant

on top of Rock Hill, overlooking the Salton Sea

lake called Lake Cahuilla, which dried up and was replenished multiple times over a period of 3,000 years. Each occurrence of Lake Cahuilla lasted as much as 600 years. It is estimated that the last time the natural lake existed was sometime in the 16th century.

Then in 1905, a series of manmade dams and levees on the Colorado River burst their seams, and water flowed into the Imperial Valley for almost two years. The resulting manmade lake, dubbed the Salton Sea, was originally freshwater and filled with trout and other fish from the Colorado River. However, the Salton Sea gradually became saltier over the next century due to agricultural runoff, evaporation, and the lack of replenishing freshwater. Today, the Salton Sea is 25 percent saltier than the ocean. Freshwater fish did not survive; saltwater fish, including sargo, tilapia, mullet, and corvina, were introduced in the 1950s.

Start your trip at the wildlife refuge headquarters. Rock Hill Trail begins by the observation platform, just to the left of the building. You can't see the sea at first, but shortly the trail turns right and curves around some turbines, and soon you're looking at a freshwater marsh, lined with cattails, on the Salton Sea's edge. You can see Rock Hill off in the distance; that's the overlook point where this trail ends.

Trace along the edge of the sea, watching the parade of bird life. Migrating geese and ducks, including snow geese and Ross geese, come to feed on the neighboring croplands. Blue herons and black-crowned herons wade in the freshwater marsh. White pelicans and gulls circle over, dive into, and perch on the sea's surface. Other types of wildlife also make an appearance: migrating butterflies and bats stop here on their way to South America. Literally hundreds of bunny rabbits can be seen hopping along the edges of the hiking trail. It's a busy place.

At the base of Rock Hill, you face a brief uphill climb. The panoramic view from Rock Hill is surprising. In your field of vision are the Chocolate Mountains to the north, the Orocopia Mountains to the west, and the Little San Bernardino Mountains toward Joshua Tree to the north. Most impressive of all, from this height you gain a revealing perspective on the immensity of the Salton Sea.

Information and Contact

There is no fee. A free map and brochure is available at the refuge visitors center. For more information, contact the Sonny Bono Salton Sea National Wildlife Refuge, 906 West Sinclair Road, Calipatria, CA 92233, 760/348-5278, website: www.pacific.fws.gov/salton.

Directions

From Indio, drive south on Highway 111 for approximately 50 miles to the turnoff for Sinclair Road, four miles south of Niland. (If you reach Calipatria, you've gone too far.) Turn right on Sinclair Road and drive six miles to the Sonny Bono Salton Sea National Wildlife Refuge visitors center, at the intersection of Sinclair Road and Gentry Road.

© ANN MARIE BROWN

Resources

SOUTHERN CALIFORNIA HIKING CLUBS

Looking for some friends to hike with? Check out these Southern California hiking clubs:

Ivy League Association of Southern California, Hiking Group
www.ivy.hiking.info

Jewish Outdoor Adventures
www.jewishoutdooradventures.com

Outdoors Club
www.outdoorsclub.org

San Gorgonio Wilderness Association
www.sgwa.org

Angeles Chapter of the Sierra Club
(Los Angeles and Orange Counties)
www.angeles.sierrraclub.org

Los Padres Chapter of the Sierra Club
(Santa Barbara and Ventura Counties)
www.lospadres.sierraclub.org

San Diego Chapter of the Sierra Club
(San Diego and Imperial Counties)
www.sandiego.sierraclub.org

San Gorgonio Chapter of the Sierra Club
(Riverside and San Bernardino Counties)
www.sangorgonio.sierraclub.org

Santa Lucia Chapter of the Sierra Club
(San Luis Obispo County)
www.santalucia.sierraclub.org

Kern-Kaweah Chapter of the Sierra Club
(Kern, Kings, and Tulare Counties)
www.kern-kaweah.sierraclub.org

ACKNOWLEDGMENTS

NATIONAL PARKS, MONUMENTS, WILDLIFE REFUGES, AND RECREATION AREAS

Richard Banuelos, Pinnacles National Monument
Charlie Calligan, Death Valley National Park
Ruby Newton, Mojave National Preserve
Christine Artmann, Sonny Bono Salton Sea National Wildlife Refuge
Jean Bray, Santa Monica Mountains National Recreation Area
Joe Zarki and Cindy VonHalle, Joshua Tree National Park
Kris Fister, Sequoia and Kings Canyon National Parks
Karl Pierce, Cabrillo National Monument

NATIONAL FORESTS

Denise Alonzo, Sequoia National Forest (Tule River Ranger District)
Debe Arndt, Sierra National Forest (High Sierra Ranger District)
Judy Behrens, Cleveland National Forest (Trabuco Ranger District)
Alfredo Zarate, San Bernardino National Forest (Mill Creek Ranger Station)

STATE PARKS

Juventino Ortiz, San Luis Obispo Coast State Parks
Allyn Kaye and Gary Olson, Torrey Pines State Reserve
Michael Allan, Will Rogers State Historic Park
Paul Pettit, Antelope Valley California Poppy Reserve, Saddleback Butte
    State Park, and Providence Mountains State Recreation Area
Brian Cahill, Mount San Jacinto State Park
Fred Jee, Anza-Borrego Desert State Park
Tom Cline, Cuyamaca Rancho State Park
Andrew Zilke, Oso Flaco Lake Natural Area
Gail Berry, San Simeon State Beach

COUNTY AND REGIONAL PARKS

Debbie Goodwin, L.A. County Parks and Recreation (Vasquez Rocks
    Natural Area)
Darrell Wanner, Placerita Canyon County Park
Glenn Kinney, Wildwood Park

Don Olgin, Santa Barbara County Parks and Recreation (Nojoqui Falls County Park)
Dennis Parker, San Diego County Parks and Recreation (William Heise County Park)
Betty Zeller, Big Morongo Canyon Preserve
David Numer, Devil's Punchbowl Natural Area

INDEX

Notes

Notes

Notes

Notes

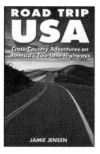